Fundamental Principles of Panamanian Foundations

Bochumer Studien zum Stiftungswesen

Herausgegeben von Karlheinz Muscheler

Band 6

PETER LANG

Frankfurt am Main · Berlin · Bern · Bruxelles · New York · Oxford · Wien

Irena Braxator

Fundamental Principles of Panamanian Foundations

PETER LANG
Internationaler Verlag der Wissenschaften

Bibliographic Information published by the Deutsche Nationalbibliothek
The Deutsche Nationalbibliothek lists this publication in the Deutsche Nationalbibliografie; detailed bibliographic data is available in the internet at http://dnb.d-nb.de.

This book was originally published in German
under the title “Grundlagen der Panama-Stiftung”

Translated by: Wendy Jane Jones

ISSN 1864-936X 6
ISBN 978-3-631-61332-0

www.peterlang.de

Table of Contents

List of Abbreviations

A.	Auflage
ABGB	General Civil Code (of Liechtenstein) dated 1 June 1811, ASW, LR 210.1
Para	Paragraph
AG	Joint stock corporation
AO	Tax Regulations
OL	Old Law (Liechtenstein law governing foundations, valid until 01.04.2009)
Art.	Article
AS	Official collection of Swiss federal laws and directives, in order of year and page number
ASW	Official collection of Liechtenstein legal regulations issued prior to 1 January 1863, as amended
Vol.	Volume
BG	Federal Act
BGB	Civil Code (of Germany) dated 18 August 1896
BGB1	Federal Law Gazette
BGE	Federal court ruling
BJM	Basler Juristische Mitteilungen (Basle legal notifications)
BV	Federal Constitution of the Swiss Confederation, SR 101
CC	Código Civil, (Civil Code of Panama)
Ccom	Código Comercial, (Commercial Code of Panama)
CP	Constitución Política de la República de Panamá (Political Constitution of Panama)
i.e.	id est
Ed.	Edition
EheG	(Liechtenstein) Marriage Act dated 13 December 1973, LGBl 1974/20, LR 212.10
ELG	Rulings by Liechtenstein's courts of justice (up to 1978)
ErbStG	Inheritance Tax Act
Etc.	etcetera
et seq/et seqq	et sequens/et sequentia
FL	Principality of Liechtenstein

FLOGH	(Liechtenstein) Supreme Court of Justice
G.	Gesetz
GB1.	Law Gazette
GBOeR	(Liechtenstein) Office of Land and Public Registration
a.a.	as amended
IPL	International private law
IPRG (IPRG)	Swiss Act governing International Private Law dated 18 December 1987
LES	(Liechtenstein) collection of rulings
LF	La Ley No. 1/84 por la cual se regulan el fideicomiso y se adoptan otras disposiciones, 5 de Enero del año 1984, Gaceta Oficial No. 19971; Law No. 1/84 dated 5 January 1984 governing trusts, published in Gazette No. 19971 (Panama).
LFIP	La Ley No. 25/95 por la cual se regulan las fundaciones de interés privado, 6 de Junio del año 1995, Gaceta Oficial No. 22804; Law No. 25/95 dated 12 June 1995 governing private-benefit foundations, published in Gazette No. 22804 (Panama)
LGBl	(Liechtenstein) National Law Gazette
lit.	litera
LJZ	Liechtensteinische Juristen Zeitung
LR	Systematic collection of legal regulations in Liechtenstein, classified in accordance with Register 1993, published by the Legal Office of the Government of the Principality of Liechtenstein
N	Note
rev.	revised
No.	Number
NL	New Law (Liechtenstein law governing foundations, valid from 01.04.2009)
OG	(Liechtenstein) High Court
OGH	(Liechtenstein) Supreme Court of Justice
OR BG	dated 30 March 1911 concerning additions to the Swiss Civil Code, Section Five: Code of Obligations, SR 220.
ÖRegV	Liechtenstein Public Register Decree dated 11 February 2003, LGBl 2003 No.66 dated 18.02.2003
PGR	(Liechtenstein) Person and Companies Act dated 20 January 1926, LGBl.1926 No.4, as amended (LR 216.0) Private Schriftenreihe von KPMG, Zurich.
PSG	(Austrian) Private Foundations Act, BGB1 1993/694
resp.	respectively

RIW	Recht der Internationalen Wirtschaft, (German trade magazine focusing on international business law), Heidelberg
RSO	(Liechtenstein) Rights Protection Act, LGBl 1923/8, LR 283.0
SR	Systematic collection of (Swiss) federal laws
SteG	(Liechtenstein) Taxation Act, LGBl 1961/7, LR 640.1
StGB	(Liechtenstein) Criminal Code dated 24 June 1984, LGBl 1988/37, LR 311.0
StGH	(Liechtenstein) State Court of Justice
TruG/TrUG	(Liechtenstein) Trust Companies Act, Law governing trust companies (incorporated into the PGR as Art.932a with own paragraph numbering)
i.a.	Inter alia
VBI	(Liechtenstein) Court of Administrative Appeal
VE	Preliminary draft of the new Swiss Foundations Act
Cf.	compare
VO	Regulation
ZGB	Swiss Civil Code dated 10 December 1907, SR 210
ZSR	Zeitschrift für Schweizerisches Recht (trade magazine focusing on Swiss law)
ZVW	Zeitschrift für Vormundschaftswesen (trade magazine focusing on issues of probate)

Section 1 Introduction / Preface

Private foundations were codified in Panama on 12 June 1995 by Law No. 25 *La Ley de Fundaciones de Interés Privado* ("LFIP"). Panama used the law governing foundations in Liechtenstein as its basis and adopted some of the wording literally. It would, however, be wrong to assume that the interpretation of Liechtenstein norms can be transferred to the Panamanian legal standards without further ado. On the contrary, future administrative and legal practice in Panama and Liechtenstein will show the extent to which the two countries adopt the same or differing approaches to administering their laws governing foundations.

The legal system in Panama is based on Roman law and is classified as a "civil law system", also known as continental law or codification. It does, however, also include numerous elements of Anglo-Saxon law ("common law"). Added to which, Panama frequently incorporates modern and current elements from other systems into its own legal system and will probably continue to do so in the future.

Since the Panama foundation that forms the basis of this work is also compared with a normal joint stock company,[1] the creation of the joint stock company **(Panama Company)** in 1927 is also worth mentioning in relation to the law governing foundations in Panama.[2] The Liechtenstein Foundation Act was by far not the only source of inspiration for the Panamanian foundation; it was also influenced to a major extent by the ideology behind the Panamanian "fideicommiss" and the Anglo-Saxon "trust".[3] Eleven years before the Foundation Act was introduced, the **Anglo-Saxon trust** was codified in Panama, in 1984,[4] and contains many similarities with the foundation that was introduced at a later date. According to the opinion of some Panamanian academics, the foundation (private foundation) represents an incorporation of the Anglo-Saxon trust into the continental legal system of civil law, which is why they call it a "continental

1 Cf. below: Section 3 Systematic Interpretation / The Incorporation of the LFIP into Panama's Legal System

2 Law No. 32 from 1927, La Ley de La Sociedad Anónima (SA).

3 Via the ratification and recognition of the trust pursuant to the Hague Convention, 1985.

4 Law No. 1 dated 5 January 1984, La Ley de Fideicomisos. (hereafter: LF). Cf. also the global recognition of trusts in the Hague Convention, 1985.

trust".[5] In light of the responsibility associated with, and functions of, asset management, **fiduciary** regulations and norms must also be considered; in both Panama and Liechtenstein these are subject to **subsidiary application**.[6]

The aim of this book is to examine the Panamanian foundation – *La Fundación de Interés Privado* – in more detail. By interpreting the articles of the law and associated rulings, and taking account of legal teachings, it aims to promote a better understanding of the legal institution of the "Panama Foundation".

---

5 *Boutin*, 2000, p.17 et seqq.

6 Cf. the description and delimitation of the foundation in Liechtenstein pursuant to OL Art.552 Para.3 PGR: "The judge shall decide in the individual case the extent to which separately administered assets (fund) shall be entitled to independence according to private law or to the character of trust property".

Section 2 Historical Interpretation / History of the Origins of the LFIP

At some point during the evolution of mankind, "man" claimed the right to individual self-awareness, started to focus on his "being", which automatically included the aspect of "*no longer being*", ventured the leap to the Gods – the "immortals" – and finally wrestled with his fate of "being mortal".[7]

By developing a legal system, individualized "man" finally searched for, and created, the tools he needed firstly to realize the symbiosis of his rebellion against mortality and his wish to continue to "rule" even after his death and, in doing so, to continue shaping the history of his family, and secondly to give him the means of making his dreams come true: First of all, he developed the *law of succession* and stipulated as an absolute right *in rem* that "the legal powers of a person, which we know as that person's assets and the sum of which constitutes the wealth of that person, do not dissolve into nothing upon the death of said person".[8]

The transfer of ownership is determined by the law or by the deceased testator. An analysis of history teaches us that the law of succession has its roots in the family in every nation, albeit with differing principles and legal norms.[9]

From a historical perspective, the evolution of the purpose of foundations can be roughly divided into five phases of European foundation law history. These are: pre-Christian ancient times, the middle ages under the influence of Christianity, the trend towards secularization in the late middle and early modern ages, the national codification in the 19th century, and the rediscovery of the foundation in modern times.[10]

Foundations not only played a significant role in the social development of Europe; early foundations emerged in **Egypt** and can still be seen today in various representations of the philosophy behind foundations, such as the "Wakf"

---

7 *Santo-Passo*, p.44.
8 *Santo-Passo*, p.44.
9 Cf. *Santo-Passo*, p.44.
10 Cf. *Schlüter*, p.36.

or "Habous".[11] These were not, however, private foundations – they were aimed at common welfare.

I. Foundation elements in ancient times

The primary element in Roman law was the will (*successio ab intestato* was deemed "undesirably makeshift").[12] One thing is certain: neither the Greeks nor the Romans created the foundation (for private or common benefit) as we know it today. Establishments and independent foundations as they are understood in modern legal terms did not exist in Greek or Roman law. The model of a legal entity was unknown to these legal systems.[13] A model or theoretical legal entity was not an aspect in Roman law. If such a model did exist at all, then only as a model of corporations.[14] Contrary to the definition of the legal entity, Roman law has always known the term of corporation as an association of individuals, where the members can change but the legal identity remains intact in spite of the altered composition.[15]

Pursuant to the **Justinian Code**, for example, institutions existed, which were dedicated to so-called *piae causae* (pious causes); these were generally public charity organizations whose activities are reminiscent of modern-day **common-benefit foundations**.[16] Other charitable institutions in the day of Justinian include the *venerabiles domus*.[17] The legal capacity of both the *piae causae* and the *venerabiles domus* was limited. On the one hand, they were granted proprietary rights, mainly in the form of privileges,[18] which virtually gave them legal entity status. On the other hand, they were comparable to, if not even treated the same as, natural persons.[19] For example, the monks (in a monastery) or the poor

---

11 Cf. *Schlüter*, p.36.

12 *Santo-Passo*, p.45.

13 *Alexander*, Introduction.

14 *Alexander*, p.4.

15 *Kaser*, RP I § 72 I.

16 See *Alexander*, p.9; Cf. also recital 19 Foundations in the middle ages (first paragraph after this heading) in this book.

17 *Alexander*, p.19 et seqq. The Codex Justinianus and the Justinian amendments are the main sources. In the first case, primarily the second and third headings of the first book. The amendments include primarily 7, 120 and 131.

18 *Alexander*, p.23. These institutions were allowed to inherit, they were allowed to accept bequests or entails, they were allowed to sign contracts and rental contracts for a maximum term of 30 years under the law of obligations.

19 *Alexander*, p.20 et seqq.

people (in an almshouse) were required to participate, just as the administrator was required to participate.[20]

In classical times, five institutions existed that demonstrated at least some elements of the concept of legally independent assets:

the *res sacrae*,
the *fiscus*,
the *hereditas iacens*,
the wealth of a prisoner of war, and
the *peculium*.

The purpose in each case remained the *pia causa* (pious cause) and they all demonstrated marked public-law characteristics, even though some of these institutions demonstrated private-law characteristics to a certain extent.[21]

A. Res sacrae

The *res sacrae* are patrimonies that are dedicated to the Gods, although two different interpretations of the scope and application existed at the same time. Accordingly, the wealth in question is the property of the Gods on the one hand, or of the state, on the other. It represents wealth whose application is targeted at, and restricted to, the *usus sacer*, the property of the Deities or Gods and an early form of foundation patrimony.[22]

B. Fiscus

The Imperial *fiscus* is a "subjugating" establishment of the Emperor which basically constituted a legally independent estate.[23] Other authors believe that the

---

20 *Alexander*, p.31.

21 *Alexander*, p.46 et seqq.

22 Cf. *Wenger*, p.63 et seq., Tituli ex corpore, and *Ulpiani*, p.22, 6: Ulpiani describes the ability of Deities to inherit in principle, and, as such, the theoretical possibility of divine property, even if the same is restricted to certain Gods.

23 Cf. *Mitteis/von Bolla/Bonfante*.

term means the person of the Emperor himself.[24] The *populus Romanus* is indicated as the legal subject of the *fiscus* as a third alternative.[25]

C. Hereditas iacens

Literally translated: a "dormant legacy". The *hereditas iacens* constitutes the entire estate left by a deceased Roman. The dormant state of the estate is terminated by the desire of the heirs to appropriate the assets.[26] As such, the assets remain in economic circulation and accessible while at the same time being preserved as a self-contained unit for the heirs. Nevertheless, this cannot be described as a subject position. The *hereditas* only assumes the function or character of a subject to overcome certain practical problems.[27]

D. The wealth of a prisoner of war

The wealth of a prisoner of war is comparable to the *hereditas iacens*. If a Roman citizen was taken prisoner during a war, he became a slave upon capture (*servus hostium*) and therefore lost his legal capacity.[28] He re-acquired all his earlier rights upon his return. His wealth remained in a subjectless state, albeit preserved, until the prisoner of war returned or died.[29] Under certain circumstances, it could be administered by a *curator*, although this was not necessarily the case. Little has changed in this respect in post-classical times.[30]

---

24 Cf. *Kaser* RP I, § 72 III 2.

25 Cf. *Hirschfeld* 1 et seqq. In late classical times, the *ius fisci* occupied a position between the *ius publicum* and the *ius privatum.*

26 Cf. *Kaser* RP I § 174 II 2 and I 2. Roman law distinguishes between family heirs (*sui heredes*) and external heirs (*extranei heredes*) in the transfer of property rights to a deceased's estate. The family heirs assume the position of heirs and, as such, acquire the heritable rights of the testator directly, by operation of law; automatically and therefore without and sometimes even against their own wishes. By contrast, the external heirs acquire the inheritance only after they have performed the act of accepting the inheritance (*adire hereditatem*). Until they do so, the inheritance remains "dormant" (*hereditas iacet*).

27 As a legal subject, representative for a person, Cf. *Alexander*, p.61.

28 Gaius I, 129

29 The death of the prisoner of war is simulated at the time of his capture.

30 Cf. *Alexander*, p.65 et seqq. and 110.

E. Peculium

The *peculium* constituted a special estate. It was placed at the disposal of a slave to allow a certain amount of economic activity. Although it remained part of the master's wealth, it was separate and, as such, independent.[31]

The so-called *ecclesiae* emerged when Christianity gained state recognition as a religion. The Christians' property was supposed to be handed over to the *ecclesiae* in the context of "returning" the wealth with the aim of avoiding the division of the assets belonging to the Christians and preserving the unity of the same. The Bishops quickly gained the sole right to access the various assets, however, which meant that the church congregations were no longer included in the dispositions.[32]

Teachings describe the "victory" of Christianity as the major **turning point in the history of foundation law**.[33] Teachings cite the *arcae*, the dormant corporate wealth in the congregations, as one of the first indicators of this turning point. These *arcae* constituted a corporate special-purpose fund dedicated to charitable tasks in the **Christian congregations**. A certain part, a certain amount of the communal wealth, is separated from the remaining assets and may only be used for the intended purposes.[34]

Dependent foundations[35] already featured in **classic Roman law**,[36] in that a congregation or association was endowed with assets on condition that they be used for a specific purpose.[37] The key element of this variation on the dependent foundation is the congregation to whom the land is assigned. It then leases it back to the founder (and former owner) and uses the interest payments from the latter for specific purposes. Pursuit of the purpose continues even after the founder and tenant has died and can be achieved by the fact that other tenants follow,

---

31 Cf. *Alexander*, p.68.
32 Cf. *Alexander*, p.40 et seq.
33 Cf. *Liermann*, p.24.
34 Cf. *Alexander*, p.115.
35 Cf. below, Section 4.II 5: Types of foundation: Real and fictitious foundations
36 Cf. below Section 4.II Types of foundation: Real and fictitious foundations. The independent foundation is the fundamental opposite of the dependent version, even to this day. Unlike the independent foundation, the dependent foundation is not an autonomous institution in terms of its legal ownership. The assets are bestowed for the purpose of the foundation and assigned to a trustee who administers them in line with the contractually defined purpose. In modern law, the legal relationships between the involved parties are governed solely by the law of obligations.
37 Cf. *Kunkel/Honsell*, p.80.

whose interest payments are again tied to the same specific purpose.[38] The *bona fides* plays an important role in this respect. This institution is the sole means of ensuring that the purpose of the foundation is pursued and achieved. It is also the *bona fides* which suggests the establishment of a **dependent foundation** by means of *fideicommissum*.[39]

The fundamental purpose of the *fideicommissum* is to comply with an informal wish of a testator for the period after his death.[40] This compliance is based solely on moral obligation.[41]

The initial recipients of bequests in ancient times were individual Deities. They were later joined by municipalities and cultic communities. Some time after that, assets were also bequeathed to various different types of corporations, such as private schools. The foundation of educational institutions was later followed by hospitals and hospices, *e.g.* inns for pilgrim travellers. The establishment of these institutions was not just motivated by the desire to promote common benefit; the associated honour of enhancing one's reputation in the public domain also usually played a role.[42] In ancient Roman times, around the 1st and 2nd centuries A.D., Roman towns were granted the right to accept bequests for the first time (thus also permitting foundations).[43]

---

38 Added to which, in the case of endowment to corporate or quasi corporate institutions, there is the risk of failing to achieve the purpose as a result of incorrect conduct by the responsible representatives with regard to the *modus* defined for the attribution (condition). The state and, in particular the *curatores rei* publicae cannot, after all, always perform the task of monitoring the pursuit of the foundation's purpose. Cf. also *Bruck*, p.54.

39 Cf. *Bruck*, p.76.

40 Cf. *Estribí*, p.11. Only Roman citizens could be appointed heirs. If the father of a family (*pater familiae*) wanted to make sure that his non-Roman citizens were taken care of after his death, he would ask a good friend to commit to an agreement (*fideicommissum cum amico*), whereby the friend would distribute pre-defined assets among those specific individuals after the death of the father.

41 Cf. *Alexander*, p.76.

42 The best known institution of this kind is the hospice affiliated to the Temple of Asklepios in Epitauros, which provided some 160 rooms to accommodate travelling pilgrims. Cf. Smith/Borgmann, Foundations in Europe: The Historical Context, in: *Schlüter/Then/Walkenhorst*, Foundations in Europe, p.4.

43 Cf. *Schlüter*, p.37.

II. Foundations in the middle ages

The *pia causa, i.e.* ecclesiastical-religious[44] and social causes, remained the focal purpose of foundations in the middle ages.[45] The principles of **Christian teachings** are motive, content, and justification behind the act of donation. Since ancient Christian times, the belief has held firm that Christ was entitled to a share of an estate and that wills that bequeathed to pious causes (*piae causae*)[46] were not just a basic principle of Christian ideology but were also good for the donor's soul.[47] The fathers of the Christian church had taught that Christians – when determining who should benefit from their wealth after death – should leave part of their estate to ecclesiastical-social causes ("the portion owing to Christ"). In doing so, they could also ensure the well-being of their own immortal souls (*pro salute animae*).[48] Both the specifications in terms of content and the transfer of wealth that formed the basis for pursuing the purpose were closely linked to the organization of the church.[49] The church itself was seen as a "divine foundation" regardless of the faithful in its congregation or care. The bishops were granted the right to monitor the execution of such final wills. If the heirs did not execute the will *ad pias causas*, the local bishop warned them and, if that did not produce the desired result, confiscated the estate in order to execute the will himself.[50]

The **Roman-Catholic church** held fast to the philosophy of dispositions being necessary *pro salute animae* and therefore advocated the permissibility of wills. In the early and high middle ages, such dispositions in favour of the church or the poor were seen to be very closely linked to confession and the receipt of the last sacraments. The church managed to succeed in being awarded responsi-

---

44 Cf. *Seifart/von Campenhausen*, 1999, p.76 ff. The term *piae causae* relates to donations for the following purposes:
Requiems pro salute animae,
To Christ, saints, the church in general or to specific churches, monasteries, hospitals and other ecclesiastical establishments, and to students,
To the poor, widows and other *miserabilies personae*, to poor girls for their dowries, to pay for the freedom of prisoners,
For public utilities (*publica utilitas*), especially for building roads and bridges,
For paying off creditors.

45 Cf. *Boehmer* (1743-54, II, X3, 26 (12)) indicates four groups: the poor, *pro anima, intuitu religionis Christianae, ab utilitatem publicam.*

46 The *piae causae* become the foundation on which the term "charities" is based in common law.

47 Cf. *Horn*, 1968, p.178 et seqq.

48 Cf. *Seifart/von Campenhausen*, 1999, p.73.

49 Cf. *Schlüter*, 2004, p.38.

50 Cf. *Seifart/von Campenhausen*, 1999, p.74.

bility to a lesser or greater extent for the execution of last wills. All issues relating to wills were fundamentally seen as being subject to ecclesiastical jurisdiction. This applied, in particular, to the **English church**. Since the church was fundamentally guided by Roman law in the middle ages, the regulations governing *piae causae* in the Justinian Code remained applicable and further developed in the canonical laws that were forming.[51]

Apart from the organization of these public institutions which were the predecessors of the public foundations, the Germanic legal system applied the principle of "*Primogenitur*" to private law issues (the first-born or oldest son was appointed heir; all other younger lines were excluded). The *family fideicommiss*, which was a form of **house rules for the nobility**,[52] emerged in Continental Europe, based on the "*Majorate*" that had been witnessed in Spain in the 16th century. The middle classes were substantially excluded from this institution. It required the approval of the sovereign, which was usually reserved for the nobility.[53]

The middle ages in England saw the emergence of the "**Trust**", which was based on Salian law.[54]

III. The late middle ages / Early modern times

The late middle ages and early modern times can be seen as the **beginning of secular foundation laws**. Up until the high middle ages, foundation law had substantially developed as part of ecclesiastical and Roman law.[55] The early modern times were characterized by the Reformation and "*Aufklärung*" (enlightenment). Foundation law become more secular, and clerical institutions and property were compulsorily transferred to secular rulers as a result. This did not, however, cause any fundamentally new approach to dealing with the issue of purpose, the *piae causae*,[56] although the purpose did lose its direct reference to the institution of the church and became a form of public welfare organization that was inde-

---

[51] A detailed explanation of the law governing the execution of wills can already be found in the *Speculum Iuris des Durantis* from the 2nd half of the 13th century (in II, part. 2 § 13); individual regulations contain the decrees of Gregor IX (1234) and the Clementines (X 3; Clem.3, 6, 1312). Cf. *Seifart/von Campenhausen*, 1999, p.74.

[52] The royal house of Liechtenstein is still subject to this regulation to this day.

[53] Cf. *Santo-Passo*, 2002, p.45.

[54] Cf. *Santo-Passo*, 2002, p.45.

[55] Cf. *Seifart/von Campenhausen*, 1999, p.80 et seqq.

[56] Cf. *Coing*, §5, recital.34 et seqq.

pendent of the church. The secular establishments were also based on canonical law.[57]

One important milestone in the development of foundations took place towards the end of the middle ages when **foundations in free towns** were established, which were largely **managed by the citizens**. The emergence of new foundations in this form, which were independent of the church, were managed by laypersons and monitored by the municipal authorities and, in particular, the town council.[58] Common-benefit foundations along these lines were set up in Nuremberg (1522), Strasbourg (1523), Mons (1525) and Lille (1527). Town dignitaries or municipal boards assumed responsibility for managing the foundations that pursued charitable goals for the benefit of the general public and especially of the town's poor and sick; at the same time, the governing bodies of the town strived to set themselves up as a supervisory authority for the foundations.[59] In some towns, such as Florence (Statutes of 1415), the town authorities centralized and made themselves responsible for the administration of all foundations[60] Further donors frequently added to the foundations as long as the municipal authorities contained their influence within boundaries. The Frankfurt **Reformation** in 1509 stipulates that trustees who administer foundations must present accounts to the town council.[61]

This development did not, however, result in any basic legislation; instead it emerged through the customary approaches of the donors to drafting their wills and through the administrative practice of the towns. The donors no longer just transferred land, capital assets and annuities straight to the church or ecclesiastical organizations. Instead they appointed executors (trustees) – who were frequently laypersons – and charged them with donating the income to the *piae causae*.[62]

The territorial states that were slowly forming followed the example of the towns and tried to take over the supervisory function for the foundations and to centralize existing institutions. This development was particularly prevalent in those countries that joined the Reformation.[63] In some cases, however, the church property (not just foundation assets but also assets belonging to dissolved monasteries) was used to create **major new secular foundations**; one prime example of this is the organization of the Chamber of Monasteries ("*Klosterkam-*

---

57 Cf. *Seifart/von Campenhausen*, 1999, p.80.
58 Cf. *Liermann*, 1963, p.169-229.
59 Cf. *Schlüter*, 2004, p.38 et seqq.
60 Cf. *Liermann*, 1963, I, p.127.
61 Cf. *Liermann*, 1963, I, p.131.
62 Cf. *Seifart/von Campenhausen*, 1999, p.80.
63 Cf. *Seifart/von Campenhausen*, 1999, p.81.

mer") in Braunschweig – Lüneburg. Meanwhile, this overall trend towards secular administration was no longer restricted to the Protestant countries; it was becoming increasingly noticeable in Catholic territories as well. The state authorities were taking over the authority of the church; a development that became official in the German Empire when the Imperial Police Ordinance ("*Reichspolizeiordnung*") came into force in 1577. The common law regulations stipulated that the sovereign was responsible for **establishing independent foundations**.[64]

These trends were legalized in **England** in the **Charities Act** of 1601.[65]

The dominance of the state and emphasis of centralized power in France were based on a claim of monopoly, which assigned all tasks aimed at benefiting the general public to the state whilst allowing a certain amount of private activity that was, however, closely monitored by the state. This development was substantially hindered by the restrictions placed on the rights of foundations and the ban on the establishment of new foundations during the reigns of Louis XIV (1638 - 1715) and Louis XV (1715 - 1774). Even the **French Revolution** did not produce any changes towards a liberalization of foundation law.[66] Quite the opposite: The restrictions placed on the *corps intermédiaires* between the people and the state as a threat to freedom were tightened further, to the detriment of foundations. Commercial and trade corporations were dissolved and any new formations banned by the *Le Chapellier Act* of 1791.[67] At the same time, the state started confiscating the foundations, which virtually eliminated the system of foundations in France.[68]

In the wake of enlightenment and liberalism, the family fideicommiss also encountered massive criticism and resistance in the 18th and 19th centuries. It was not even incorporated into the **Code Napoléon** since the authors had difficulties with this old-established benefit for the nobility in times of Liberté and Egalité. Instead, it was replaced by a new legal instrument – the "legal entity". Among the pioneers in this respect were Carl Friedrich von Savigny (1779-1861) and Otto von Gierke (1841-1921) who separated legal entities into corporations as associations of individuals, foundations as independent special-purpose funds, and establishments as independent special-purpose funds.[69]

64 Cf. *Seifart/von Campenhausen*, 1999, p.81.
65 Cf. *Seifart/von Campenhausen*, 1999, p.81.
66 Cf. *Schlüter*, 2004, p.40.
67 Cf. *Horn*, 1986, p.3190 et seq.
68 Cf. *Smith/Borgmann*, 2001, p.25.
69 Cf. *Santo-Passo*, 2002, p.45 et seqq.

Two ideas, in particular, emerged during this period:[70] Up until then, foundations had primarily been seen in conjunction with the promotion of religious causes and, as such, in connection with church institutions. Now, however, focus was shifting to secular causes. In his *Ecclesiasticcum protestantium* Protestant canonist Justus Henning Boehmer opined that donations to *pias causas* for the purpose of encouraging the Christian religion were, in practice, usually "*superstitiosae*". Donations for use in the *utilitas publica* were more useful as they benefited so many people. Boehmer particularly mentioned the workhouses and almshouses in this respect. The *utilitas publica* is not, however, just restricted to establishments such as these. Education and science are also being promoted (*e.g.* Franke Foundations in Halle, 1692 and the Senckenberg Foundation in Frankfurt a. M., 1763).

The "***Aufklärung***" was also not favourably disposed towards common-benefit foundations. The state should be responsible for any work that needed doing for the common benefit. As a result, **independent foundations** required a state permit (privilege) as "*collegia*", which regularly also specified the organization of the foundation. In addition they were subjected to close state supervision. This idea is particularly reflected in the regulations in the Prussian Statute Book (ALR) of 1794.

IV. Foundations in the 19th century

As the **modern national states** emerged, foundation laws started to diverge. Until then they had been largely standardized under the binding influence of the church. This trend was clearly visible in respect of the definition of the purpose of a public foundation. The majority of national regulations continued the tradition of classifying foundations as an instrument of private commitment to the common good. In other legal orders, the definition of defined categories of purpose was abolished. Foundations evolved into legal instruments. Although they still adhered to the definition of a relationship between the assets and the purpose, the restriction on purpose was lifted to the extent that only a negative delimitation defined which purposes were excluded on grounds of non-compliance with the legal order.[71]

Although **France** tried to **revive and widen the reach of its foundations** over the course of the 19th century, the continuing restrictions on permits and the

70 Cf. *Seifart/von Campenhausen*, 1999, p.81.
71 Cf. *Schlüter*, 2004, p.39 et seqq.

large extent to which the state exercised influence on the activities of the foundations prevented an independent system of foundations from emerging.[72]

By contrast, developments in **Germany** took a different course with the emergence of a concept that to this day forms the focus of discussions – the all-purpose foundation that conforms with the common good, whereby conformity with the common good did not relate to a specific purpose aimed at benefiting the general public but rather was aimed at excluding by means of negative delimitation those foundations that contravened the interests of the general public.[73] The recognition of foundations as legal entities became more widespread in both legal teachings [74] and legislation. Baden was the first to **codify the foundation** by means of an Act passed in 1870, which permitted **family foundations**, in addition to foundations that served public causes.[75] One of the characteristics of the **liberal constitutional state in the 19th century** was the freedom enjoyed by donors in Germany to define the purpose of their foundations; the definition of the foundation's purposes constituted a discharge of property and was free of any state restrictions.[76] The distinction between corporations and foundations was defined anew, both in Germany and Switzerland.[77] The new definition also played a role in the legislation of the 19th century, for example, by forming the basis for Bluntschli's "**Code of Private-Law Statutes for the Canton of Zurich**" (1854-1856) and for Saxony's law on legal entities dated 15 June 1868.[78]

Around the turn of the century, **Switzerland** banned the fideicommiss (Art. 335 Para. 2 ZGB) and permitted foundations only to support destitute members of the family or to provide dowries, in addition to the idealistic purpose.[79] The country was nevertheless a **pioneer in terms of foundation law** as it implemented the first German-language codification of foundation law in 1853,

---

72 Cf. *Schlüter*, 2004, p.40.

73 As such, this criterion should only be interpreted as a general statutory reservation according to the opinion prevailing today in: *Seifart/von Campenhausen*, 1999, § 8, recital 56.

74 The so-called Städel case was the starting point: In his will, J.F. Städel, a Frankfurt merchant, had left his estate to a foundation that had not yet been established; his family claimed that they were entitled to the inheritance since a legal entity in the shape of a foundation did not exist as an heir at the time of death; the case triggered widespread discussion about the nature of a legal entity, details of which are explained in *Richter/Germann*, 1998, pp.427, 430.

75 Pursuant to §36 of this Act. Cf. *von Campenhausen*, 1998, p.40.

76 Cf. *Schlüter*, 2004, p.41.

77 Cf. *Seifart/von Campenhausen*, 1999, p.82.

78 Law and Ordnance Gazette for the Kingdom of Saxony 1868, p.315-330.

79 Cf. *Santo-Passo*, 2002, p.45 et seqq.

in the Canton of Zurich.[80] The Zurich Act permitted the **establishment of a foundation vested with legal capacity** by means of legal transactions between living individuals and by means of wills, a state permit was not needed although the foundation was subject to overall supervision by a state or municipal authority.[81]

Austria's laws provided for foundations for common-benefit, charitable causes and/or "intangible" family foundations for emergencies or "mixed" foundations for family members as beneficiaries, in addition to the definition of general purposes (§ 2 BSTFG). The lack of any real significance that was afforded to foundations at this point in time was, however, visible upon closer analysis of the ABGB, which was passed in 1812 and only devotes 2 paragraphs to foundations (§26 and §646).[82]

Unlike the states on the Continent, legal developments relating to foundation purposes were much more consistent in **England** – and, on the same basis, in the **United States** as well. This continuity was visible both in the form and the purposes of the institution. The legal form of the *trust* formed the basis for establishment, while the common-benefit purposes were clearly defined. The rights of common-benefit foundations are based on the *Charitable Uses Act 1601*. This regulation that came into force in 1601 still forms a central element of English and US-American foundation laws to this day.[83]

V. Foundations in modern times

Discussions in **France** at the end of the 20th century resulted in a codification of foundation law and to the introduction of **corporate foundations**, a form of charitable commitment for business enterprises that had been unknown until then.[84] Foundations were expressly recognized for the first time by the French Act of 23 July 1987.[85]

Foundation law was also reformed in **Italy** when the banks were converted into common-benefit foundations, the system of concessions was replaced by a

80 Cf. *Künzle*, 2002., p.1.
81 Cf. *Seifart/von Campenhausen*, 1999, p.83.
82 Cf. *Santo-Passo*, 2002, p.45 et seqq.
83 Cf. the ruling on Income Tax Special Purposes Commissioners v. Pemsel (1891) A.C. 531, 583, together with further details explained in *Schlüter*, 2004, p.41 et seqq.
84 With regard to the suggestions for reform: Conseil d'État, Rendre plus attractif le droit des fondations, p.133 et seqq.
85 Cf. *Schlüter*, 2004, p.94; *Loi No. 87-571 du 23 Julliet 1987 sur le développment du mécénat*, Text from Allard, Les Fondations, Guide pratique et juridique, p.125 et seqq.

system of normative regulations and the emergence of **joint foundations** which were based on the involvement of several donors provided new momentum.[86]

The Principality of **Liechtenstein**, whose legal system was largely defined by **Austria**, was the only country in which the family fideicommiss survived; new regulations for this institution were defined in Section 4/Title 14 (Art. 829-833) when Liechtenstein drew up its own new Persons and Companies Act (PGR) in 1926. However, the degree of significance that the author attached to the institution of the family fideicommiss is visible from the number of legal norms – a total of 5 articles.[87] In the same year, the small country also stipulated a form for **private foundations** (family foundations), which has proven to be the **optimum legal institution** for resolving succession in the case of private estates.[88]

A possible harmonization of foundation law in the **European Union**[89] is the central issue that foundations face in the future.[90] A project conducted by the Hamburg-based Max Planck Institute for foreign and international private law compared the legal aspects of the foundation laws prevailing in the EU member states, Switzerland, Liechtenstein, the USA and eastern European countries in order to identify a possible approach to reforming or harmonizing[91] foundation law within the EU. Based on its comparison of the legal structures, the project aims to develop a **European Foundation**[92] along the lines of the European joint stock corporation. The legal comparison, which was commissioned in 1997 by the EU

---

86 Cf. *Schlüter*, 2004, p.42.

87 *Santo-Passo*, 2002, p.46.

88 To this day, some 100,000 registered private foundations are assumed to exist. Since they are not entered in the Public Registry, it only possible to glean the exact number from the tax income that is published by the Liechtenstein tax authorities, based on the assumption that these tax-privileged foundations take advantage of the tax privilege and only pay the annual tax of 1,000 Swiss Francs.

89 Based on Art. 95 and 308 EU Treaty.

90 Cf. *von Hippel*, p.32.

91 This European Foundation project is being conducted in collaboration with the Institute for Foundation Law at Bucerius Law School, Hamburg, under the leadership of Prof.Peter Rawert and Prof.Rainer Walz, and with the support of further institutions, such as the Bertelsmann and Zeit Foundations, Compagnia di SanPaolo and the European Foundation Centre. Cf. *von Hippel*, p.33.

92 Cf. the preamble in the planned EU Directive "This model law for the **European Foundation** is intended to promote Foundations in Europe (especially within the European Union). European Foundations shall exemplify generally accepted best practice in their activities and administration, especially in following high accountability standards and serving the public interest and therefore benefit from a favourable tax status, especially for cross border relationships."

Commission,[93] reveals a need for action within the EU. And yet even trying to start harmonizing the codification of foundation law is proving to be difficult, not least because private-law foundations can pursue causes that differ totally from each other. By the same token, other types of foundations exist alongside private foundations throughout Europe – common-benefit, family, corporate, and joint foundations, to name just some.[94] Trying to capture this confusing diversity of foundation types in a harmonized legal context throughout Europe would seem to be difficult.[95] It raises problems in terms of both legal comparability and the desired EU harmonization. [96]

93 Cf. memorandum by the EU Commission dated 06.06.1997 on the promotion of common-benefit associations and foundations in Europe, p.241.

94 Cf. Rawert, p.115.

95 Even at a level within the EU states. In Germany, for example, the federal states are responsible for foundation law, and the German federal legislator only has restricted legislative powers pursuant to Art.70 Para.1 Basic Constitutional Law. As such, following its modernization, the German Civil Code (BGB) only provides rudimentary regulations governing private foundations and refers to the foundation laws enacted by the German federal states. Cf. *Andrick/Sauerbaum*, p.256 et seqq.

96 Cf. permanently updated information on the website of the European Foundation Centre: www.efc.be (the planned Directive is currently in its third draft).

Section 3 Systematic Interpretation / The Incorporation of the LFIP into Panama's Legal System

The foundation is an institution that is affected by various fields of law. In certain aspects, it is affected by civil law,[97] family law,[98] tax law,[99] international private law[100] and international criminal law.[101]

The private foundation is rooted in Panama's Constitution (Constitución Nacional), where Article 39 permits and recognizes the establishment of legal entities (companies, associations and foundations) which do not contravene the law or are immoral. Associations that are inspired by the ideology and theory of the superiority of a single race or ethnic group are not recognized.[102]

I. Foundations and family law

Panama's new family law[103] from 1994 (Código de la Familia) mentions Articles 84, 85, 88, 92, 94, and 98 in conjunction with foundations, together with Articles 10 and 11 from the Section on international family law.

---

97 Subsidiary application of civil law; the function and administration of the Foundation Council, the Foundation Charter and other documents, the regulations for gifting assets to the foundation.

98 The name "family foundation" already implies that the foundation in question relates to family estates, family members, the regulation of successors, etc.

99 Foundations enjoy special benefits in the tax system.

100 Extraterritorial impacts of the foundation and associated recognition of the foundation abroad.

101 In conjunction with tax evasion and money laundering. Which forms the subject of various international treaties.

102 Cf. Moreno, p.24. The original wording of Art. 39 in the Constitution is as follows: "Es permitido formar companías, asociaciones y fundaciones que no sean contrarias a la moral o al orden legal, las cuales pueden obtener su reconocimiento como personas jurídicas. No se otorgará reconocimiento a las asociaciones inspiradas en ideas o teorías basadas en la pretendida superioridad de una raza o de grupo étnico, o que justifiquen o promuevan la discriminación racial."

103 Law. No. 3 dated 27 April 1994, Código de la Familia.

The assets of a family should unite with the assets of a foundation in cases where the law provides for enhanced privileges and enhanced protection (of the assets) when creating a legal entity. This can be interpreted as an invasion of foundation regulations into family law, or as a harmonization between the two legal fields. The issue is therefore a subsidiary application of foundation law wherever endowments or family assets require protection.[104]

The foundation therefore constitutes a reaction to such legislation that does not satisfactorily govern the protection of the family from various perspectives. This shows that the institution of the foundation is of strong social significance and does not serve the purely economic purposes that are so often unfortunately claimed.

II. Foundations and international private law

Recognition of foreign foundations

Both the Foundation Act, in Art.28 – 36 LFIP, and Panama's Trust Act[105] contain norms from international private law. These norms primarily govern the recognition of foreign foundations in Panama and vice-versa. Art.28 LFIP stipulates that foundations which are established in a legally valid form and compliant with a foreign law must be recognized by the LFIP and, in consequence, can adhere to the dispositions of the Foundation Act.

Art.28 LFIP does not define the fields of law and jurisdictions to which this stipulation of recognition refers. No restrictions are placed on the jurisdictions. The regulation governing recognition is of a general nature. The foundation in question can be a Liechtenstein foundation or a foundation that is equivalent to a Liechtenstein foundation. This Article leads us to the principle of continuity or redomiciliation, or to the principle of change of domicile and change of jurisdiction, which result in a change of the applicable laws as a consequence of the "change in nationality" of the foundation.

---

104 This is the case, for example, when minors need protection or when the family unit as such, or the cohesion of the family, requires support.

105 Law No. 1 dated 5 January 1984, La Ley de Fideicomisos

In cases where the domicile is changed pursuant to Art.28 LFIP, all of the responsibilities, rights and obligations that applied prior to the change in jurisdiction remain in force, as do any court actions instigated against these foreign foundations or pending court actions initiated by these foundations abroad. Pursuant to Art.31 LFIP, such rights and obligations are not affected by the change in jurisdiction.

Art.28 LFIP is inconceivable without Art.29 LFIP, which stipulates the following: Foundations that wish to change their domicile must present a resolution adopted by the responsible governing bodies. Such a resolution must contain the following:

Name of the foundation and date of its establishment.
Details of the registration, excerpt from the commercial register in the country of origin.
Declaration containing the explicit desire to continue the legal existence of the foundation as a Panamanian foundation.
All of the formalities required to establish a foundation.

In addition to these formalities, the following documents must also be enclosed:[106]

A copy of the formation deed, which must explicitly include the desire for continuity in Panama, together with any amendments.
A power of attorney granted to a Panamanian lawyer who has been engaged to perform the transaction.

Finally, the foundation is entered in the Public Registry, in the Section for

Private Foundations ("Sección de Fundaciones de Interés Privado").[107]

The change of domicile must, of course, also be permissible in the country of origin as it would otherwise be out of the question.

A distinction must be made between the continuation under these conditions and the liquidation of a foundation. The change of domicile of a foundation does not constitute its liquidation. This means that the responsibility of the Foundation

106 Cf. Art. 30 LFIP.
107 Cf. Art. 33 LFIP.

Council or any other individuals who acted on behalf of the foundation is not rescinded. Equally, any legal action pending against the foundation remains in force. This is regulated in Art.31 LFIP: Both the acquired responsibilities, rights and obligations of the foundation and any court proceedings instigated against the foundation or by the foundation itself, remain in force despite a change of domicile or jurisdiction, without these rights and obligations being affected by the change of legal norms.

The issue of a change in domicile is linked to the principle of autonomy of will, to the principle of the freedom to choose the jurisdiction. This autonomy of will is specified in Art.32 LFIP: Foundations established in compliance with the Foundation Act can be moved or placed under other laws or jurisdictions, together with the wealth that constitutes their assets, on condition that such action is provided for by the formation deed or Bylaws of the foundation. This means that a Panamanian foundation can subject the regulation of its internal relationships and administrative activities (*e.g.* by the Foundation Council, the Protector and/or the beneficiaries) to a foreign legislation, together with its assets, if applicable.

As such, two fundamental aspects are addressed: the will to move to a different jurisdiction, and the legal recognition on the part of both jurisdictions and the associated subjecting of the foundation to the new legal regime. This again shows the similarity between foundations and trusts, which can also freely choose "their" legal system. This tolerance towards foreign laws is one of the major advantages of the Panamanian foundation. One caveat does, however, exist in regard to the choice of jurisdiction: The exception based on Art.6 of the Civil Code (Código Civil), whereby conflicts arising in conjunction with real estate located in Panama are always governed by Panamanian law in line with the principle of "*lex rei sitae*".

Let us remain on the subject of conflicts and the international regulation of the same in conjunction with the principle of autonomy of will and with regard to the jurisdiction resp. the authority to exercise jurisdiction. Art.36 LFIP stipulates that any and all conflicts for which the procedure is not specifically defined in the Foundation Act must be resolved in general court proceedings and according to subsidiary legal norms.

In addition, the formation deed or Bylaws can specify that all disputes can be resolved by a court of arbitration or by arbitrators.[108]

[108] The stipulation of this arbitration can be institutionalized or it can be chosen on an "ad hoc" basis that is subject to defined criteria. In doing so, any nature of ruling can emerge as long as it is, of course, not illegal.

The rules of procedure that are binding for the arbitration court or the arbitrators can be stipulated *mutatis mutandis*. The guidelines issued by public and well-known arbitration centres[109] are often used as role models, as are international treaties, such as the Panama Convention from 1975[110] or the New York Convention from 1958, which was ratified by Panama in 1983. The benefits of an arbitration court lie in its separation from general, proper, customary state jurisdiction, together with its flexibility, specialization, and the confidentiality that is often demanded by the involved parties. If the Foundation Charter or Bylaws do not contain any relevant stipulations, the norms of the Civil Code (Código Civil) apply.[111]

III. Foundations and international criminal law

Art.34 LFIP contains norms that regulate the unjustified and unlawful use of a private foundation. To avoid any possible criminal offences, their function is subject to all of the legal norms contained in Government Ruling No. 468 from 1994 together with any and all other norms aimed at combating money laundering.

Art.34 LFIP permits the use, not just of national legal norms but also of international treaties relating to this field, irrespective of whether these are unilateral, multilateral[112] or of a regional nature.[113]

IV. The foundation compared with a Panamanian joint stock corporation and a fideicomiso (TRUST)

Panamanian joint stock corporation

Panamanian joint stock corporations came into being with the enactment of Law No. 32: 'La Ley de la Sociedad Anónima' in 1927. A joint stock corporation con-

---

109 Arbitration centres at the International Chamber of Commerce in Paris or the International Arbitration Centre in Stockholm.

110 Convención de Panamá governs arbitration issues in the Latin American region.

111 The criterion that determines the responsible court is the domicile or registered office of the legal entity. This is defined as the place where the administration is controlled and management and is therefore the seat of the Foundation Council in the case of Panamanian foundations.

112 Such as the Vienna Convention of 1988.

113 Such as the treaty between Panama and the United States. Cf. 'Mutual Assistance Treaty in Penal Cases' (TALM) from 1991.

stitutes a contract that becomes effective vis-à-vis third parties upon its creation, *i.e.* its incorporation, whereas pursuant to Art.4 LFIP a foundation constitutes a unilateral act of free will by the founder.

A joint stock corporation issues shares which serve to determine who can exercise control over, or who holds title to, the company. A foundation does not issue shares; the control and procedure for exercising control are defined in the Foundation Charter or the Bylaws. A foundation does not have owners or shareholders. Once the founder has established the foundation, that founder parts company with his assets pursuant to Art.10 LFIP. The beneficiaries do not hold any rights of ownership either, pursuant to Art.18 Para.4 LFIP they are only entitled to make claims on the foundation.

A joint stock corporation pursues a commercial objective,[114] whereas a private foundation attempts to give its assets a specific purpose. Pursuant to Art.3 LFIP, private foundations are banned from pursuing any form of commercial purpose.

A joint stock corporation is governed by commercial law. A foundation is subject to civil law pursuant to Art.2 LFIP.

Panamanian trust

As is also the case in Liechtenstein, Panama allows the legal institution of the Anglo-Saxon trust, which demonstrates huge parallelisms to the foundation.

The option of setting up trusts of an Anglo-Saxon nature in Liechtenstein has given the Principality of Liechtenstein a leading edge over the rest of Continental Europe since 1926. The wealth provided by the founder of a trust is administered by a trustee in the country of domicile on behalf of either the trustor or his beneficiaries. These trusts become legal entities in their own right without having to be entered in Liechtenstein's Public Register. In addition, the laws of a different country can be specified when setting up the trust.[115]

The Republic of Panama legally defined the Trust, 'El Fideicomiso' in 1984.[116]

Pursuant to this Law, the Trust constitutes a contract (Trust Deed) pursuant to which the settlor (el fideicomitente) transfers title to his assets to the trustee (el

[114] Its aim is to generate as much economic profit as possible, which is then distributed among the shareholders.
[115] Cf. Art. 931 PGR, and *Lazard*, 2003, p.13.
[116] Law No. 1 of 1984, La Ley de Fideicomisos.

fiduciario) so that the latter can administer the same for the benefit of certain beneficiaries (los fideicomisarios, los beneficiarios) or the settlor himself.

A trust is not a legal entity; it is merely a specific agreement between the settlor and the trustee. By contrast, the foundation is indeed a legal entity with all the specific characteristics of a legal entity (capital, governing bodies, etc.). As such, it can enter into obligations towards third parties or agree other contracts directly on its own behalf and at its own risk.

Unlike a foundation, a trust does not require entry in the commercial register in Panama since the contract only governs special assets that are administered by the trustee. By contrast, a foundation must be entered in the Public Registry pursuant to Art.4 LFIP and it is this registration that produces the required constitutive effect.

Nevertheless, the two legal institutions have much in common: The same assets can be used as the object for both institutions. The motives behind establishing and founding the two institutions are the same, and they pursue the same purpose. Both are secretive and very confidential by nature. Both the foundation and the trust constitute an instrument for tax planning purposes[117] and for protecting assets.

Both institutions are intended to preserve the assets (conservación). And, last but not least, both can be set up inter vivos or mortis causa.

The fact that the trust is much more diversified than the foundation is worth mentioning in that as many trusts can exist as purposes are conceivable. The settlor and the founder also resemble each other to a certain extent; both have expressed the will to endow their assets to an institution for a specific, usually family-related, purpose and, in doing so, to part company with their wealth. As already mentioned, the assets in question are independent – the trustee holds legal title in the one instance, whereas they constitute the capital assets of the foundation in the other.[118]

---

[117] A trust does not pay any taxes in Panama; a foundation pays an annual tax of USD 150.

[118] The foundation holds title to the endowed assets as a legal entity. The Foundation Council has no rights of ownership; it is bound by the statutes and bylaws. In the case of a trust, the trustee is also bound – by the trust deed and the letter of wishes – although he holds title.

Section 4 Basic principles of the LFIP

A private foundation can serve any number of interests. It is an instrument that can be used for tax planning, asset management, asset protection and estate planning purposes.[119]

Private foundations are usually set up for the following purposes:[120]

- Separating the foundation's assets from the founder's wealth, holding and administering the founder's wealth, simplifying the beneficial utilization of the assets, protecting against the assets being broken up.
- Ensuring compliance with the wishes of the founder in respect of the investment of his wealth.
- Private investments.
- Investments in companies.
- Succession planning and business protection, avoidance of complications caused by deaths in the family, protection against profligate heirs and their creditors.
- Avoidance of creditor recourse.
- Possibility of exemption from and/or minimization of inheritance tax, income tax, capital gains tax, wealth tax.
- Statute of limitations on challenges to foundations following an endowment:[121]
- by individuals with entitlement to a statutory share of the inheritance
- by creditors of the founder
- Compensating deficits in state activities, protection against political instability.
- Pursuit of long-term objectives.
- The founder can ensure that he is remembered after his death.

---

119 *Clauss/Blockwitz*, 2003, p.1; *Häusler*, 2003, p.119.

120 Cf. *Künzle*, 2002, p.5.; Cf. also *Hoop*, 2002, p.67 and 71.

121 Thwarted, on the one hand, because the assets of the foundation were attributed to the founder and, on the other hand, because limitation periods do not commence.

I. Definition of the term "Foundation"

Literally translated, La Fundación de Interés Privado is a "foundation of private interest". Private foundations are governed by Law No. 25 dated 12 June 1995 (La Ley No. 25/95 por la cual se regulan las fundaciones de interés privado, LFIP 25/95). The Notes pertaining to the Law also refer to the law governing trusts (LF), the Civil Code (CC) and the Commercial Code (CCom).[122]

The Panamanian Foundation Act provides the following definition of a foundation: "For such purpose, it shall be required the **endowment of a patrimony** for the **purposes** expressly provided in the Foundation Charter".[123]

This wording permits a **very broad definition** of foundations.[124] The subsequent Art.2 LFIP does, however, immediately and explicitly exclude public foundations.[125]

---

[122] Cf. Boutin, 2000, p.18.

[123] Art.1 Para.2 LFIP. In addition, the first paragraph in Art.1 LFIP stipulates that one or several natural persons or legal entities may set up a foundation on their own behalf or on behalf of others in conformity with the provisions of the Foundation Act.

[124] It extends farther than the laws in **Liechtenstein**, where OLArt.552 Para.1 PGR and NLArt.552 §1 Para.1 PGR regulate the definition and delimitation and at the same time classify foundations as real and fictitious, independent and dependent. A **real** foundation can be defined as an independent legal entity to whom the founder transfers title to assets for a specific purpose. (Cf. *Künzle*, 2002, p.14; Cf. *Quaderer*, 1999, p.53.) This (real) type of foundation is frequently classified as a legal entity and established in Liechtenstein. A **fictitious** foundation is defined in OLArt.552 Para.2 PGR as an endowment of assets without legal character. Prof. Dr. Karl Kohlegger (former President of the FL OGH) has the following to say about Liechtenstein foundations: "Legislation in Liechtenstein wanted to use the foundation to provide a legal institution which, on the one hand, supported the philosophy that people at the height of their creativity could reserve part of their wealth for special purposes, which could include providing security for family members against the vicissitudes of life, supporting common-benefit or charitable causes, or ensuring that the name and activities of the founder continued to be linked with charitable deeds and institutions even after his death". (*Santo-Passo*, 2002, p.47; *Kohlegger*, 1990, p.60.)
Under **Swiss** law, a foundation is an establishment. It is distinct from a company (an association of individuals) and is not defined by law. From the wording of Art.80 ZGB it is possible to derive that the (private-law) establishment is a special-purpose fund with its own legal character, which resembles the definition of a (private-law) foundation. In the context of the same Article (Art.80 et seqq. ZGB), a foundation is seen as a patrimony that is defined by an individual for a permanent purpose that is stipulated by the same individual in such a way that the patrimony is separated from the legal rights of the founder and assumes it own legal identity. (Cf. *Künzle*, 2002, p.5 and 6; *Sprecher/von Salis-Lütolf*, 1999, NO. 1 and 3; Cf. *Riemer*, 1981, Syst. Part N 13 and 15).

As is also the case in Liechtenstein,[126] Panamanian[127] teaching offers different definitions of a foundation. The following definition of a foundation would seem to be most expedient in respect of Panamanian foundation law:

A foundation is a patrimony endowed by one or several natural persons or legal entities – the "founder(s)" – for a specific purpose. As a result of the endowment, the patrimony – known as the "foundation assets" – acquires independence. Its administration is entrusted to an executive body – the "Foundation

---

According to the statutory definition in **Austrian** law, a private foundation is deemed to be a legal body to which the founder has endowed assets that are used, administered and utilized to perform a permissible purpose that is defined by the founder. The private foundation is an estate without an owner; it has no shareholders, participants, owners nor does it confer property rights of any nature. (Cf. *Eiselberg*, 2002, p.166.)

German legislation has not statutorily defined or protected the term 'foundation'. Closer inspection reveals that different definitions are used for 'foundations' in German discussions: a generic term that encompasses several different legal forms that call themselves 'foundation' and a more closely defined term that refers to the BGB foundation with legal capacity. The more closely defined term 'foundation' is initially characterized by §§80 et seqq. BGB and thus restricted to a specific legal form that is described as a legally independent special estate. (Cf. *Soergel/Neuhof*, 2000, §80 BGB recital 1 et seqq., *von Hippel*, 2002, p.22 et seqq.) According to the Federal Association of German Foundations (*Bundesverband Deutscher Stiftungen*), 2001, p. IX, "foundations" – in the broad sense of the word – are all organizations that call themselves 'foundations', irrespective of their actual legal form. A civil-law foundation reflects the statutory concept of foundations. As already mentioned, it is not statutorily defined but is generally understood to be an organization with legal capacity, which does not comprise an association of individuals, and which pursues specific purposes defined by means of a foundation transaction with the help of patrimony which has been permanently endowed to it.

As already mentioned in the historical development of the **French** legal system, a system of foundations is still extremely underdeveloped in this country. Pursuant to Art.18 Para.1 of the Act dated 23 July 1987, a foundation is deemed to be the legal act of one or several natural persons or legal entities irrevocably donating property, rights or other assets for a non-commercial pupose that is in the interests of the general public. Cf. *Schlüter*, 2004, p.96; *Loi No. 87-571 du 23 Juillet 1987 sur le développement du mécénat*, Text from Allard, Les Fondations, Guide pratique et juridique, S.125 et seqq.)

As is also the case with the French and German systems, **Italian** law organizes foundations in the form of private-law legal entities. Pursuant to Italian law, foundations are independent organizations that are endowed with their own assets for the purpose of pursuing an independent cause. The definition of the foundation in the *Codice Civile* does not restrict the purposes of a foundation to purely common-benefit causes. Nevertheless, the use of a foundation to pursue private-benefit purposes is excluded, according to general opinion. (Cf. *Galgano*, Le associazione, le fondazioni, i comitati, 1996, p.185 et seqq., *Barbetta*, 1999, p.200, *Rescigno*, 1989, p.490 et seqq., *de Giorgi*, 2001, p.386.)

Council" – for the purpose of ensuring compliance with the intentions of the founder – the founder's wishes – for the benefit of one or several natural persons or legal entities – the "beneficiaries". In order to acquire legal character, it must be entered in the Panamanian Foundation Register using a Foundation Deed as defined by the provisions of the LFIP Law.

In **Anglo-Saxon** circles, a foundation is a common-benefit institution that is endowed with its own assets and which uses the income from these assets to pursue a specific (common-benefit) purpose. The historical concept for the endowment of wealth for a specific purpose is based on the *trust*. To this day, many foundations are organized in line with this legal form. The forms in which a *trust* are used, however, extend far beyond the structural objectives of a public foundation. Cf. *Siederer*, 2002, p.40 et seq., *Jones*, 1998, p.173 et seqq., *Brauch*, 2001, p.27 et seqq.) The **future EU Foundation** of the European Union shall only be used for charitable purposes and shall be defined as following in Art.1, Sub-Title 1.1: "European foundations are separate and independently managed entities with their own management bodies; they are endowed with irrevocable assets, rights or other means of generating income, they do not have any members and they serve a public, charitable purpose". Sub-Title 1.2. then goes on to list the purposes that are deemed to be 'public, charitable'. (Cf. *European Foundation Project*, 2004, Part 1, Title 1, Sub-Title 1.1. and 1.2.).

[125] Art.2 LFIP: "**Delimitation** of private foundations vis-à-vis traditional common-benefit and charitable foundations and vis-à-vis public foundations:
Private foundations shall be governed by the Foundation Charter and its regulations, as well as by the provisions of this law and other applicable legal and regulatory provisions.
The provisions of Title II, Book I of the Civil Code shall **not** apply to private foundations".

[126] Rolf Santo-Passo sees a foundation as an independent legal entity whose purpose is to pursue a clearly defined cause using the assets endowed by the founder; such assets to be administered by the Foundation Council for that specific purpose and on behalf of the beneficiaries. (Cf. *Santo-Passo*, 2002, p.48.)
In his work "Tolley's Tax Havens", Eugen Heeb describes the foundation as "a fund which has been endorsed for a specific purpose and acquires an independent legal status". (Cf. *Heeb*, 1990, p.336.)
Markus Wanger takes a more restricted view of private foundations in that he sees them as a legal entity or a fictitious corporation under the control of the law whose purpose is to pursue a specific defined cause. (Cf. *Wanger* 1993, p.60)
At the conference in Geneva ("Hot Topics in the World of Trusts", which took place on 14 November 1994), Herbert Oberhuber described them quite simply as an "autonomous fund with legal character" or "a patrimony organized as a corporate body" or a "special-purpose fund elevated to the status of a legal entity". The assets which are earmarked for a specific purpose become independent and acquire their own legal character. These independent assets no longer form part of the private wealth of the founder and, instead, form the assets of a separate legal entity – the foundation. The foundation exists solely to implement the wishes of the founder as defined in the Foundation Charter and the bylaws. In order to implement the wishes of the founder,

Irrespective of the public or private-law nature of a foundation, it is always a unilateral legal transaction.[128] The founder is the only and sole person who acts.[129]

The fundamental and essential elements (*essentialia negotii*[130]) of a private foundation are as follows:[131]

- **Will of the founder: The will of the founder to form the foundation**. The foremost fundamental principle of the Foundation Act is the freedom granted to everyone to establish a foundation and to determine its purpose.[132]
- **Organization**: In the broadest sense of the word, the organization relates to all executive bodies and individuals who are involved in the foundation,[133] in a narrower sense, the organization only represents the Foundation Council, its formation and tasks, and the Protector (optional). Legal recognition of the foundation is dependent on the organization.

---

the foundation uses its executive bodies. As such, these bodies do not primarily define their own wishes but rather they execute the wishes of the founder. (Cf. *Santo-Passo*, 2002, p.61.)

127 Rogelio Tribaldos-Alba defines a foundation as a corporate body with legal capacity, that is established as a separate entity from the founder and manages itself independently, which is not subject to the restrictions of provisions governing charitable or common-benefit causes and which has acquired international recognition. (Cf. *Tribaldos-Alba*, 1999, p.18.)
Gilbert Boutin describes it as a "protective regime for proprietary assets". It is a legal entity with the task of acquiring assets and ensuring that they are preserved and administered in line with the wishes of the founder. Passive perfection is the goal; the only aim being to preserve and protect the wealth of the founder. Any activity of a speculative nature is excluded. It is an institution that is created through the will of the founder, a unilateral act of private law, the impacts of which become visible during the founder's life and/or after his death. (Cf. *Boutin*, 2000, pp.17, 20, 21 et seqq.)

128 Acto Unilateral.

129 Cf. *Boutin*, 2000, pp.17, 20, 21 et seqq.

130 In order to ensure the validity of a trust, common law specifies three material aspects, which are absolutely essential as the establishment of the trust would otherwise be void: a) Certainty of **intention**. b) Certainty of **subject** (*i.e.* indirectly, the intended purpose and c) Certainty of **object**. Cf. Tolley's, Administration of Trusts, Section A.1.1. 'Nature of a Trust', Eighth edition, London 2002, published by STEP (Society of Trust and Estate Practitioners, London).

131 Cf. *Estribí*, 2002, p.17; *Ferreira*, 1998, p.15.

132 Cf. *Morgan*, 1992, p.7.

133 The founder, the Foundation Council as the administering body, the beneficiaries, the Protector, any lawyers that may be needed.

- **Assets as an independent patrimony**: Panama's law stipulates a minimal start-up capital of USD 10,000.[134]
- **Private interest and a specific, defined and non-commercial purpose**: A Panamanian foundation must be established for a specific purpose, must benefit one or several persons or bodies (individuals, family, or company), and may not serve any public or state interests. The purpose of a foundation is the separation of a patrimony from the wealth of the founder. The intention behind the establishment must not be of a commercial business nature.[135]

The endowment of the patrimony is seen as a 'donation', *i.e.* it influences the relinquishment of the '*animus sibi habendi*'; the founder relinquishes all rights to dispose of the assets. In the case of independent patrimonies, in particular, the fact that they do not belong to anyone, *i.e.* that they have no 'owner' is frequently overlooked. So if an involved party, such as the founder, acts as if he owns the patrimony, the transaction is fictitious at best.[136]

The foundation is therefore a permanent, lasting institution that allows the founder to realize ideas and define objectives and to pursue these for a long time, even after his death; ideas and objectives that the founder wishes to implement in connection with his capital and wealth.

II. Types of foundations

1. Public and private foundations

Foundations are primarily and globally sub-divided in line with the purposes they pursue. This fundamental classification of foundations into public and private foundations exists in Panama, as well.

Public foundations have been in existence since before 1995, *i.e.* before the emergence of the private foundation. These public foundations are the so-called "*Fundación Pública sin Fines de Lucro*", which translates as: Public foundation without profit or acquisition objectives. This type of foundation is only defined

---

134 Cf. Art.5 Para.2 LFIP. Unlike Liechtenstein, a private foundation is first registered in Panama, *i.e.* first acquires status as a legal entity, before the assets are transferred. In the case of Liechtenstein foundations, the procedure is exactly the opposite; a foundation cannot be established without proof of the foundation's assets. Cf. in more detail below.

135 Cf. Art. 3 LFIP.

136 *Santo-Passo*, 2002, p.50.; Cf. FL OGH 2C 133 95-70 dated 8 January 1998, LES 1998, 111.

in a few Articles in the Panamanian Civil Code[137] and may only be used for charitable, ecclesiastical and common-benefit causes. The Panamanian government must permit (grant a concession for) the establishment (the Government and Justice Ministry, *Ministerio de Gobierno y Justicia* is responsible). Once established, the foundation is subject to state supervision. Moreover, the foundation assets must be located in the country. This shows that this type of foundation is utterly unsuitable for purposes of private asset management.[138] Article 2 LFIP explicitly states that the regulations governing public foundations are not applicable to private foundations. [139]

The founders of public and private foundations differ as a result of the act of establishment. The former are established by law, ordinance or official notification; the latter by a private act of endowment.

The private foundation, which forms the subject of this book, was brought to life by the law governing private foundations (LFIP). This law does not, however, provide any further classification of private foundations, such as is the case in Liechtenstein or other countries. As such, it only acknowledges one private foundation which acquires legal character as a legal entity the moment it is entered in the Public Registry.[140]

2. Common-benefit and private-benefit foundations

The distinction is governed by the purpose pursued by the foundation. The former serve the common good, *i.e.* provide common benefit, whereas the latter serve personal, private purposes. They can be of both private-law and public nature. Most of the public foundations in Panama are common-benefit foundations.[141]

Private-benefit foundations are "private institutions" which serve to regulate the founder's succession or protect the assets of private individuals. These foun-

---

[137] Book V, Title 2, Art. 64 et seqq. CC.

[138] Cf. *Ferrer*, p.5: "...the new private foundation does not have anything to do with the traditional foundation of **public interest**, known through the centuries in civil law countries and which is normally used for charitable purposes or other humanitarian reasons".

[139] Art. 2 LFIP 25/95: "Private foundations shall be governed by the Foundation Charter and its regulations, as well as by the provisions of this law and other applicable legal and regulatory provisions. The provisions of Title II, Book I of the Civil Code shall **not** apply to private foundations".

[140] Pursuant to Art.1 LFIP.

[141] Pursuant to Art.64 CC. Cf. also *Ferrer*, p.5: "...foundation of public interest... which is normally used for charitable purposes or other humanitarian reasons".

dations are usually anchored in their own laws. Their purpose benefits only a limited circle of defined or definable people (family, clubs, company employees). Family foundations represent the most important group of private-benefit foundations.[142] This book concentrates on this type of foundation, with particular focus on the Panamanian private foundation.

By contrast, common-benefit foundations are "institutions that serve the common good" and pursue common-benefit, social, charitable, cultural, scientific or other purposes aimed at benefiting the general public. Most countries acknowledge common-benefit foundations and have firmly anchored them in their legislations.[143]

3. Revocable and irrevocable foundations

The founder's option of revocation is an important aspect in international relationships since it allows the founder to retain control over the foundation. From a tax perspective, the recognition of the institution as a foundation may be questioned, as may the issue of transparency.

The fundamental irrevocability of a foundation provides a serious answer to all of the issues surrounding the recognition of the foundation and the certainty of the founder's intention. The establishment of a foundation should, after all, not serve to manipulate or simulate with the aim of circumventing legal norms.

Panamanian foundation law stipulates that **all private foundations are irrevocable**, with the exception of the following cases:[144]

- If the Foundation Charter has not been entered in the Public Registry.
- If the revocation is explicitly regulated in the Foundation Charter.

---

142 *Seifart/von Campenhausen*, 1999, p.3.

143 Cf. above, §2 Historical Interpretation / History of the Origins of the LFIP

144 Art.12 LFIP: "Revocation of foundations: Foundations shall be irrevocable except in the following cases:
If the foundation charter has not been registered at the Public Registry.
If the foundation charter provides otherwise.
For any of the causes of revocation applicable to donations.
The transfers of assets made to foundations shall be irrevocable by the person who made the transfer, unless it is expressly stated otherwise in the act of transfer of such assets."

- If grounds for revoking the donation arise.[145] A revocation of the donation can be demanded in Panama[146] if a) the recipient of the donation no longer complies with the conditions set by the donor, *i.e.* if the beneficiary no longer complies with a condition set by the founder, or b) if the recipient has committed a criminal offence against the person, the honour, or the wealth of the donor, or the donor's spouse, predecessors or successors, *i.e.* if the beneficiary has committed a crime against the founder.

A founder who has established a foundation by virtue of his last will also has the exclusive and unlimited right to revoke the foundation.[147] After his death, the heirs shall have no right to revoke the creation or transfer of assets to the foundation, even if it has not been entered in the Public Registry before the death of the founder.[148]

---

145 The issue of revoking a donation clearly demonstrates the close link between the foundation and the donation. After all, it represents the basis, the fundamental philosophy of the foundation. Moreover, this Article 13 LFIP is a good example of the subsidiary application of the Panamanian (but not only Panamanian) Civil Code for interpreting foundation law.

146 Pursuant to Art.964 et seqq. CC.

147 Art.13 LFIP: "Foundations created by testamentary dispositions, rights to revoke the same: In addition to the foregoing provisions, if a foundation has been created to be effective at the time of death of its founder, he / she shall have the exclusive and unlimited right to revoke it. The heirs of the founder, after his / her death, shall have no right to revoke the creation or transfer of assets to the foundation, even when it has not been registered at the Public Registry before the death of the founder."

148 This Article was adopted from the former Liechtenstein law, OLArt.559 PGR (Revocation):
1) Revocation of the foundation is admissible only:
1. if a foundation has not yet been entered in the Public Register, in as much as existence ensues only in the event of such entry;
2. in the event that registration of the foundation is not necessary and the foundation should become effective in law during the founder's lifetime, up to the time of conclusion of registration;
3. in the case of foundations formed by way of last will and testament or contract of inheritance, in accordance with the relevantly applicable rules under the law of inheritance.
2) In the case of testamentary dispositions, the founder personally has an unrestricted right of revocation but not, on the other hand, the heirs after the founder's death, not even if the foundation is not yet entered in the Public Register.
3) Likewise, the heirs do not have a right of revocation where in the case of the foundation inter vivos the founder certainly drew up the deed but died before the foundation was entered in the Public Register.
4) Revocation expressly reserved in the foundation deed or the reserved amendment of the deed or of the articles is admissible at any time.

4. Mortis causa and inter vivos foundations

Panamanian foundation law makes provision for both types of foundations.[149] The private foundation can be established to come into existence the moment it is formed (inter vivos) or not until after the death of the founder (mortis causa). A mortis causa foundation can be established as follows:

- By means of a private deed, drafted and signed by the founder. The founder's signature must be certified by a public notary at the place of constitution,[150] or
- Directly before a public notary at the place of constitution (public deed).[151]

Compliance with the requirements of foundation law is, however, mandatory for both types of constitution.[152]

Irrespective of whether a foundation is established by private or public deed, it does **not** need to comply with the regulations in the Panamanian Civil Code

---

The new law governing foundations in Liechtenstein also adopted this regulation in NLArt.552 §30 PGR:
1) The founder may in the foundation deed reserve for himself the right to revoke the foundation or to amend the declaration of establishment. These rights cannot be assigned or bequeathed. Should one of these rights be exercised by a direct representative, this shall require as pecial power of attorney referring to this transaction.
2) If the founder is a legal entity, it cannot reserve for itself the rights in accordance with para.1.
3) If the rights in accordance with para.1 are exercised by an indirect representative (§ 4, para.3), the legal consequences shall revert directly to the founder.

149 Art.4 LFIP: "Private foundations can be created inter vivos or mortis causa. Formalities for the creation of wills shall not apply to foundations mortis causa:
Private foundations may be constituted to become effective at the time of constitution or after death of their founder, in either of the following manners:
1. By private document subscribed by the founder whose signature shall be authenticated by a public notary at the place of constitution.
2. Directly before a public notary at the place of constitution.
In either case, the constitution of the foundation shall comply with the formalities established in the present law for the creation of foundations.
In case of a foundation being created to become effective after the death of the founder, whether by public or private document, the formalities required for the execution of wills shall not apply."

150 Art.4 Para.1 No.1 LFIP.

151 Art.4 Para.1 No.2 LFIP.

152 Art.4 Para.2 LFIP.

that govern the drafting of wills[153] in order to become legally effective after the death of the founder.[154]

Art.13 LFIP also addresses a mortis causa foundation. As mentioned above, a mortis causa foundation is deemed to be irrevocable from the instance of the founder's death, even if it has not been entered in the Public Registry. It therefore comes into existence the moment the founder dies and the entry in the Public Registry only serves a declaratory purpose.[155]

5. *Real and fictitious foundations*

These types of foundations are addressed in detail in European law.[156] The classification as a real/independent or fictitious/dependent foundation or additional/subsequent donation is based on the recognition or non-recognition of the legal character of a foundation.[157]

Real foundations are recognized as (independent assets and) legal entities with no distinction being made between any public or private purpose they might pursue.[158]

---

153 Unlike Switzerland, for example, where the regulation pursuant to Art.493 ZGB differs.

154 Cf. *Ferrer*, p.6: "The second part of the Article is intended to say that when foundations are created to take **effect after the death** of the founder, that is, with testamentary intentions, they will have to comply with all of the formalities of the law on foundations, but **shall not be required** to follow additionally the formalities established in the **Civil Code** of Panama for the making of a valid will. The legislators considered the formalities required to draft a valid will to be rather ancient and cumbersome. Consequently, to have to follow the formalities required to create a private foundation, and then in addition the ones established in the Civil Code to make a valid will, seemed to the drafters of the law to be too demanding on the party wanting to create a foundation of private interest with testamentary effects."

155 Cf. *Boutin*, 2000, p.22

156 A strict distinction is made between "fictitious foundations" and "real foundations" since one of the foremost characteristics of the act of establishing a foundation is that it represents the **intended** donation of assets to a future legal entity.

157 Cf. *Spielvogel*, 1998, p.69 et seqq. Additional donations are assets transferred to an existing foundation by third parties at a later date, whereas teaching defines assets transferred by the founder himself at a later date as subsequent donations. These are not legal transactions *sui generis*. Depending on the structure, they are, *e.g.*, donations, inheritances or legacies, to which the respective statutory provisions are applied.

158 Cf. *Consultation Report*, 2004, pp.20 and 66.

Fictitious foundations constitute a donation of patrimony for a specific purpose but without legal character.[159] Fictitious foundations do not feature in Panamanian legislation.

6. *The ecclesiastical foundation*

All ecclesiastical foundations are public foundations.

They are devoted to social, charitable, religious and ecclesiastical causes, and perform pastoral tasks which can be contained within the church or extend beyond it.[160] Panamanian law does not stipulate any particular regulations for ecclesiastical foundations, *i.e.* like any other public foundation, they must be entered in the Public Register and are subject to state supervision.

7. *Staff welfare foundations*

By the same token, Panama does not stipulate any particular regulations for welfare foundations. Unlike other types of private foundations, the purpose of such foundations is to provide benefits for employees or their families for capital accumulation purposes.[161] The benefits in question are primarily intended for use in case of old age, death or invalidity.[162] Staff welfare foundations are very rare in Panama. Mandatory benefit provision by employers is foreign to the country, private provision is voluntary.

---

159 Cf *Künzle*, 2002, p4; Cf *Riemer*, 1981, Syst. Part N 421 and 422 et seqq.; *Sprecher/von Salis-Lütolf*, 1999, No. 17.

160 Cf. *Spielvogel*, 1998, p.37 et seqq; Cf. also OLArt.553 Para.1 PGR. The NLArt.552 §2 Para.2 PGR places ecclesiastical foundations on a par with common-benefit foundations:
2) A common-benefit foundation within the meaning of this Section is a foundation whose activity according to the declaration of establishment is entirely or predominantly intended to serve common benefit purposes in accordance with Art.107, Para.4a, unless it is a family foundation.
Art.107 Para.4a PGR: Where the Act refers to non-profit making (common-benefit) or charitable purposes, this shall include such purposes the fulfilment of which is of benefit to the general public. In particular, there is deemed to be a benefit to the general public if the activity serves the common good in a charitable, **religious**, humanitarian, scientific, cultural, moral, sporting or ecological sense, even if only a specific category of persons benefits from the activity.

161 Cf. *Clauss/Blockwitz*, 2003, p.2.

162 *Ferreira*, 1998, p.11.

8. Corporate foundations

Corporate foundations exist in two main types:[163]

- If it directly manages the company itself, it is known as a 'corporate management foundation'.
- If it only manages the company indirectly by means of a substantial stake (membership) in a legal entity that directly manages the company, it is known as a 'holding foundation'.

The material factors for designation as a corporate foundation are firstly the patrimony (the company), and secondly the purpose. Depending on the purpose, the corporate foundation can be established as a public (*e.g.* ecclesiastical) or a private (family) foundation.[164]

The corporate foundation is as old as the institution of foundations itself, as witnessed by those hospitals, schools, old people's homes, etc., that were run by foundations.[165]

The motives for establishing a private corporate foundation can be very diversified: If a founder has a large number of heirs and wants to protect his company from contradicting individual interests, or to avoid the company being carved up in the succession or restructured by the successors, if the existing heirs do not have sufficient capabilities or the willingness to manage the company, or in the absence of any heirs at all, etc. By establishing a holding foundation, the founder can define the control mechanisms for the relevant company over the long term since the foundation does not have an owner and transferable rights of membership therefore do not exist. [166]

Panamanian law does not regulate corporate foundations. Although a private foundation may not engage directly in business, it may pursue commercial, *i.e.* private-benefit purposes.[167] As such, it can be used as a corporate foundation to regulate succession by means of stakes held in companies.

---

[163] Cf. *Spielvogel*, 1998, p.51.
[164] Cf. *Clauss/Blockwitz*, 2003, p.3.
[165] Cf. *Lanter*, 2000, p.86.
[166] *Spielvogel*, 1998, p.52.
[167] Cf. commercial purpose of Panamanian foundations in §4 of this book.

9. Maintenance foundations

The purpose of maintenance foundations, which are also known as family maintenance foundations, is to pay annuities in retirement or in the case of an accident, illness, or death. Maintenance foundations are permitted both in Panama and in Liechtenstein, as is also the case with family trusts, unlike France, Germany, Switzerland and Austria, who banned this legal institution from their legal systems on the grounds of it being 'aristocratic'.[168]

10. Family foundations

Panamanian law does not expressly mention the family foundation. Equally, neither the LFIP nor Liechtenstein distinguishes between a pure and a mixed family foundation.[169]

Generally speaking, a family foundation is an interesting estate planning tool since it offers the option of planning across several generations whereas testamentary provisions do not directly extend beyond the next generation. In addition, the family wealth can be protected from the beneficiaries/heirs themselves, *i.e.* from an all too casual use of the assets, thus preserving it for use by future generations.[170] Private foundations pursuant to Panamanian law are ideal for this purpose.

---

168 Cf. *Santo-Passo*, 2002, pp.48 and 61.

169 Cf. OLArt.553 Para.2 and 3 PGR: 2) A family foundation is a pure family foundation where the foundation assets are continuously connected with the purpose of defraying the expenses for the upbringing and education, outfitting or support of the relatives of one or several designated families, or with similar purposes.
3) It is a mixed foundation where assets so donated serve additional or supplementary ecclesiastical or other purposes outside the family."
Cf. also NLArt.552 §2 Para.4 No. 1 and 2:
1. pure family foundations; these are foundations whose assets exclusively serve the defrayal of costs of upbringing or education, provision for or support of members of one or more families or similar family interests;
2. mixed family foundations; these are foundations which predominantly pursue the purpose of a pure family foundation, but which, in addition, also serve common-benefit or other private-benefit purposes.

170 *Clauss/Blockwitz*, 2003, p.2.

III. Constitution

The formation of a foundation is a unilateral legal act, which does not require confirmation and which can be performed by either a native of the country or a foreigner.

The entire structure and organization of the foundation is defined in a publicly accessible document – Acta Fundacional / Foundation Charter – and in a private document called the "Bylaws" or "Regulations".

Since Panama, unlike Liechtenstein, does not require the filing[171] of the Foundation Charter with the Public Registry, the structure for establishing a foundation is more simply and clearly defined than is the case in Liechtenstein.[172] It solely requires the registration of the foundation in the Public Registry.

---

[171] In the context of OLArt.554 PGR in conjunction with NLArt.557 PGR. Liechtenstein permits the relatively simple constitution of a foundation pursuant to OLArt.557 Para.2 PGR: " **... pure and mixed family foundations and foundations whose beneficiaries are defined or definable, acquire legal character without being entered** in the Public Registry".
OLArt.553 Para.2 PGR defines which foundations must be declared as pure family foundations: "A family foundation is a pure family foundation where the foundation assets are continuously connected with the purpose of defraying the expenses for the upbringing and education, outfitting or support of the relatives of one or several designated families, or with similar purposes."
OLArt.553 Para.3 PGR defines which foundations must be declared as mixed family foundations: "It is a mixed foundation where assets so donated serve additional or supplementary ecclesiastical or other purposes outside the family."
The old PGR does not define, resp. specifically classify foundations where the beneficiaries are defined or definable. This norm is missing from the old PGR despite its significance in term of legal consequence, *i.e.* the creation and acquisition of legal character.
The new Liechtenstein Foundation Act makes provision for exactly the same regulation: Cf. NLArt.552 §14 Para.1 and Para.5 in conjunction with §4 Para.4 PGR.

[172] The old PGR system provides the following in Section A. 'Definition and Delimitation', Section III. 'Deposition': "To ensure observance of the obligation to register, to prevent foundations with unlawful or immoral purposes and to avoid circumvention of possible supervision, the foundation deed including all amendments of the foundation's articles and/or certified copy of the testamentary disposition or the deed of inheritance must be deposited by the Foundation Council or the legal representative and/or the probate court with the Office of Land and Public Registration at the time a foundation is formed, insofar as an application for entry does not ensue otherwise" (OLArt.554 PGR).
The old PGR does not clearly or systematically distinguish between the regulations for 'deposited' foundations versus 'registered' foundations. On the contrary: Pursuant to OLArt.554 PGR, the Foundation Charter must be deposited unless an application is submitted for its registration.

The registration is an important feature of the foundation structure. As such, two phases can be defined when setting up a foundation.

The old PGR system further provides for both registration and deposition in Section B. 'Constitution', Section III. 'Creation': "The foundation only comes into existence when entered in the Public Register as Foundation Register" (OLArt.557 Para.1 PGR). Ecclesiastical foundations, pure mixed family foundations and foundations whose beneficiaries are defined or definable acquire legal character **without being entered** in the Public Registry (OLArt.557 Para. 2 PGR).
The wording of the execution ordinance for the Public Registry equally does not distinguish between the legal systems. Section 9 'Foundation' cites 3 Articles – 'Constitutional documents; Auditing' (Art.89 OeRegV), 'Registration' (Art.90 OeRegV) and 'Supervisory Authority' (Art.91 OeRegV). The old PGR does not provide a clear distinction between the deposited and the registered foundation in terms of the submission of the formalities required to establish the foundation.
The wording of Art.89 OeRegV under the heading 'Constitutional documents; Auditing' is as follows: "The following documents must be submitted together with the application for first-time registration of a foundation to the Office of Land and Public Registration (OLArt. 554 and 556 PGR):
a certified copy of the Foundation Charter, the testamentary disposition or the inheritance contract;
any regulations that govern the organization and representation of the foundation, unless these regulations are included in the documents listed in a);
a list of the members of the administration, with indication of first and surnames, nationality, domicile or registered office resp. corporate name and domicile of the members of the Foundation Council or other representatives of the foundation (OLArt.556 Para.2 PGR);
the record of the constitution of the administration unless already indicated in the Foundation Charter or regulations.
The Office of Land and Public Registration verifies compliance with the prerequisites for establishing a foundation (OLArt.555 PGR).
Any subsequent amendment to the Foundation Charter or regulations must be notified to the Office of Land and Public Registration, with the exception of amendments that must be entered directly at the instruction of the relevant supervisory authority.
If the Foundation Charter is merely **deposited** (OLArt.554 PGR), the deposition is noted in the company register, together with the name of the foundation, its domicile and its representative.
Any amendment to the foundation purpose of a **non-registered** foundation must also be notified to the Office of Land and Public Registration (OLArt.554 PGR)."
The wording of Art.90 OeRegV under the heading 'Registration' provides a clearer definition: "The entry of the foundation shall contain the following information:
-the date of constitution;
-the name;
-the domicile;
-the purpose; and
-the organization, the representation and the signatory formalities."

A. Steps to set up a Panamanian foundation

The constitution of a Panamanian foundation can be split into two main phases:

Steps prior to entry in the Public Registry

Steps following entry in the Public Registry

1. Steps prior to entry in the Public Registry

Panama's foundation law gives founders two choices for establishing a foundation under Panamanian law: through a third party[173] or by the founder, himself.[174]

a. The founder commissions a third party to set up the foundation:[175]

When establishing a private foundation, a distinction is made between the beneficial founder (the person who actually provides the assets) and the legal founder (trustee). The beneficial founder of a private foundation in Panama can be a local or foreign natural person or legal entity. He can act on his own behalf or in a fiduciary capacity, through the legal founder. As such, foundations can also be established on a fiduciary basis by individuals not domiciled in Panama. Generally, the beneficial founder is not publicly known, for reasons of anonymity, and the foundation is established on a trust basis. The Bylaws can, and generally do, specifically determine that the fiduciary founder automatically loses all rights conveyed by the legal act of constitution once the foundation is established. This eliminates any need for considerations about the type of legal relationship following the constitution of the foundation[176] between the beneficial and legal founders in respect

---

Given the surprisingly clear formulation of the requirements in the old PGR and the OeRegV, one could almost assume that Panama's Art.5 LFIP and its enumeration principle was used as the basis for Art. 90 OeRegV. The new foundation law in Liechtenstein also adopted the LFIP regulation and its enumeration principle (Cf. NLArt.552 §14 Para.5 in conjunction with §20 for private-benefit, deposited foundations, and §14 Para.4 in conjunction with §19 for foundations subject to mandatory registration).

173 Pursuant to Art.1 Sent.1 LFIP.

174 Pursuant to Art.1 Sent.1 LFIP in conjunction with Art.4 LFIP.

175 Cf. Art.1 Sent.1 LFIP. "... (acting) on his own behalf or through a third party ..."

176 For example, a contract governing the mandate, authorization, contractual relationship, trust or fiduciary relationship.

of the act of constitution. Pursuant to Art.1 Sent.1 LFIP, the fiduciary founder is, after all, acting on behalf of the founder. He is acting in his own name but for the account and risk of the beneficial, real founder.

The regulation pursuant to Art.1 LFIP corresponds to the provision in Liechtenstein's OLArt.555 Para.1 PGR. The new law governing foundations in Liechtenstein explicitly provides for direct and indirect representation (Cf. NLArt.552 §14 Para. 2 and 3 PGR). If the founder is not setting up the foundation by testamentary disposition, he drafts the Foundation Charter himself or commissions a third party to do so.[177]

b. The founder establishes the foundation himself by drafting the Foundation Charter himself:[178]

As such, Panamanian foundation law supports the spontaneous conduct of the founder by clearly regulating the constitution formalities. No approval of any sort is required by an official body.[179]

A Panamanian foundation is established by the founder drafting the regulations for the foundation in compliance with the formalities pursuant to Art.5 LFIP anywhere in the world and having his signature certified by a notary public.[180]

---

177 OLArt.555 Para. 1 PGR stipulates that a Liechtenstein foundation can be established by means of a deed on which the signatures of the founders (new: the founder) are certified, by testamentary disposition or by deed of inheritance. Cf. NLArt.552 §15 PGR.

178 Art.1 Sent.1 LFIP in conjunction with Art.4 Para.1 LFIP.

179 This regulation deviates from its Liechtenstein counterpart in that OLArt.554 PGR already stipulates official supervision for foundations, even if they are only deposited and not registered: "To ensure observance of the obligation to register, to prevent foundations with unlawful or immoral purposes and to avoid circumvention of possible supervision, the foundation deed including all amendments of the foundation's articles and/or certified copy of the testamentary disposition or the deed of inheritance must be deposited by the foundation council or the legal representative and/or the probate court with the Register Office at the time a foundation is formed, insofar as an application for entry does not ensue otherwise." The new law governing foundations in Liechtenstein adopted this regulation in NLArt.552 §21 PGR.

180 Art.4 Para.1 No.1 LFIP. The regulation corresponds to the provision in Liechtenstein's OLArt.555 Para.1 PGR: "The formation of a foundation ensues in the form of a deed on which the signatures of the founders are certified, by testamentary disposition or by deed of inheritance." NLArt.552 § 14 Para.1 and 2 PGR provides for the same regulation.

The founder can also consult a notary public directly and constitute the foundation together with the notary public.[181]

The formalities governing wills and testamentary dispositions pursuant to Art.4 Para.3 LFIP are abolished in their entirety if the founder determines that his foundation shall be established upon his death.[182]

The Bylaws are the basic document governing a Panamanian foundation.[183] Panamanian foundation law stipulates that a foundation is only guided by its regulations, Bylaws and by the law. Art.5 defines the obligatory content of this constitution document:

- The name of the foundation
- The initial capital
- The members of the Foundation Council and their residential addresses
- The domicile of the foundation
- The name and domicile of the local representative
- The purpose of the foundation

---

181 Art.4 Para.1 No.2 LFIP.

182 Art.4 Para.3 LFIP. In case of a foundation being created to become effective after the death of the founder, whether by public or private document, the formalities required for the execution of wills shall not apply.

183 Cf. Art.4 Para.2 in conjunction with Art.5f LFIP. This regulation corresponds to Liechtenstein legislation although the latter stipulates two-fold requirements – one for deposited and one for registered foundations.
Deposited foundations are regulated in Liechtenstein pursuant to OLArt.555 Abs.2 PGR: "The foundation deed or the articles must contain the name and domicile of the foundation, its purpose or object, the designation of the foundation council members and the method for appointing another foundation council as well as a provision concerning the application of the assets in the event of the dissolution of the foundation."
Registered foundations are regulated in Liechtenstein pursuant to OLArt.556 PGR:
"1) The foundation's application to register in the Foundation Register must be recorded by all the members of the Foundation Council personally or submitted in writing in certified form, whereby the application must be accompanied by a certified copy of the foundation deed.
2) The entry and publication, which may ensue by announcement on the court notice board, must contain: the name (name of the firm), address and purpose of the foundation, the date of the formation deed, the names and addresses and/or the name and domicile of the firm of the foundation council members and/or of other representatives.
3) If necessary, entry and publication may also be undertaken by order of the Government as supervising authority by virtue of the foundation deed, possibly by the Register Authority ex officio upon notification by the Probate Authority or upon petition of the Beneficiaries." The new law governing foundations in Liechtenstein also adopted this regulation (Cf. NLArt.552 §§19 and 20 PGR).

- The procedure for designating the beneficiaries
- The right to amend the Bylaws
- The duration of the foundation
- The procedure for liquidation and distribution of the assets
- Any and all other provisions that are important for the founder and are legally permissible

c. Name of the foundation

The name of the foundation can be in any language but must be composed of letters from the Latin alphabet.[184] It may not conflict with, *i.e.* be identical or similar to, the name of an already existing foundation.[185] The word 'foundation' must be suffixed to the name chosen by the founder to clearly identify the foundation as a legal entity.[186]

Panamanian law does not allow for any reservations of names when establishing a foundation, unlike other jurisdictions (*e.g.* when setting up a joint stock corporation in the British Virgin Islands).

d. Initial capital

The statutory foundation capital may be denominated in any currency in the Bylaws as long as it is equivalent to at least USD 10,000 (ten thousand).[187]

The statutory foundation capital does not have to be paid in, as is also the case in Liechtenstein.[188] The confirmation of capital payment is not required when applying for registration in the Public Registry.

---

184 Art.5 Para.1 No.1 LFIP.

185 Art.5 Para.1 No.1 LFIP.

186 Art.5 Para.1 No.1 Sent.2 LFIP.

187 Art.5 Para.1 No.2 LFIP.

188 Proof of capital is only required in Liechtenstein for the legal forms of joint stock corporation, establishment and trust company. Cf. OLArt.122 Para.1 and Para.2 PGR in conjunction with OLArt.207 PGR. No proof of capital is demanded for foundations that are only deposited with the Office of Public Registration pursuant to OLArt.554 PGR in conjunction with Art.89 Para.4 OeRegV: "If the Foundation Charter is merely deposited (OLArt.554 PGR), the deposition is noted in the company register, together with the name of the foundation, its domicile and its representative." The new law governing foundations in Liechtenstein adopted this regulation (Cf. NLArt.552 §20 Para.2 No.11 PGR and §19 Para.3 Sent.3 PGR).

e. The members of the Foundation Council and their residential addresses

The names and addresses of the members of the Foundation Council must be disclosed pursuant to Art.5 Para.1 No.3 LFIP. This regulation corresponds to the provisions in Liechtenstein law.[189]

f. The domicile of the foundation.

The statutory domicile of the foundation must be registered pursuant to Art.5 Para.1 No.4 LFIP.[190] This regulation corresponds to the provisions in Liechtenstein law.[191]

g. The name and domicile of the local representative

The local representative (Agente Residente) should not be confused with the legal (fiduciary) founder.[192] The representative is nominated by the founder in the Bylaws. Legislation demands that he must be a lawyer or a law firm with his/its

---

[189] Cf. OLArt.556 Para.2 PGR: "The entry (must contain) ... the representatives, whereby the names and addresses or registered office and domicile of the members of the Executive Board or any other representatives must be indicated" together with the version of this norm in Art.89 Para.1 lit.c) OeRegV: "The list of members of the administration with indication of the first and surnames, nationality, domicile or registered office resp. corporate name and domicile of the members of the Foundation Council or other representatives of the foundation" in conjunction with Art.90 Para.1 lit.e) OeRegV: "the organization, the representation and the signatory formalities." The new law governing foundations in Liechtenstein adopted this regulation (Cf. NLArt.552 §20 Para.2 No.6 PGR and §19 Para.3 No.6 PGR).

[190] The domicile of the foundation frequently does not just mean the place where it is registered. It can just as easily be the place where the foundation is administered or the place where the Foundation Council is domiciled, although these places should be consistent. Pursuant to Art.5 Para.1 No.4 LFIP, the place of registration determines the "nationality" of the foundation, *i.e.* to which jurisdiction it is subject; in this case, to Panamanian law.

[191] Cf. OLArt.554 PGR in conjunction with Art.89 Abs.3OeRegV: "If the Foundation Charter is merely deposited (OLArt.554 PGR), the deposition is noted in the company register, together with the name of the foundation, its domicile and its representative.", together with Art.90 Para.1 lit c) OeRegV: "The entry of the foundation shall contain the following information: ... the domicile;" The new law governing foundations in Liechtenstein adopted this regulation (Cf. NLArt.552 §20 Para.2 No.2 PGR and §19 Para.3 No.2 PGR).

[192] Art.1 Sent.1 LFIP stipulates that the person establishing a foundation does not necessarily have to be the real founder. In addition, Art.10 LFIP permits any third party to voluntary donate assets to the foundation.

domicile and/or registered office in Panama and must be registered as a lawyer in the Public Registry.[193] He is responsible for reviewing the constitution documents.[194] He must sign the Bylaws before they are registered.[195] Generally, he is responsible for legally reviewing any and all changes to the foundation and for ensuring the registration of the same. This function differs from that of a legal representative in Liechtenstein.[196]

The local representative officiates as the postal address in Panama and is responsible for all correspondence with the Panamanian authorities. He pays the annual fees and receives himself an annual fee in return for his services. He regulates all actions brought against the foundation that are subject to Panamanian jurisdiction. Basically, the local representative is responsible for performing all actions of the foundation in connection with Panamanian territory.

The local representative is, however, not the representative of the foundation. The foundation is represented by any legal entity or natural person designated by the founder or the Foundation Council (*e.g.* the founder himself, the Protector, an uninvolved third party, or other people with signatory powers).

In this respect it is important to note that the local representative has a duty of care[197] which obligates him to know enough about his client at all times.[198]

h. The purpose of the foundation

The purpose of a foundation is its defining characteristic. It embodies the intention of the founder in respect of the desired utilization of the donated assets.

Since there is no need for official approval,[199] a Panamanian private foundation can pursue a virtually unlimited diversity of purpose. For example:

---

[193] Numeral 1, Art. 1, Decreto 147 de 1966.

[194] Cf. Art.5 Para.1 No.5 Sent.1 LFIP.

[195] Cf. Art.5 Para.1 No.5 Sent.2 LFIP.

[196] In Liechtenstein, it is the Office of Land and Public Registration itself that verifies compliance with the requirements for establishing a foundation, pursuant to Art.89 Para.2 OeRegV. In addition, prior to issuing official confirmation to the applicant, the Office of Land and Public Registration notifies the supervisory authority of the registration of the foundation and obtains confirmation that the latter has assumed responsibility for supervising this foundation, pursuant to Art.91 OeRegV.

[197] Pursuant to Decree (Decreto ejecutivo) No.468 dated 19 September 1994.

[198] In the sense of "Know your Customer". Cf. also Art.34 LFIP.

[199] The purpose of the foundation is only reviewed by the local representative pursuant to Art.5 Para.1 No.5 Sent.2 LFIP when he reviews and signs the bylaws.
This regulation in Panama deviates from the provisions in Liechtenstein law, whereby even deposited, non-registered foundations are subject to official review pursuant to OLArt.554 PGR: "To ensure observance of the obligation to register, to prevent foun-

- Foundation to govern direct succession (with testamentary regulation).
- Foundation to govern indirect succession, *i.e.* during his lifetime, the founder is the only beneficiary; after his death, he is replaced by the vested beneficiaries he has appointed.
- Foundation for direct family maintenance (family maintenance foundation).
- Foundation for indirect, conditional family maintenance, *i.e.* the founder defines criteria and issues instructions in respect of how his family shall benefit, resp. how the estate earmarked for his family shall be administered, both during his lifetime and in the event of the founder's death. This is the most commonly known type of "family foundation".
- Foundation for general educational purposes, *e.g.* the foundation guarantees the academic education of the beneficiaries.
- Foundation for specific educational purposes, *i.e.* to support the education of family members who work in the founder's company, wish to further their education, and take on responsibility in the family company.
- Foundation with a fixed lifelong personal annuity for the beneficiaries, *e.g.* with or without inflation protection (linked to the national consumer price index).
- Foundation with a variable lifelong annuity for the beneficiaries resulting from the variable income generated by the underlying assets that are managed by a bank. This foundation serves the function of a private old age pension scheme. Once the founder has paid the capital into the foundation, the beneficiaries benefit from the income.
- Foundation for general tax optimization purposes.
- Foundation for specific tax optimization purposes as part of the carve-out of the founder's wealth. Since Panamanian foundations are totally exempt from tax as long as the assets are located abroad, resp. the source of the wealth originates abroad, pursuant to Art.27 LFIP.[200/201]

---

dations with unlawful or immoral purposes and to avoid circumvention of possible supervision, the foundation deed including all amendments of the foundation's articles and/or certified copy of the testamentary disposition or the deed of inheritance must be deposited by the foundation council or the legal representative and/or the probate court with the Register Office at the time a foundation is formed, insofar as an application for entry does not ensue otherwise." The new law governing foundations in Liechtenstein adopted this regulation (Cf. NLArt.552 §19 Para.5 and §20 Para.2 No.3 and 9 in conjunction with §21 PGR).

200 Article 27 LFIP defines the tax privilege afforded to Panamanian foundations:
"Tax privilege: The acts of constitution, amendment or extinction of the foundation, as well as the act of transfer, transmittal or encumbrance of assets of the foundation and the income arising therefrom, or any other act in connection therewith, shall be ex-

- Foundation for the purpose of general asset management as part of a family planning schedule, *i.e.* the foundation protects and administers the wealth of one or more families.
- Foundation for the purpose of protecting assets, with the result that the wealth brought into a foundation cannot be confiscated or pledged, nor may legal action be brought to enforce its utilization to fulfil personal obligations of the founder or the beneficiaries.
- Foundation to guarantee an obligation, *i.e.* the foundation can be held liable for an obligation or debts of the founder or a person designated by the founder.
- Foundation to support general charitable causes or for the benefit of the general public.
- Foundation to support a specific charitable cause. The beneficiary can be a cancer association, an orphanage, an art museum or any other institution that serves the common good, or an institution that serves a social purpose.

The broad definition of the purposes reflects the liberal stance that Panama has adopted towards foundations.

The only statutory requirement that must be complied with pursuant to Panamanian law is stipulated in Art.3 LFIP which states that a foundation must not pursue commercial or profit-oriented goals. This regulation corresponds to the provisions in Liechtenstein law.[202] As such, foundations are banned from per-

empt from all taxes, contributions, duties, liens or assessments of any kind, provided they relate to
1. Assets located abroad.
2. Money deposited by natural or juridical persons whose income does not derive from a Panamanian source or is not taxable in Panama for any reason.
3. Shares or securities of any kind issued by corporations whose income is not derived from a Panamanian source, or which are not taxable for any reason, even when such shares or securities are deposited in the Republic of Panama.
The transfer of immovable property, titles, certificates of deposit, assets, funds, securities or shares carried out by reason of the fulfilment of the objectives of the foundation or the termination of the same, in favour of relatives within the first degree of consanguinity or the spouse of the founder shall be exempted from all taxes."

201 This is due to the fact that Panama has adopted the principle of territorial taxation, *i.e.* taxes are only payable in the country by institutions that are designed to protect assets (instituciones de proteccion de activos), such as trusts, foundations or joint stock corporations. Panama does not apply the principle of double taxation (Panama no usa el criterio de doble tributacion).

202 The only restriction imposed on the purpose of a foundation in Liechtenstein is stipulated in OLArt.107 Para. 5 PGR, pursuant to which the purpose may be neither immoral nor illegal: "Associations and establishments, including foundations, that pur-

forming any commercial or profit-generating activities as a business enterprise.[203] The joint stock corporation is there to perform commercial activities. Panamanian legislation wished to follow the example of Liechtenstein[204] in not allowing the two forms to compete and, instead, strives to ensure that they com-

---

sue immoral or illegal purposes may not, by law, acquire legal character." (OLArt.107 Para.5 PGR). The new law governing foundations in Liechtenstein adopted this regulation (Cf. NLArt.552 §20 Para.4 No.1 in conjunction with §21 PGR).

203 Cf. Art.3 LFIP. Foundations in Liechtenstein may pursue a commercial (benefits or considerations) or non-commercial purpose. Pursuant to OLArt.552 Para.1 PGR, engaging in commercial business is permitted in two cases:
- when such activity serves to achieve the non-commercial purpose (distributions to beneficiaries without any service in return), or
- when the type and scope of participations held by the foundation necessitate commercial management.
The new law governing foundations in Liechtenstein also adopted this regulation (Cf. NLArt.552 §1 Para.2 PGR).

204 Pursuant to OLArt.552 Para.2 PGR, a foundation in Liechtenstein may only undertake commercial activities provided such activity serves its non-commercial purpose or the type and scope of the participations held require the facilities of a commercial business. The new law governing foundations in Liechtenstein also adopted this regulation (Cf. NLArt.552 §1 Para.2 PGR).
The reform of Liechtenstein foundation laws also stipulated new regulations governing the rights of the founder, the foundation governing bodies or third parties to implement changes. This is especially important in respect of a change in the purpose; only the founder may change the purpose provided he has reserved the right to do so in the Foundation Charter. This right is neither transferable nor hereditary. (Cf. NLArt.552 §4 Para.2 PGR) A foundation governing body or third party may only change the purpose if provision to do so is explicitly included in the Foundation Charter and if the purpose proves to be unachievable, impermissible or unreasonable, for example, or if the circumstances have changed such that the purpose acquires a quite different meaning or effect and the foundation no longer fulfils the wishes of the founder (OLArt. 566 Para.1 PGR, NLArt.552 §16 Para.2 No.5 PGR).
In the event that the Foundation Charter does not entrust such change of purpose to a governing body or third party and the aforementioned circumstances arise, a judge may – on petition by the involved parties or *ex officio* – change the purpose of the foundation by administrative action. (Cf. NLArt.552 §33 et seqq. PGR)
In the event that the founder has established the foundation for the purpose of fulfilling an obligation to a third party, who receives assets from the foundation free of charge, the founder may explicitly reserve the right for this third party (indirect founder) to change the purpose of the foundation in the Foundation Charter. (Cf. NLArt.552 §30 Para.1 PGR)
The reform in Liechtenstein does not, however, amend the purpose of "administering and utilizing assets for beneficiaries" (Cf. NLArt.552 §1 in conjunction with §25 PGR). As such, distributions can clearly still be made unconditionally to beneficiaries, even after the reform of the Liechtenstein law (Cf. NLArt.552 §2 Para.4 PGR).

plement each other. Nevertheless, a foundation may engage in commercial activities as long as they are not of a daily, customary nature or it may act as a holding company and own shares in a commercial company and also invest its assets to generate profits. These activities are always permitted when such an action is unexpected, coincidental and/or occasional and is not performed as a commercial business enterprise.[205] Within this framework it can set up partnerships or private equity funds for investment purposes or manage funds incepted by pre-defined companies. The income may, however, only be used for the purposes defined in the Bylaws. So a foundation may not, itself, act as a commercial enterprise but may perform the function as a holding company.[206]

i. The procedure for designating the beneficiaries

The Bylaws define in detail the beneficiaries and the regulations applying to the beneficiaries.[207]

j. The right to amend the Bylaws

The right to amendment is confirmed several times over in Panamanian foundation law: in Art.5 Para.8, Art.6 and Art.7 LFIP.[208]

---

205 For example, if the founder owns a building which he brings into the foundation and – pursuant to instructions in the bylaws – this building must be sold after x years and the proceeds distributed to the beneficiaries. This is a one-off transaction and does not constitute a commercial business enterprise.
The following would, however, be deemed a commercial business-oriented enterprise: If – pursuant to the founder's instructions – the foundation were to regularly purchase and sell real estate and to distribute the proceeds from these real estate transactions to the beneficiaries.

206 Cf. Ferrer, Notes on Art.3 LFIP, p.5.

207 Cf. Section Specimen Texts / Templates, Unpublished Documentation. Sample bylaws in German and English.

208 Art.5 No.8 LFIP: "The Foundation Charter shall contain: ... the reservation of the right to modify the Foundation Charter when deemed necessary."
Art.6 LFIP: "Entry of the Foundation Charter in the Foundation Register:
The Foundation Charter, as well as any amendment thereto, may be drafted in any language with characters of the Latin alphabet, and must comply with the regulations regarding registration of acts and titles at the Public Registry, for which purpose it must be certified by a public notary of the Republic of Panama.
If the Foundation Charter or its amendments are not written in Spanish, the same shall be certified by a public notary of the Republic of Panama, together with its Spanish translation by a certified public translator."
Art.7 LFIP: "Amendments to the Foundation Charter:

k. The duration of the foundation

Since no restrictions are imposed by law on the "useful life" of a foundation, it is usually established for an indefinite period. The founder may make the termination of the foundation subject to a condition or event.

l. The procedure for liquidation and distribution of the assets

This norm defines the conditions for any liquidation of the foundation, together with regulations governing the distribution of the assets and/or liquidation proceeds of a liquidated foundation.[209]

m. Any and all other provisions that are important for the founder and are legally permissible

This is where the reserved rights are defined, especially those of the founder, for example the right to amend the Bylaws or regulations, to allow the founder to adapt his foundation to new or changed circumstances.

In addition, the following definitions are common in practice: the designation of the Protector(s); the procedure for resolving conflicts between the subjects of the foundation; the designation of the legal representatives of the foundation if this is not the Foundation Council; the procedure for dismissing members of the Foundation Council, etc.These additional regulations are enormously important for avoiding problems, conflicts or other disputes.

Although the Bylaws may be drafted in any language (Latin alphabet), a Spanish translation is necessary for entry in the Public Registry pursuant to Art.6 LFIP.[210] It has become common practice in Panama to draft the Bylaws in sev-

---

Any amendment to the Foundation Charter, when permitted, shall be executed and signed in accordance to the provisions of the Foundation Charter itself. The relevant agreement, resolution or act of amendment shall contain the date in which it was carried out, and a clear indication of the name of the person or persons executing such amendments, whose signatures shall likewise be authenticated by a notary public at the place of execution of the document."

209 Art.5 Para.10 LFIP: "The destination to be given to the estate of the foundation and the manner of liquidation such estate in the event of dissolution."

210 Art.6 LFIP: "Art.6 LFIP: "Entry of the Foundation Charter in the Foundation Register:

The Foundation Charter, as well as any amendment thereto, may be drafted in any language with characters of the Latin alphabet, and must comply with the regulations regarding registration of acts and titles at the Public Registry, for which purpose it must be certified by a public notary of the Republic of Panama.

eral languages – Spanish and English, German or French (depending on the native language of the founder). The Bylaws of a Panamanian foundation are very closely linked to Liechtenstein practice and therefore sometimes seem surprisingly similar.

The option to amend the Bylaws forms a mandatory part of their content.[211] Generally, the Foundation Council has the authority to amend them. The founder may, however, reserve this right for himself.[212] Art.7 LFIP defines in detail the content requirements for such amendments. The local representative must submit the Amendment Deed to the Public Registry.

Unlike Liechtenstein, where a foundation can be established either on the basis of a Foundation Charter and the Bylaws or on the basis of a single document (*i.e.* the Bylaws include the Foundation Charter), Panamanian foundation law only recognizes a single founding document that contains both the Foundation Charter and the Bylaws.[213] The practical advantage of the two separate documents as regulated in Liechtenstein (and not recognized in Panama) is that any changes to the Foundation Council do not automatically result in changes to the Bylaws.[214]

The single Foundation Charter containing the Bylaws is the basic document governing a Panamanian foundation. This was specifically desired by Panamanian legislation.[215]

If the Foundation Charter or its amendments are not written in Spanish, the same shall be protocolized by a public notary of the Republic of Panama, together with its Spanish translation by a certified public translator."

211 Cf. Art.5 Para.8 LFIP.

212 In the context of Art.7 LFIP. Pursuant to the new law governing foundations in Liechtenstein, a judge will be authorized in future – on petition by the participants or *ex officio* – to amend the contents of the Foundation Charter with regard to the purpose of the foundation to reflect changes in circumstances, unless the Foundation Charter authorizes any other governing body or third party to implement such amendment (NLArt.552 §31 and §33 PGR).

213 Art.5 LFIP.

214 This separation as regulated in Liechtenstein seems to be reflected in the revised foundation law as well: Pursuant to OLArt.555 PGR, the Foundation Charter of a Liechtenstein foundation must contain the name and domicile of the foundation, its purpose or object, the designation of the Foundation Council members and the method for appointing another Foundation Council as well as a provision concerning the application of the assets in the event of the dissolution of the foundation. The revised law extends the content of the bylaws to include the duration of the foundation (NLArt.552 § 16 Para.1 No.6 PGR).

215 Cf. FERRER, p.8: "Consequently, we have created under **one title and one public deed** the Foundation Charter, which in turn contains the information normally includ-

As such, Panama has eliminated the discussion (which frequently arises in Liechtenstein) as to whether the Foundation Charter takes precedence over any other formal sources of the founder's intention.[216] The latest reform of the law governing foundations in Liechtenstein seems to be following Panama's example with regard to clarifying in more detail the constitution formalities.[217]

n. The Foundation Charter is entered in the Public Registry.

All Panamanian foundations must be entered in the Public Registry. This is not the case in Liechtenstein, which distinguishes between deposited and registered

---

ed in the Act of Constitution and the Statutes, as the terms are known and used in Liechtenstein."

[216] Liechtenstein does not automatically rank the Foundation Charter and the bylaws in respect of the Foundation Charter taking precedence over the bylaws. Instead, it remedies the issue based on which documentation was drafted in the necessary form by the founder in the course of constitution. Precedence is determined solely on the basis of the origin. These documents rank equally and require interpretation in the event of contradictions, as is also the case with contradictory provisions in other documents governing legal transactions. As such, the hierarchy of the documentation depends on its origin and not on its name.

[217] OLArt.552 PGR offers a list of examples of possible foundation purposes ("especially") and the latest revision of the section governing foundations in NLArt.552 §2 PGR aims to expand this catalogue of examples. The following purposes are listed for consideration: common-benefit, cultural, scientific, family and ecclesiastical purposes, the administration and utilization of assets for beneficiaries, and the preservation and support of companies. A process to reform the PGR in the Principality of Liechtenstein was launched to eliminate or at least contain the misuse of foundations. It aims to protects the characteristic features of the foundation and prevent it from being diluted down to company status. As such, when establishing a foundation in future, the purpose will be an *essentialia negotii* in the Foundation Charter that must be sufficiently defined or definable. Foundations whose purpose is solely defined as the management of their assets and the unconditional distribution of income to specifically designated beneficiaries do not demonstrate a specific purpose for which the estate was endowed to the foundation and for which the income is to be utilized. Such a foundation does not correspond in any way to the definition of a foundation as accepted in the neighbouring countries (FLOGH ruling dated 02.12.1966). So if the purpose of a foundation is not defined specifically enough, the foundation risks losing its legal character.
If it is allowed to retain its legal character, it is – at the very least – threatened with non-recognition by jurisdictions in other countries (*e.g.* in Switzerland, Cf. BGE 115 Ib 555; BGE 108 II 398; ZH OGer. SIZ 85 (1989) 85 No. 13).

foundations.[218] The mandatory registration pursuant to Panamanian legislation increases legal certainty. The individuals involved in setting up the foundation bear more responsibility and third parties are better protected since the names and addresses of the Foundation Council members are registered.

Pursuant to Article 9 LFIP, a foundation acquires legal character as soon as its Foundation Charter is entered in the Private Foundations section of the Public Registry. Publication of the registration is not required.

In most cases in Liechtenstein, foundations also have to wait for registration in the Public Register to become legal entities.[219] Ecclesiastical, pure and mixed family foundations and foundations with defined or definable beneficiaries acquire legal character without registration (OLArt.557 Para.2 PGR).[220] The following information is published on the court notice board following registration: Name, domicile, purpose, date of constitution deed, organization and representation incl. names and residential addresses (OLArt.556 Para.2 PGR).[221]

In Liechtenstein, the assets must first be brought into the foundation before the foundation can be entered in the Register and thus acquire legal character,[222]

---

218 Cf. OLArt.554 PGR for deposited foundations and OLArt.556 and 557 PGR for registered foundations. The new law governing foundations in Liechtenstein also adopted this regulation (Cf. NLArt.552 §§19 and 20 PGR).

219 OLArt.557 Para.1 PGR: "The foundation only comes into existence when entered in the Public Register as Foundation Register." The new law governing foundations in Liechtenstein also adopted this regulation (Cf. NLArt.552 §14 Para.4 PGR).

220 The revised PGR demands the registration of ecclesiastical foundations, whereas foundations with defined or definable beneficiaries acquire legal character provided such the purpose of such foundations is not primarily to benefit the general public (NLArt.552 §14 Para.4 and 5 PGR).

221 This Article was abolished in the reformed law and replaced with a reference to pertinent regulations governing the Public Register (NLArt.552 §19 PGR).

222 Pursuant to Art.122 PGR, the proof of capital constitutes an "*essentialia negotii*" in Liechtenstein: Paying in the capital is a prerequisite for acquiring legal character:
1) The minimum capital or minimum assets must be at least 50,000 Swiss francs in the case of joint stock corporations and other associations whose capital is divided into shares, and at least 30,000 Swiss francs in the case of companies with limited liability and associations whose capital is not divided into shares.
1a) The minimum capital or minimum assets can be registered in local currency, or in Euros or US Dollars. In this case, the minimum capital or minimum assets must be at least 50,000 Euros or 50,000 US Dollars in the case of joint stock corporations and other associations whose capital is divided into shares, and at least 30,000 Euros or 30,000 US Dollars in the case of companies with limited liability and associations whose capital is not divided into shares.
2) The minimum capital and minimum assets must be fully paid in and/or incorporated." (Art.122 Para.1-2 PGR).

whereas in Panama, the opposite is the case: The foundation is first registered and the assets then incorporated.

Contracts between the foundation and third parties will not be recognized if the foundation is not registered (since it then, by law, does not exist).

In Panama, all public documentation relating to the foundation must be entered in the Public Registry. It must not be deposited, as is the case in Liechtenstein law.[223]

Any third party can, on request, obtain an excerpt from the foundation's entry in the Registry, which can then be translated, certified and apostilled. This is important in terms of legal certainty as it ensures, for example, that signatories are actually authorized to sign. The excerpt contains the following minimum information:

- The name of the foundation
- The name of any fiduciary founder
- The members of the Foundation Council, together with their residential addresses if requested
- The representation of the foundation
- The foundation capital
- The domicile and duration of the foundation
- The number and date of registration
- The date of issue and the issuing authority.

Panama has signed the Hague Convention on "Apostilles" dated 5 October 1961 governing the international certification of documents, which permits documents to be recognized simultaneously in various countries with just one certification.

The new law governing foundations in Liechtenstein also adopted this regulation (Cf. NLArt.552 §16 Para.1 No.3 PGR).

223 This raises the interesting legal question in the case of **deposited** foundations in Liechtenstein that do not comply with the requirements of Art.122 PGR (minimum capital and/or minimum assets, etc.). The consequence of Art.122 PGR would be the dissolution, even of a deposited foundation, on grounds of lack of assets:
"3) In the event that the minimum capital (minimum starting capital) drops below the specified amount, members or creditors may file an **application for dissolution** to the court on pertinent grounds. The same applies in the absence of the required number of members in non-contentious civil proceedings.
4) The law interprets capital as a denominable sum of money and assets as any property or rights that are only denominated in monetary terms for accounting or other purposes." (Art.122 Paras.3 and 4 PGR).

2. *Steps following entry in the Public Registry*

a. *Payment of the registration and annual fees*

Once the foundation is registered, it becomes liable for taxation and must pay a registration and annual fee.[224] This regulation corresponds to the provisions in the Principality of Liechtenstein where, upon registration/deposit,[225] the payment of a registration fee[226] and an annual tax becomes mandatory.[227]

The registration tax in Panama is determined by the amount of statutorily determined foundation capital. Since the approved, authorized and not paid-in capital of a foundation usually amounts to the standard USD 10,000, the tax derived on the basis of this capital is 50 USD.[228]

The annual fee for a Panamanian foundation is USD 250[229] and must be paid within three months of registration. Late payment of tax obligations incurs a fine of USD 50.[230]

b. *The regulations are drafted*

As is also the case with Liechtenstein law, the law governing foundations in Panama demands that regulations ("reglamento") be drafted in addition to the

---

224 Cf. Art. 8 LFIP: "Registration and annual taxes: Every private foundation shall pay registration fees and annual taxes equivalent to those established for corporations in Articles 318 and 318A of the Fiscal Code. The procedure and form of payment, the surcharge for late payment, the consequences of non-payment, as well as all the complementary dispositions of the legal precepts previously cited, will also be applicable to private foundations."

225 Just depositing a foundation also invokes an invoice for about 600 Swiss francs from the Public Register in Liechtenstein.

226 in Liechtenstein 200 Swiss francs

227 in Liechtenstein 1000 Swiss francs p.a., resp. 1 o/oo of the foundations assets, payable in advance.

228 This regulation corresponds to the provisions in Liechtenstein, where – again – the registration fee increases in line with, resp. is directly dependent on, the statutorily determined foundation capital.

229 The Balboa is the national currency of Panama. It is fixed to the USD. 1 Balboa is equivalent to 1 USD. When the Panamanian foundation law came into effect in 1995, the annual tax initially amounted to USD 150 but was subsequently increased in 2002 through Amendment No. 61 to the Fiscal Code dated 26 December 2002. The tax amendment came into force on 1 January 2003.

230 Prior to the tax amendment in 2003, the fine amounted to 30 USD.

constitution document, the Bylaws.[231] Although the Bylaws constitute the documentary basis, they are never the only document on which the administration of the foundation is based. The law does not prescribe the required content of these regulations. The founder can issue them and define their content at his own discretion. He uses them to govern specific and detailed matters and requirements that are not **destined for the public domain**. This means that no details concerning beneficiaries or benefits are registered in Panama.[232]

The regulations generally govern the following issues:

- The designation and hierarchy of the beneficiaries The procedure to be adopted if a beneficiary is eliminated or no further beneficiaries are available. The procedure for notifying beneficiaries. Regulations and special conditions that the beneficiaries must comply with.
- Specific and defined assets to be incorporated into the foundation and the specific distribution of the same to, or utilization by, the beneficiaries.
- The powers of authority, restrictions on competencies and control of the Foundation Council and the founder.
- Activities of the foundation both during the life, and after the death, of the founder.
- The procedure for amending the regulations.

The Bylaws are subject to mandatory registration as a public document, whereas the regulations are private. They are drafted by the Foundation Council. The regulations can be registered in the interests of enhanced legal certainty. The founder can engage a notary public to certify the signatures on the regulations. The same procedure applies to amendments of the regulations as to the drafting of the same.

c. The initial capital / assets are brought into the foundation

The foundation's wealth is nothing less than the aggregate of assets and rights whose title is transferred by the founder or by third parties to the foundation and which is administered by the Foundation Council in accordance with the Bylaws

[231] Pursuant to Art.81 Para.1 ZGB, Switzerland also only stipulates the mandatory certification of the Foundation Charter and even then only when a foundation is established *inter vivos*. Nowadays, the simple written form is generally deemed sufficient when drafting valid regulations. This regulation corresponds to the provisions in both Liechtenstein and Panamanian law.

[232] Cf. Section Specimen Texts / Templates. Unpublished Documentation. Sample regulations in German and English.

and regulations.[233] The estate can comprise transferable assets of any kind; national (Panamanian) or foreign, movable or immovable assets;[234] including future assets or regular income and/or payments. Wealth can also exist in the form of rights and/or obligations, stocks and/or dividends. The important factor is the ability to denominate the foundation's estate in monetary (pecuniary) terms. The estate of a foundation cannot, however, include objects that cannot be traded or are not suitable for trading (fuera de comercio), since no title of ownership to them can be acquired.

Pursuant to Art.5 Para.2 LFIP, the indication of the initial capital in the Bylaws is mandatory. It may be denominated in any legally acceptable currency but must amount to the equivalent of USD 10,000, at least.[235] This regulation corresponds to the provisions in Liechtenstein.[236] There is no need to provide evidence of this amount to the Public Registry in Panama prior to establishment of

---

233 OLArt.558 PGR defines the donations to the foundation, once it has been constituted, in Liechtenstein:
"1) When the foundation has come into existence, the founder or the third party, upon demand of the Supervising Authority, the representative of public law or of interested parties, is required to transfer to the foundation the assets mentioned in the deed of foundation.
2) Rights, for whose transfer a declaration of assignment is sufficient, devolve by operation of the law upon the foundation on coming into existence.
3) Where the foundation only becomes effective on the death of the founder or after the termination of a firm or legal entity, the said foundation shall be deemed to have been in existence already before the death or termination of the founder for the donations of the founder or third party.
4) The donation of assets may also be effected, in particular, by the establishment of a contractual relationship to the founder or third party according to which the founder or third party undertakes to donate annually or at certain intervals a fixed or variable sum or other assets (donation of periodical payments).
5) In case of doubt, the investment of assets shall ensue pursuant to the regulations concerning trust investments." (OLArt.558 Paras.1-5 PGR)
The new law governing foundations in Liechtenstein also adopted this regulation (Cf. NLArt.552 §16 Para.1 No.3 PGR).

234 Immovable assets (land and buildings) on Panamanian soil must be transferred to the foundation by means of a public deed, which must be entered in the Public Registry.

235 Pursuant to Art.122 Para.1 PGR, the minimum capital in Liechtenstein is 30,000 CHF. The new law governing foundations has adopted this regulation (Cf. NLArt.552 §13 PGR).

236 The former law in Liechtenstein did not require the indication of capital of a Liechtenstein foundation although, in practice, the Public Register refused to accept applications for registration if the capital was not included in the Foundation Charter and bylaws. The new law governing foundations in Liechtenstein has taken a similar approach to regulating this issue (Cf. NLArt.552 §16 Para.1 No.3 PGR).

the foundation. This regulation also corresponds to the provisions in Liechtenstein.[237]

Founders prefer not to disclose the real assets of their foundations for reasons of discretion and confidentiality. Legislation has recognized this fact and regulated it accordingly: The initial capital does not have to be physically paid in by the founding individuals or third parties, neither on or after establishment of the foundation; it merely needs to be recorded as the initial capital in the Bylaws. Art.10 LFIP merely stipulates that the assets destined for the foundation be transferred to the foundation as soon as it has been established. These assets do not, however, have to amount to USD 10,000. Equally, the assets can be increased at any time without any need to notify Panama, *i.e.* to register the same. As such, the actually existing foundation capital remains concealed from the general public. This raises the question as to whether such a liberal solution does not encourage potential misuse.

In the event that a founder wishes to establish a foundation upon his death, the donations (of assets) promised by the founder on his death to the foundation are payable, pursuant to Art.10 LFIP. [238]

The donation of assets to a foundation becomes due immediately after the establishment of the foundation. "Once a foundation has acquired juridical personality, the founder or any third party who has acquired an obligation to contribute assets to the foundation, either by himself/herself or at the request of another person with interest in the foundation, shall formalize the transfer to the foundation of the assets which they agreed to transfer."[239]

Once the estate has been donated, it/the foundation capital constitutes assets that are independent of the other assets belonging to the founder. It is therefore legally separated and deemed to be independent and may only be used for the purpose indicated in the Bylaws; legal action can no longer be brought against it to satisfy personal obligations of the founder or the beneficiaries.

---

[237] If a foundation in Liechtenstein is **registered**, the capital must be paid in for the foundation to acquire legal character (Art.122 Para.2 PGR). The Public Register demands the provision of corresponding evidence of the capital. In the case of **deposited** foundations, the proof of capital does not have to be presented to the Public Register although the obligation to pay in the capital remains (Cf. NLArt.552 §20 Para.2 No.11 PGR).

[238] Art.10 Sent.2 LFIP: "Donation of assets: ... When the foundation is constituted to be effective at the time of death of its founder, it shall be deemed to have existed prior to the death of the founder with respect to the donations which he/she may have made to the foundation."

[239] Art.10 Para.1 LFIP.

The protection of the foundation's estate as a special fund is provided in full by the law itself: "The assets of the foundation constitute a separate special fund that is independent of the founder's other assets."[240]

As such, the assets of the foundation may not be subject to any precautionary action or measure, unless such action or measure is related to fulfilling the purposes or objectives of the foundation, or of the legitimate rights of the beneficiaries of the foundation.[241]

In no case shall such assets be held liable for the personal obligations of the founder or of the beneficiaries.[242]

These assets may not be seized or attached except in the case of obligations incurred, or damages caused by virtue of actions taken in fulfilment of the purposes or objectives of the foundation, or of legitimate rights of the beneficiaries of the foundation.

This means that the founder or any third party, who has transferred assets to the foundation, loses title of ownership to these assets.[243]

The transfer of assets to foundations is irrevocable for and by the person making the transfer, unless expressly stated otherwise in the deed documenting the transfer.[244]

IV. Organization of the foundation

A. The founder

Although the founder is not an official governing body of a Panamanian foundation, he must be mentioned in connection with the organization of the foundation since his reasons for establishing the foundation are important for other statutorily specified governing bodies and participants. Although not a governing body, his position influences the foundation from the very first moment of its existence.

---

240 Art.11 Para.1 LFIP.

241 Art.11 Para.2 LFIP.

242 Art.11 Para.3 LFIP.

243 Nevertheless, the founder can still determine how the assets he has donated are used. Various possibilities exist: the founder can be a member of the Foundation Council, the founder can be given power of attorney authorizing him to manage the foundation's assets, or the founder assumes the function of Protector and controls these assets, although this exercise of control may result in tax disadvantages for the founder in other countries.

244 Art.12 Para.2 LFIP.

The founder must be sane and capable of action and judgement.[245]

When establishing a foundation, the law gives the founder as much freedom as he likes to define the required conditions, restrictions and rules. The founder can exert permanent influence on the administration of the foundation if this is explicitly specified in the Bylaws, by reserving rights for himself or by having himself appointed Foundation Council or Protector during the act of constitution.[246] Generally speaking, however, founders do not take advantage of this right.[247]

Irrespective of whether the founder reserves rights for himself in the Foundation Charter, he can, by law, demand the dismissal of one or several members of the Foundation Council on pertinent grounds in a court of law.[248]

The founder has the following rights and obligations:

- To establish and revoke the foundation.[249]
- To determine the content of the Bylaws and regulations and to alter the purpose of the foundation.[250]
- To transfer the assets to the foundation.[251]
- To belong to the Foundation Council,[252] to nominate or dismiss members of the Foundation Council.[253]

---

245 Cf. Art. 297 Código Civil: "capacidad para actuar en el mundo jurídico." Pursuant to Panamanian law, people who are incapable of judgement, minors, deaf mutes or blind people who cannot express their intentions may not act as founders.

246 Cf. Art.18 and Art.21 LFIP.

247 Normally, the founder appoints a third party as Foundation Council and agrees a management contract with that person (authorization, fiduciary, trust contract, freelance service agreement) in which the Foundation Council undertakes to only act in accordance with the founder's instructions. This contract is, however, governed solely by the law of obligations; it does not possess any statutory power. Breaches of the contract result in contractual liability, but not D&O liability. Cf. *D. Loretz*, Diss. No. II. lit. E. 1. bb.

248 Cf. Art.23 LFIP.

249 Cf. Art.1 and Art.4 in conjunction with Art.12 Para.1 No.2 and Art.13 LFIP: To revoke the foundation at any time if he has established it to come into existence "post mortem" (Art. 13 LFIP) or if he has specified accordingly in the constitution documents (Art.12. Para.1 No.2 LFIP).
This regulation corresponds to the provisions in Liechtenstein law (Cf. OLArt. 559 Para. 4 PGR, see also revised foundation law, NLArt.552 §22 PGR).

250 Cf. Art.7 LFIP. This regulation was adopted by Liechtenstein in the new Art.552 §30 PGR when the foundation law was revised.

251 Cf. Art.10 LFIP. Both the initial capital and any subsequent donations to the foundation's assets, at any time and without notifying Panama.

252 Cf. Art.5 Para.3 LFIP.

253 Cf. Art.21 and Art.23 LFIP.

- To appoint the Protector and to define the latter's rights and obligations.[254]
- To appoint one or several supervisory bodies.[255]
- To designate third parties or himself as the beneficiaries of the foundation.[256]

Neither Liechtenstein nor Panamanian foundation law prescribes any strict regulations governing the structure of a foundation's organization. The founder is entitled to specify the structure in the constitution documents.[257]

As already mentioned, the founder of a Panamanian foundation can be either a natural person or a legal entity. This is new in Panamanian law; previously only natural persons were accepted and recognized as the founders of a legal entity.[258]

Although the founder can himself act as the "Beneficial Founder" of the foundation, he generally prefers fiduciary constitution on grounds of anonymity. As such, the foundation is set up by a fiduciary – the "Nominee Founder" or "Legal Founder".[259] The relationship between the beneficial and the legal founders is generally deemed to constitute an authorization contract containing both a power of attorney and a mandate, on the basis of which the legal founder executes the constitution of the foundation.

Panamanian law does not contain any provisions for a possible assignment of the founder's rights from the fiduciary to the beneficial founder. Here it is necessary to resort to Liechtenstein teachings and jurisdiction.

The former law in Liechtenstein does not, however, specifically define the legal nature of the founder's rights, either, or the legal consequences resulting from the same. In the past, this has resulted in different court rulings and, consequently, in legal uncertainty.[260] The amended law governing foundations in

---

[254] Cf. Art.24 LFIP.

[255] Cf. Art.19 LFIP in conjunction with Art.24 LFIP.

[256] Cf. Art.5 Para.7 and Art.24 Para.2 No.9 LFIP.

[257] This structure may vary, depending on the defined purpose. In the case of commercial administration of the foundation's assets, the consequences may differ from one country to the next: Foundations in Liechtenstein may, exceptionally, also engage in commercial business enterprises (OLArt.557 Para.3 PGR and NLArt.552 §1 Para.2 PGR), which necessitates the appointment of an auditor who must present annual reports on the accounts and administration of the foundation to the tax authorities; a legal requirement that is not known in Panama.

[258] See, *e.g.*, Art.1 of the law governing joint stock corporations.

[259] The OGH in Liechtenstein rejects any distinction between beneficial and legal founders. Cf. the proposed revision of the foundation law dated 10 September 2004, p. 38.

[260] In its ruling dated 1.7.1996 (6 C 410/91-20), the Supreme Court of Justice in Liechtenstein concluded that the rights reserved for the founder could be freely assignable, otherwise transferred and bequeathed. In a ruling dated 6.12.2001 (1 Cg 378/99-50), the OGH took a different stance, deciding that the reserved rights of the founder were entirely personal rights. Such rights of determination were apparently foreign to the

Liechtenstein does not alter the rights of the founder. It does, however, distinguish them more clearly from the rights of the Foundation Council.[261] Both jurisdiction and teaching argue on whether, and the extent to which, these determination rights of the founder are "transferable" or can be also be granted to a third party.[262]

---

nature of foundations and needed to be interpreted restrictively. As such, they could not be separated from the person of the founder and transferred from this legal position.

261 Cf. new Art.552 §4 and §24 PGR.

262 The Liechtenstein amendment is based on the opinion that determination rights of the founder (the right to revoke the foundation and the right to alter the purpose of the foundation) would completely obliterate the distinction between foundation and company if they did not cease to exist upon the death of the founder and instead could be freely transferred and bequeathed. As such, the new Art.552 §22 PGR still stipulates that the founder can alter the purpose of the foundation as he likes and can revoke the foundation at any time. These rights are neither transferable nor hereditary. In the event that the founder has established the foundation for the purpose of fulfilling an obligation to a third party, who receives assets from the foundation free of charge, the founder may explicitly reserve these rights for this third party (indirect founder) in the Foundation Charter. If the founder reserves these determination rights for himself, he can exercise them unconditionally and without restriction as long as he remains with the borders of legality and morality. The founder may also reserve other rights of amendment, such as rights regarding the organization of the foundation. The new Art.552 §30 PGR aims, however, to explicitly regulate those determination rights that can be solely reserved for the founder.
Particular analysis is required, in particular, when the foundation is established by a legal entity and, especially, on a fiduciary or quasi-fiduciary basis, in view of the potentially long duration and the free transferability of the shares in the legal entity. Following the OGH ruling dated 6.12.2001, the founder's rights were supposed to be assigned solely to the fiduciary (legal) founder in the case of foundations established on a fiduciary basis. In this respect, a possible Para. 3 of OLArt. 559a PGR with the following wording was discussed during the amendment of the foundation law: "If and to the extent that the determination rights are reserved for a legal entity, these reserved rights cease to exist if the legal entity is dissolved or in any case 30 years after the establishment of the foundation."
The proposed Para. 2 of OLArt.559a PGR focused on the issue of whether the exercise of the amendment rights reserved for the founder can be reserved solely for the fiduciary founder or whether the fiduciary founder can also include a clause in the Foundation Charter that authorizes the client to make amendments as well. The government in Liechtenstein believes that the reserved amendment rights can be transferred to the client since the fiduciary establishment of a foundation reflects the intentions of the client, and not of the fiduciary founder. The option of wording the Foundation Charter to authorize the client to exercise a free right of revocation or amendment of the purpose is therefore not only materially consistent with the purpose

B. The beneficiaries

Although the beneficiaries do not constitute a governing body of a foundation, they nevertheless play an important role.[263] The beneficiaries are those individuals[264] who benefit from the foundation. They do not, however, constitute owners or creditors of the foundation. As such, they can only assert rights against the foundation that are specified in the Bylaws, regulations and/or resolutions adopted by the Foundation Council. Beneficiaries can be natural persons or legal entities and can include the founder himself. The beneficiaries must be specified in a defined or definable manner. Usually, they are only named in the regulations, but not in the Bylaws, for reasons of discretion and are, therefore, not disclosed to the general public.

The beneficiary rights can be of a widely diverse nature and can be conditional, limited, irrevocable and/or revocable, etc. The rights and obligations arising from the beneficiary status are determined by the law, the Bylaws and the regulations.

The rights can be divided into two groups:

1. Rights with characteristics of a material legal nature: Receipt of benefits in the shape of assets and income,[265] receipt of information about the economic status of the foundation.[266] This also includes the planned tax exemption for beneficiaries in Panama.[267]

---

of the foundation, it also does not materially affect the sense and purpose of the "non-transferability of the founder's rights".

The new law governing foundations in Liechtenstein ultimately adopted the former regulation (Cf. NLArt.552 §4 Para.3 PGR).

263 Simply because it makes no sense to establish a foundation from which nobody benefits.

264 Panamanian law does not, however, permit animals to be designated as beneficiaries, although this is perfectly possible in some Anglo-Saxon countries. Art.5 Para.7 and Art.18 Para.1 No.3 and 4 LFIP talk about "persons" and – pursuant to Art.38 Código Civil – the term only means human beings or legal entities.

265 Pursuant to Art.18 Para.1 No.4 LFIP: "To deliver to the beneficiaries of the foundation the assets, properties or resources designated for them by the Foundation Charter or its regulations."

266 Pursuant to Art.18 Para.1 No.3 LFIP: "To inform the beneficiaries of the foundation or the economic situation of the same as provided by the Foundation Charter or its regulations."

267 Beneficiaries do not pay taxes when transferring real estate whenever a) the beneficiary is a first-degree relative of the founder (e.g. from father to son or vice-versa) or b) the beneficiary is the spouse of the founder (Law No. 106, passed in 1974, and Law No. 31, passed in 1991).

2. Rights with characteristics of an administrative nature: Taking court action to enforce administrative measures: In the event of infringements of their interests and rights, the beneficiaries may take action against, and hold the Foundation Council liable.[268] This can even result in the dismissal of the Foundation Council.[269]

The beneficiaries may contest any and all resolutions, administrative actions or measures by hte Foundation Council that infringe their benefits.

Pursuant to Panamanian law, the rights of the beneficiaries are strictly personal.[270] The constitution documents can, however, determine otherwise. For example, they can explicitly specify the beneficiary must waive its right to compensation, that the beneficiary may pledge, assign or sell his beneficial rights, or that any beneficiary who contests his beneficiary rights through legal action loses them, etc.[271]

Art.14 LFIP specifies[272] that the **inheritance laws** that are applicable at the domicile of the founder or the beneficiaries **do not have any influence** on the

---

268 Cf. Art.26 LFIP. "Any beneficiary of the foundation may object to acts of the foundation which damage his or her rights or interests by denouncing such circumstance to the Protector or other supervisory body, if any, or if there are none, by directly instituting the corresponding judicial action before the appropriate court of the domicile of the foundation."

269 Pursuant to Art.23 LFIP: "Active legitimation for dismissing or appointing members of the Foundation Council:
The founder or the beneficiaries may instigate legal action to remove the members of the Foundation Council. If the beneficiaries are disabled or minors, the application for dismissal of the Foundation Council members can be filed by whoever exercises patriae potestas or legal guardianship over them, as the case may be. The judgement of the court decreeing the removal shall also appoint new members to replace the former, who must be persons with sufficient capacity, qualifications and recognized moral standing to administer the assets of the foundation in accordance with the purposes established by the founder."

270 The reverse is the case with Anglo-Saxon trusts where the law primarily regulates the assets of the trust and the administration of the same by the trustee.

271 Here again, the regulations in Liechtenstein can be adopted when drafting regulations for a Panamanian foundation. OLArt.567 Para.3 PGR and NLArt.552 §36 PGR permit a founder to explicitly state in the bylaws that none of the income from the foundation's assets can be taken from the beneficiary in the event of compulsory execution or bankruptcy. Moreover, the founder is at liberty to specify that second or third beneficiaries do not receive any rights of inspection or control.

272 Article 14 was adopted by Panama based on the trust rights prevailing in Caribbean jurisdictions and in Jersey and Guernsey. Cf. Ferrer, p.13.

validity of the foundation.[273] The only governing elements are the provisions in the constitution document and the regulations. This means that a judge in Panama must solely and exclusively respect the wishes of the founder.[274] Liechtenstein law differs in this respect,[275] as it does indeed observe **entitlements to statutory shares.**[276] In this respect it is, however, important to mention that foundation assets, which are located in a state (not Panama) where entitlements to statutory shares are recognized and, as such, enforceable, may be subject to confiscation, irrespective of the Panamanian law governing foundations.

C. The Foundation Council

1. Definition and composition

The Foundation Council is responsible for administering the foundation.[277] As such, the Foundation Council is an executive body that is charged with administering the foundation. It must fulfil the wishes of the founder. As an administrative body, it possesses powers of discretion and decision making.[278] Its members

---

273 Art.14 LFIP: "Entitlements to statutory rights: The existence of legal provisions regarding inheritance, at the place of domicile of the founder or the beneficiaries shall not affect the foundation or its purposes in the manner provided in the Foundation Charter or its regulations."

274 The intention of the founder when setting up the foundation is all that matters.

275 In its ruling dated 7.3.2002 (1 Cg 145/99-75 – LJZ 2003, 100), the Supreme Court of Justice in Liechtenstein (OGH) contradicted the widespread opinion that the establishment of a Liechtenstein foundation could enable the circumvention of statutory shares in other countries. Cf. also Künzle, Revision of Liechtenstein Foundation Laws, Section: "No circumvention of foreign statutory shares by FL foundations", Private 2004, p.22.

276 The heirs (whose statutory shares are at risk) are mentioned in OLArt.560 Para.1 PGR and NLArt.552 §38 PGR, where they are given the opportunity to contest the foundation as they might a donation. Prior to the amendments, OLArt.552 Para.4 PGR generally referred to the law governing trust companies (TruG §78-133) as long as its norms did not contradict the nature of foundations. Unless the bylaws or regulations specify otherwise with regard to the beneficiaries or the benefit, the founder is assumed to be the sole beneficiary in application of §105 Para. 1 TruG and legal succession in accordance with inheritance law regulations is presumed. Cf. *Bösch*, LJZ 2003, p.55 et seqq.

277 Art.17 Para.1 LFIP: "Foundation Council: The foundation shall have a Foundation Council whose powers or responsibilities shall be established in the Foundation Charter."

278 Cf. Art.17, 18 and 19 LFIP.

represent the foundation vis-à-vis third parties, the state and the administration.[279]

Panamanian law stipulates that the Foundation Council must be comprised of a minimum of 3 natural persons or one legal entity.[280] The two can also be combined at will. The legal entity can be a joint stock corporation, other company or even a bank. All members of the Foundation Council can be from Panama or abroad; neither a professional qualification nor a domicile in Panama is required.[281] The founder may belong to the Foundation Council.[282]

2. Appointment of the Foundation Council

The appointment of the Foundation Council is a mandatory part of the Bylaws. The Bylaws do not, however, have to specify the procedure for appointing the Foundation Council.[283]

---

[279] The responsibilities of the Foundation Council can be delegated to others: To the Protector: the Protector can administer the foundation directly (e.g. signatory power for the foundation's bank account), or indirectly by controlling the files and documents of the Foundation Council.
To third parties: A system of completely indirect administration where a third party who is not part of the foundation system can govern the assets of the foundation. This can be achieved with a general power of attorney, for example.
To the founder: The law permits membership of the founder on the Foundation Council.

[280] Art.17 Para.2 LFIP: "Unless the Council is a juridical person, the number of members of the Foundation Council shall be no less than three (3)."

[281] This is regulated differently in Liechtenstein where an obligatory minimum number of Foundation Council members is now stipulated by law (Cf. NLArt.552 §24 Para.2 PGR). Pursuant to Art.180a PGR, however, at least one member of the Foundation Council must be a citizen of Liechtenstein, domiciled in Liechtenstein (foreigners with residence permits are equally permitted) and must actively pursue the profession of a lawyer, auditor or trustee. These minimum requirements aim to prevent misuse and to ensure that the Liechtenstein authorities have an addressee whom they can reach. Apart from this restriction, the Foundation Council can be composed at will. Since 1.4.2009, Liechtenstein therefore no longer permits one single member of the Foundation Council.

[282] This regulation as defined in Art.5 Para.3 LFIP corresponds therefore to Liechtenstein provisions where the founder is equally permitted to sit on the Foundation Council. By contrast, Austrian foundations may neither appoint legal entities nor beneficiaries or their spouses or relatives up to the third degree to the Foundation Council.

[283] Cf. Art.5 Para.3 LFIP. "The Foundation Charter shall contain: ... A complete and clear designation of all members of the Foundation Council, to which the founder may belong, including their addresses."

The founder appoints the first Foundation Council. Subsequently, the founder can determine who may dismiss from and/or appoint members to the Foundation Council and under which conditions.[284]

3. Rights and obligations

The Foundation Council can be organized as an administrative body that must supervise and execute the wishes of the founder without itself playing any role in the decision-making process, or it can be granted powers of discretion and decision making. The founder makes this decision when establishing the foundation and specifies it in the Foundation Charter.

If this specification is missing in the Foundation Charter or Bylaws, the standard obligations and competences as defined in Art.18 LFIP apply to the Foundation Council.[285] Generally speaking, its task is to administer the assets of the

---

[284] The founder can choose between the form of coopting that is also practised in Liechtenstein, whereby the Foundation Council members choose their own successors, or the delegation process provided in Art.24 Para.2 Nos.4, 5 and 6 LFIP: "The Foundation Charter or its regulations may provide for the constitution of supervisory bodies, which may be composed of natural or juridical persons, such as auditing companies, Protectors of the foundation, or other similar entities. The powers of the supervisory entities shall be established in the Foundation Charter or its regulations, and may include, among others, the following:

...To appoint new members of the Foundation Council by reason of temporary or permanent absence, or for the expiration of the period for which they were appointed.

... To appoint new members of the Foundation Council in replacement of existing members.

... To increase or reduce the number of members of the Foundation Council.

[285] Cf. Art.18 LFIP. "Rights and Obligations of the Foundation Council:

The Foundation Council shall be responsible for carrying out the purposes or objectives of the foundation. Unless otherwise specified in the Foundation Charter, the Foundation Council shall have the following general rights and obligations:

1. To administer the assets of the foundation in accordance with the Foundation Charter.

2. To carry out acts, contracts or lawful business which are convenient or necessary to advance the purposes of the foundation, and to include in such contracts, agreements and other instruments or obligations such clauses and conditions as are necessary or convenient and not contrary to the law, to bonos mores, or to public order and which are in accordance with the purposes of the foundation.

3. To inform the beneficiaries of the foundation or the economic situation of the same as provided by the Foundation Charter or its regulations.

4. To deliver to the beneficiaries of the foundation the assets, properties or resources designated for them by the Foundation Charter or its regulations.

5. To carry out all such acts or contracts which are permitted to the foundation by the present law and by other applicable legal or regulatory provisions."

foundation for the benefit of the beneficiaries and in accordance with the Bylaws and regulations.[286] Art.18 LFIP defines the following obligations for Foundation Councils:

---

[286] The amendments to the law governing foundations in Liechtenstein re-addressed the issue of the rights conferred on the governing bodies of the foundation or on third parties in NLArt.552 §31 PGR. The Foundation Charter must explicitly confer the right to change the organization (or the purpose). As such, a governing body of the foundation or a third party can only amend the contents of the Foundation Charter or can only draft additional deeds based on the Foundation Charter if the founder has explicitly conferred this right in the Foundation Charter (New Art.552 §31 and 32 PGR). This is of no concern to a change in the organization that does not affect the purpose of the foundation.
Rather, the governing body of the foundation that is entrusted with the power of amendment – which is usually the Foundation Council – is obligated to ensure that the structure of the organization best serves the cause of realizing the inherent purpose of the foundation. If problems arise in this respect the provisions governing supervision in OLArt. 565 PGR, NLArt.552 §33-35 PGR, become applicable. The responsible governing body can make the amendment to the Foundation Charter contingent on court approval (NLArt. 552 §35 PGR). By the same token, pursuant to Art.552 §33-35 PGR, the court can amend the organization of the foundation by administrative action on petition by a participant or *ex officio* if the existing structure is no longer adequate or the capability of the foundation to function seems to be at risk and unless the Foundation Charter has entrusted a different governing body or third party with the amendment of the organization. This regulation complies with the formerly applicable OLArt.565 Para.1 PGR: "After hearing the foundation's supreme authority and those persons, whose rights are affected, the Government, upon application of one of the participants or ex officio, may change the foundation's organization by administrative action, if this is required urgently, in order to preserve the assets or safeguard the foundation's purpose and insofar as the foundation deed or the articles has/have not entrusted another body or a third party with the changing of the organization. In opposition to such amendment orders, the participants may lodge an appeal with the Administrative court."
If an organization is not envisaged, or the envisaged organization is inadequate, the supervisory authority must take the necessary administrative action in non-contentious civil proceedings and, if required, have the measures entered in the Public Register in the case of foundations that are not subject to government supervision and where the participants have applied for court intervention (New Art. 552 §35 PGR). If these measures cannot be satisfactorily implemented, for instance because of insufficient assets, the supervisory authority or the judge must donate the assets to another foundation that pursues as similar a purpose as possible, unless the founder objects or a provision in the Foundation Charter explicitly does not permit the same.
On the other hand, granting a governing body or third party the power to freely amend the purpose of the foundation in the Foundation Charter would be critical. The New Art.552 §35 PGR therefore provides that a foundation governing body or third party may only change the purpose if, for example, the purpose proves to be unachievable, impermissible or unreasonable, or if the circumstances have changed such that the

a. Administration of the assets.[287]
b. Conclusion of any and all legal transactions to achieve the purpose of the foundation in compliance with all laws, morals and public order.[288]
c. Provision of information to the beneficiaries about the financial condition of the foundation.[289]
d. Delivery of benefits to the beneficiaries in accordance with the Bylaws and regulations.[290]
e. Conclusion of any all agreements or actions that are legally permitted for the foundation.[291]

These actions entitle it to a fee that is usually payable annually.[292]

4. Liability of the Foundation Council

The obligations and duties of the Foundation Council are primarily determined by the Bylaws.[293] If the Bylaws specify that the Foundation Council may only act upon approval by another governing body (*i.e.* is bound by instruction), its

---

purpose acquires a quite different meaning or effect and the foundation no longer fulfils the wishes of the founder. In order to ensure that the founder's wishes are carved in stone, only the founder should have the right to freely change the purpose but not the governing bodies or third parties and equally not the supervisory authority. Moreover, if governing bodies or third parties had the right to implement changes this would give the foundation closer resemblance to a company. Such far-reaching powers for governing bodies of a foundation are fundamentally inconsistent with the nature of a foundation. This would, in turn, only create legal uncertainty with regard to the issue of the founder's rights and, moreover, would result in the powers of the founder and the governing bodies intermingling, which could encourage the misuse of foundations.
The new Article resolves this issue by stipulating that changes to the organization must be explicitly regulated in the foundation documents and that changes to the purpose are only permissible on qualified grounds, which must be indicated.

287 Art.18 Para.1 LFIP.

288 Art.18 Para.2 LFIP.

289 Art.18 Para.3 LFIP.

290 Art.18 Para.4 LFIP.

291 Art.18 Para.5 LFIP.

292 The lump sum that is payable annually to the Foundation Council is about 3,000 USD. This flat rate is joined by hourly expenses, which are charged at a rate of max. 300 USD/hour. If the Foundation Council attends meetings in locations other than its domicile, it is entitled to reimbursement of the corresponding travel expenses. In the case of longer absences, the Foundation Council charges "man days" at a rate of 1,500 USD/day.

293 Art.30 LFIP is only applicable in a subsidiary sense: "Salvo que se disponga otra cosa en el acta fundacional o en sus reglamentos, el Consejo de Fundación deberá..."

liability is governed by Art.19 LFIP. If the Foundation Council is empowered to administer the foundation on its own (*i.e.* is not subject to instruction), Art.20 LFIP applies.

a. Foundation Council that is bound by instructions

Pursuant to Art.19 LFIP, a Foundation Council that may only act or has only acted upon approval by another governing body is exempted from liability and responsibility.[294] The act of appointing a governing body or a natural person with decision-making powers in the unpublished regulations and the ensuing contractual obligation on the Foundation Council constitutes a contractual engagement that is grounds for liability exemption.[295]

---

294 Art.19 LFIP: "Protector:
The Foundation Charter may provide that, in order to exercise their powers, the members of the Foundation Council must obtain the prior authorization of the Protector, a different governing body as specified by the founder, or the majority of the founders.
The members of the Foundation Council shall not be held liable for the loss or deterioration of the assets of the foundation or for the damages caused by their decisions, provided that the above mentioned authorization has been duly obtained."

295 This regulation differs from Liechtenstein law, where a contractual engagement does not constitute the exemption from liability of the Foundation Council. In Liechtenstein, a foundation cannot be held responsible for criminal actions that have been committed by the Foundation Council. This does not apply to administrative criminal law, e.g. tax law, customs law, which holds associations, incl. foundations, responsible.
As such, Art.111 Para.4 PGR should be observed, according to which: "Within the boundaries of their legal capacity and capacity to act, associations are moreover responsible under criminal law for impermissible actions that a governing body or other representative as designated in the bylaws commits in the performance of its administrative function, subject to a general **right of recourse** to the **perpetrator**."
As far as the administration of the foundation's assets is concerned, the procedure for such administration must always be defined in the regulations. The regulations must also specify the powers and obligations of the Foundation Council with regard to the investment of assets (OLArt.561 Para.1 PGR, NLArt.552 §25 PGR). If the bylaws raise any doubts with regard to the investment of assets, such investment must comply with the provisions governing fiduciary investments, pursuant to OLArt.558 Para 5 PGR.
Fiduciary investments are regulated in Art.913 PGR. This has raised a problem of interpretation as to whether assets that are wholly owned by a foundation may be foreign assets at all, since Para.4 of this Article specifies that this provision is not applicable for foreign assets (*D. Loretz*, Diss. p.63 et seqq). Nevertheless, the duty to preserve, improve and insure the assets lies with the trustee (based on the referenced norm in OLArt.552 Para.4 PGR), and therefore also with the Foundation Council in the pursuit of the foundation's purpose and in accordance with the principles of good

b. Foundation Council that is not bound by instructions

Pursuant to Art.20 LFIP, the Panamanian Foundation Council should act with the due diligence of a good father.[296] This duty of care by the "Bonus Pater familias" is one reason for the exemption from liability or the restriction of liability to culpable negligence.[297] This wording is reminiscent of Liechtenstein provisions for Foundation Councils, which are liable for careful business management and representation.[298] It is liable for damages caused culpably by its failure to fulfil its obligations,[299] irrespective of whether intentional or negligent.[300]

---

business management that takes account of the circumstances, even if their actions contradict the bylaws (§28 Para. 1 TrUG).

296 Cf. Art.20 LFIP: "Accounts:
Unless the Foundation Charter or its regulations provide otherwise, the Foundation Council must render accounts of its administration to the beneficiaries and, where applicable, to the supervisory entity.
If the Foundation Charter or its regulations contain no provision in this regard, accounts must be presented annually
If the accounts so rendered are not objected within the time specified in the Foundation Charter or its regulations, or, if the Charter does not regulate the matter, within ninety (90) days from the date the accounts were received, they shall be deemed to have been approved, for which purpose the above mentioned period of ninety (90) days must be indicated in the report rendering the accounts.
On the lapse of such period or upon the approval of the accounts, the members of the Foundation Council shall be free of liability for their administration, unless they had failed to act with the diligence of a '**bonus pater familias**'.
The above mentioned approval **does not** exonerate the members of the Foundation Council vis-à-vis the beneficiaries or third parties having an interest in the foundation with respect to damages caused by **gross negligence or fraud** in the administration of the foundation."

297 Culpa leve.

298 Pursuant to Art.182 Para.2 PGR:. "Rights and obligations: ... (The administration) shall diligently manage and promote the enterprise of the legal entity and shall be **liable** for observing the principles of **diligent management** and representation."

299 Pursuant to Art.220 Para.1 PGR: "Liability for management and control:
The persons entrusted with the management and control of a company shall be liable for any damage arising from their failure to perform their obligations."

300 Pursuant to Art.218 Para.1 PGR: "Accountability of legal entities and similar associations / Nature of the default: The governing bodies of a legal company and similar associations **shall be liable** for any damage they have caused to the association if they have acted **with intention or negligence**." **Minor negligence** is excluded (Cf. NLArt.552 §24 Para.6 PGR).

The statute of limitations in Panamanian civil law is 7 years for members of a Foundation Council, whereas in criminal law, the periods are determined by the nature of the crime and are 6 years maximum.[301]

The exemption from liability of the members of a Panamanian foundation does not, however, apply vis-à-vis the beneficiaries or third parties in the case of damages suffered during the administration of the foundation as a result of gross negligence or fraud.[302]

In this respect, Panamanian law[303] stipulates the mandatory preparation and presentation of annual accounts by the Foundation Council to the beneficiaries and the supervisory body/Protector and provides a three-month (90 day) period in which the beneficiaries may contest the accounts. These periods are not, however, mandatory and can be otherwise defined by the founder in the Bylaws. The annual report must indicate this period.[304]

5. Appointment and dismissal of the Foundation Council

Pursuant to Art.21 LFIP, the founder may reserve the right for himself or other individuals to dismiss, remove and appoint or designate new members to the Foundation Council.[305] This regulation corresponds to Liechtenstein law,[306] since OLArt.555 Para.2 PGR was used as the basis.[307]

---

301 In Liechtenstein, the statute of limitations commences upon commitment of the damaging act and runs for 2 years, or 10 years in the case of intentional actions (Art.226 Para.1 PGR).

302 Art.20 Para.5 LFIP: "The above mentioned approval **does not** exonerate the members of the Foundation Council vis-à-vis the beneficiaries or third parties having an interest in the foundation with respect to damages caused by **gross negligence or fraud**."

303 Both liability and accounting procedures are regulated in Art.20 LFIP.

304 This accounting regulation corresponds to the provisions in Liechtenstein. The obligation to prepare annual accounts is specified in NLArt.552 §26 PGR and in Art.923 and Art.923a/§35 PGR.

305 Art.21 LFIP: "Founder's right to remove and appoint Foundation Council members: The founder may reserve for himself/herself or for other persons, in the Foundation Charter, the right to remove the members of the Foundation Council as well as the right to designate or add new members."

306 "The foundation deed or the articles must contain the name and domicile of the foundation, its purpose or object, the designation of the Foundation Council members and the method for appointing another Foundation Council as well as a provision concerning the application of the assets in the event of the dissolution of the foundation." (OLArt.555 Para.2 PGR) The new law governing foundations in Liechtenstein also adopted this regulation (Cf. NLArt.552 §20 PGR).

307 Cf. Ferrer, p.17: "This article (21 LFIP) refers to the right of removal or designation of new members of the Foundation Council. Article 555 of the Liechtenstein law also

If the Bylaws or regulations of a Panamanian foundation do not contain any provisions regarding the rights or reasons to dismiss or remove Foundation Council members, such members can be dismissed by the court in the following instances:[308]

- Conflicts of interest between the beneficiaries or the founder and the member of the Foundation Council.[309]
- If the Foundation Council is not administering the assets as a good father would.[310]
- In the event of conviction for a crime and/or violation against private property or public faith,[311] whereby temporary suspension is effected during the court proceedings.[312]
- For incapacity or impossibility to administer the foundation.[313]
- In the case of insolvency or bankruptcy proceedings.[314]

The petition for dismissal can be filed by the founder and/or the beneficiaries. Minors or disabled beneficiaries are represented by those individuals who hold "patriae potestas" or legal guardianship. In the event that a court removes a

---

expresses the need to determine in the act of constitution how a new member of the Foundation Council can be appointed if someone resigns, dies or is removed. Some family foundations give this right to third parties or to remaining members of the Council in case of resignation of anyone of them."

308 Art.22 LFIP: "Right to remove members of Foundation Council by judicial proceeding:
If the Foundation Charter or its regulations contain no provision regarding the right and causes for removal of the members of the Foundation Council, said members may be removed by means of summary judicial proceedings for the following causes:
1. When their interests are incompatible with the interests of the beneficiaries or of the founder.
2. If they do not administer the assets of the foundation with the diligence of a bonus pater familias.
3. If they are convicted of a crime against private property or public faith. In such case, while the criminal proceedings are taking place, the temporary suspension of the member on trial may be decreed.
4. For incapacity or impossibility to carry out the objectives of the foundation, from the time such causes arise.
5. For insolvency or bankruptcy proceedings."

309 Art.22 Para.1 No.1 LFIP.

310 Art.22 Para.1 No.2 LFIP.

311 "Fé Pública / Public Faith" Cf. *Estribí*, p.25.

312 Art.22 Para.1 No.3 LFIP.

313 Art.22 Para.1 No.4 LFIP.

314 Art.22 Para.1 No.5 LFIP.

member of the Foundation Council, the ruling also includes the appointment of a new member to the Foundation Council who has sufficient expertise, capacity, wealth, authorization, skill, qualification and recognized moral standing.[315]

D. The Protector

The institution of a Protector was influenced by practice in Anglo-Saxon countries. The Protector is a person whom the founder trusts to monitor the proper fulfilment of the objectives and purposes of a foundation and to protect the interests of the beneficiaries. Panamanian foundation law does not prescribe any requirements for this function. As such, the Protector can be a natural person or a legal entity, Panamanian or foreign. The founder can stipulate professional requirements or simply entrust a friend or member of the family with this office. By the same token, the founder can also establish several governing bodies as Protectors, each of which can have various functions or public offices. The function of the Protector can be paid or not.

The responsibilities of the Protector should, however, be defined in the By-laws or regulations. Panamanian law list some of the Protector's rights and responsibilities as examples:[316]

---

[315] Art.23 LFIP.

[316] Art.24 LFIP: "Supervising bodies:
The Foundation Charter or its regulations may provide for the constitution of supervisory bodies, which may be composed of natural or juridical persons, such as auditing companies, protectors of the foundation, or other similar entities.
The powers of the supervisory entities shall be established in the Foundation Charter or its regulations, and may include, among others, the following:
1. To ensure the fulfilment of the foundation's purposes by the Foundation Council and to protect the rights and interests of the beneficiaries.
2. To require the Foundation Council to render accounts.
3. To modify the objects and purposes of the foundation when their fulfilment becomes impossible or too burdensome.
4. To appoint new members of the Foundation Council by reason of temporary or permanent absence, or for the expiration of the period for which they were appointed.
5. To appoint new members of the Foundation Council in replacement of existing members in the event of temporary or accidental absence of any of them.
6. To increase or reduce the number of members of the Foundation Council.
7. To approve the acts done by the Foundation Council pursuant to the Foundation Charter or its regulations.
8. To act as custodian of the assets of the foundation and to oversee the application thereof to the objects or purposes contained in the Foundation Charter.

- The Protector monitors the fulfilment of the foundation purposes by the Foundation Council and protects the rights and interests of the beneficiaries.[317]
- He demands the presentation of annual accounts by the Foundation Council and approves the same.[318]
- He may modify the objectives and purposes of the foundation if their fulfilment or achievement proves to be impossible or burdensome.[319]
- He may elect new members to the Foundation Council in the event of temporary or permanent absence or expiry of the period of office, and he may increase or reduce the number of members.[320]
- He administers the assets of the foundation and oversees the application of the same in fulfilment of the foundation purpose.[321]
- He may remove existing and appoint new beneficiaries if so provided in the Bylaws or regulations.[322]

Panamanian law does not contain any provisions with regard to installing or dismissing a supervising body. The founder should therefore ensure that the procedure for appointment and grounds for dismissal are regulated in detail in the constitution documents (Foundation Charter and Bylaws).

V. Supervision and control

Panamanian foundation law does not make provision for any state supervision.[323] This is demonstrated by the status held by Panamanian foundation in the legal

---

9. To remove beneficiaries of the foundation and to add new beneficiaries in accordance with the provisions of the Foundation Charter or its regulations.

317 Art.24 Para.2 No.1 LFIP.

318 Art.24 Para.2 No.2 and 7 LFIP.

319 Art.24 Para.2 No.3 LFIP.

320 Art.24 Para.2 No.4, 5 and 6 LFIP.

321 Art.24 Para.2 No.8 LFIP.

322 Art.24 Para.2 No.9 LFIP.

323 In Liechtenstein, the founder can define in the bylaws that a family foundation be subject to official supervision by the Liechtenstein government (a function that is performed by the Office of Land and Public Registration) (OLArt.564 Para.2 PGR, NLArt.552 §29 PGR). Through the Office of Land and Public Registration, the government then has a right to control whether the foundation's assets are being administered and used for the intended purpose; it implements suitable measures and, as such, can also dismiss the Foundation Council. The new law governing foundations in Liechtenstein stipulates in NLArt.552 §29 that any participant – which therefore in-

system.[324] As is also the case with private stock corporations, the foundation is not subject to any direct state supervision or control.[325] By contrast, Art.26 LFIP regulates conflict situations that are resolved by a judge, as is also the case with private disputes.[326]

As such, the founder is responsible for establishing supervisory and control procedures for his foundation and equipping the relevant bodies with various functions and rights. He can elect **controlling bodies, family councils**, governing bodies with court functions and advisory functions, or similar governing bodies.[327]

---

cludes a governing body of the foundation – can lodge complaints with a judge on the aforementioned grounds.

324 Cf. Ferrer, p.21: "This...is very clear and states that if a beneficiary sees that the foundation is being managed by the Foundation Council with negligence or fraud, or is simply not following the objectives established by the Foundation Charter, he or she has the recourse of complaining to the Protector, if appointed. If not, he or she has the right to initiate legal action to stop such wrongful management."

325 Indirectly via Art.34 LFIP: "Prevention of misuse, measures to combat money laundering: To avoid the undue use of private foundations, all the provisions in Executive Decree No. 468 of 1994 and any other legal disposition in force aimed at combating money laundering arising from drug trafficking shall be applied to their operations."

326 Art.26 LFIP: "Any beneficiary of the foundation may object to acts of the foundation which damage his or her rights or interests by denouncing such circumstance to the Protector or other supervisory body, if any, or if there are none, by directly instituting the corresponding judicial action before the appropriate **court** of the domicile of the foundation."

327 Art.24 LFIP does not impose any restrictions. This is similar to Liechtenstein law. OLArt.561 PGR provides for the establishment of these supervisory and control bodies, as does the currently applicable amendment, pursuant to NLArt.552 §27 and §28 PGR: The foundation's governing bodies, such as the Foundation Council, the audit authority and similar bodies, as well as the type of administration and representation, etc., are determined in the Foundation Charter. In addition, the Foundation Charter can also provide for the appointment of further governing bodies, such as Protectors, curators and advisory boards.

Panama aims to regulate the general risk of misuse solely through the norm for combating money laundering as defined in Art.34 LFIP.[328]

---

328 Liechtenstein takes a different approach: International criticism spotlights the lack of transparency of Liechtenstein foundations. On the one hand, legitimate protection of privacy must be ensured, while on the other hand such protection is only legitimate if appropriate measures are in place to reduce any risk of misuse to a minimum. This lack of transparency is a topic for discussion since all of the important information about the client (client profile) is known; it is just not accessible to the general public. This information must be disclosed to the authorities in certain circumstances (e.g. in criminal proceedings).
The risk of misuse is eliminated by means of "self-administration under the supervision of the Office of Land and Public Registration" and the powers of control conveyed on these institutions. In addition to the company-law component, the legislation governing money laundering and due diligence should also be mentioned; in Liechtenstein this legislation is compliant with international standards. The amendment of the law governing foundations in Liechtenstein aimed to establish a balance between the protection of privacy on the one side, and the public interest on the other.
This is primarily resolved by a catalogue of exemptions from mandatory registration. The amended NLArt.552 §21 PGR stipulates that all foundations are subject to supervision by the government in the form of the supervisory authority, a function that is performed by the Office of Land and Public Registration. (Old law permitted the following exceptions:
1. Pure and mixed family foundations;
2. Foundations with defined or definable beneficiaries provided that such foundations die not primarily aim to benefit the general public;
3. Foundations for preserving and supporting companies in which the foundation holds stakes provided that such foundations do not primarily aim to benefit the general public;
The one thing the foundations for which former foundation law provided exceptions have in common is that they are primarily restricted to providing for specific or certain specifiable families or for a firmly defined circle of people without aiming to benefit the general public.)
The amendment abolished the former Para.2 in Art.564 PGR, which stipulated the following: The foundation deed may also subject other foundations to government supervision.
Secondly, such supervision only aims to ensure that the foundation and the donated assets are administered and/or utilized in accordance with the purpose. Public supervision is obviously needed and expedient if the purpose of a foundation and the beneficiaries are only defined in a general sense.
The above-mentioned first paragraph of OLArt.564 PGR and NLArt.552 §35 PGR indicate that those foundations that are not voluntarily subject to government supervision are subject to judicial supervision (Cf. OLArt.567 Para.1: "in the case of foundations not subject to the supervision of the government, the judge may, on the application of participants, exercise the powers granted to the government as the supervisory authority in non-contentious civil proceedings"), which was adopted by the new foundation law in Liechtenstein in NLArt.552 §35 PGR.

VI. Dissolution / Liquidation / Deregistration

Unlike Liechtenstein law, the law governing foundations in Panama has been guided in this respect by the norms regulating stock corporations by stressing the definition of a) who has adopted the resolution of dissolution, b) who is executing the liquidation of the assets, and c) who is applying for deregistration from the Public Registry.

The grounds for **dissolving** a foundation are listed in Art. 25 LFIP:[329]

The Office of Land and Public Registration must notify the government of any and all foundations under its supervision.

The new paragraph 1 of NLArt.552 §21 PGR aims to establish a preventive supervision procedure. Accordingly, all foundations that are subject to mandatory supervision shall be forced to engage an independent auditing company in accordance with the law governing auditors and auditing companies. This auditing company would act as the link to the supervisory authority and would have to submit an annual report highlighting any deficits that have occurred and/or confirming that the conduct of the foundation has been free of deficits. The supervisory authority could then intervene if it became aware of any deficits. The appointment of an auditor must be notified to the Office of Land and Public Registration together with the presentation of confirmation that the engagement has been accepted. Mention should also be made here that the government can waive the appointment of a recognized auditor on application (new Art.552 §27 Para.5 Sent.1 PGR). This would primarily be the case for smaller common-benefit foundations without much wealth who would therefore like to avoid the unreasonably high cost if the business activity can be otherwise sufficiently supervised. The European Foundation draft also makes provision for an auditor, the appointment of which is, however, only mandatory from a certain size onwards.

Anyone interested in the administration and utilization of the assets for the intended purpose and the income from, or application of, the assets and public legislation can lodge a complaint against any contradictory administration and utilization of the assets by the governing bodies of the foundation.

The new Para.3 of NLArt.552 §29 PGR lists a new catalogue of the powers held by the supervisory authority, which makes the former seem very scant. The supervisory authority is now authorized to issue the following reasonable orders:

- Control and dismissal of the governing bodies of a foundation,
- Execution of extraordinary audits,
- Issuance of binding instructions to the governing bodies,
- Invalidation of resolutions adopted by the governing bodies,
- Binding interpretation of the Foundation Charter. (The same powers are granted to the supervisory authority in Swiss law pursuant to Art.84 Para.2 ZGB. Similar powers are also included in the Liechtenstein PGR explicitly for trusts pursuant to Art.919 Para.6 and trust companies pursuant to Art.932a §150 PGR.)

The former law in Liechtenstein stipulated a hearing of the participants prior to any decision by the supervisory authority or Administrative Court. The amended law replaces this provision with the option for participants to file complaints with the Administrative Court against government rulings.

- Expiry of the duration defined in the Bylaws or regulations.[330]
- The purpose has been fulfilled or cannot be fulfilled.[331]
- Insolvency, indebtedness, bankruptcy.[332]
- Loss of assets, insufficient assets.[333]
- Revocation[334] of the foundation.[335]
- Any other reason indicated in the Bylaws, regulations or legislation.[336]

The new paragraph 6 of NLArt.552 §29 PGR stipulates the powers of the government to issue decrees. This aims to empower the government to issue decrees in future to transfer the actions without prejudice to the option of recourse to legal process to an official body for independent regulation and to enforce more detailed provisions to govern the supervisory procedure and related fees.

329 Art.25 LFIP: "Dissolution: The foundation shall be dissolved:
1. On the date in which the foundation must come to an end in accordance with the foundation charter.
2. On the accomplishment of the ends or purposes for which it was created or if their fulfilment becomes impossible.
3. If it becomes insolvent, incapable of making payments, or it has been judicially declared to be subject to bankruptcy proceedings.
4. On the loss or total extinction of the assets of the foundation.
5. On its revocation.
6. For any other reason established in the foundation charter or in the present law."

330 Art.25 Para.1 LFIP.

331 Art.25 Para.2 LFIP.

332 Art.25 Para.3 LFIP.

333 Art.25 Para.4 LFIP.

334 Following its establishment, a Panamanian foundation is irrevocable; equally, the transfer of assets cannot be revoked. It can only be revoked under certain circumstances:
a. If it was established as a testamentary disposition and revoked during the life of the founder (Art.13 LFIP).
b. If the bylaws or regulations make explicit provision for revocation (Art.12 Para.1 No.2 LFIP).
c. As long as the foundation has not been entered in the Public Registry (Art.12 Para.1 No.1LFIP).
d. If the donation can be revoked on grounds of ingratitude (Art.12 Para.1 No.3 LFIP), which is permissible pursuant to Book III, Section IV, Title VI of the Civil Code:
• If the foundation no longer fulfils the conditions specified by the founder (Art. 964 Código Civil);
• If the foundation commits a crime (through actions by the Foundation Council) against the founder (Art. 965 Código Civil).
The assets of a foundation can only be revoked in one instance, if such provision is explicitly included in the foundation documents (Art.12 Para.2 LFIP).

335 Art.25 Para.5 LFIP.

336 Art.25 Para.6 LFIP.

The law provides for founders to define further reasons for **dissolving** their foundations in the Bylaws or regulations.[337] He can, for example, make the **termination** of a foundation dependent on a condition or event.[338] Equally, the foundation law provides for the definition of exact regulations to govern the dissolution and liquidation, such as who makes the decision to dissolve and liquidate the foundation, how the process must be executed and what happens to the assets.[339]

---

337 As already provided in Art.5 Para.10 LFIP if the Foundation Charter or bylaws are amended.

338 Art.5 Para.9 LFIP.

339 The grounds for dissolving a Liechtenstein foundation were listed in OLArt.568 PGR. The amendment to the foundation law has eliminated the enormous legal uncertainty surrounding previous practice. In the case of registered foundations, they were deleted from the Register, on the one side, on the basis of a declaration of lack of assets by the responsible governing body, while at the same time legislation decreed that they remained in existence as long as the assets of the foundation remained *de facto* existent. Conversely, foundations that were dissolved by act of law due to lack of assets were not deleted from the Public Register and therefore remained in existence. The legal uncertainty surrounding deposited foundations was no less severe in the past. Legal opinions – and legal rulings – in Liechtenstein diverged on the issue of the legal consequences if a foundation were simply dissolved due to lack of assets and assets were subsequently to be identified after all. Some claimed that the foundation had then not ceased to exist at all but had continued to exist. Others claimed that subsequent liquidation would then have to be executed, during which the foundation – which was officially no longer existent – had legal character.
The first paragraph of the draft amendment to OLArt.568 PGR adopted the Austrian practice as stipulated in §35 PSG and is worded virtually identically to Panamanian Art.25 LFIP.
The new law governing foundations in Liechtenstein now provides for a regulation in NLArt.552 § 39 that is similar to Panamanian foundation law pursuant to Art.25 LFIP. The provisions address reasons as to when a foundation must be dissolved based on a resolution of dissolution as adopted by the Foundation Council (unless otherwise specified in the Foundation Charter, the resolution must be adopted unanimously by the Foundation Council pursuant to NLArt.552 §39 Para.3 PGR) or whether the dissolution is based on a judicial order (without the Foundation Council adopting a resolution of dissolution). The second paragraph then regulates when the Foundation Council must adopt a resolution of dissolution and when this is not necessary. A resolution of dissolution does not need to be adopted by the Foundation Council in cases of official liquidation or dissolution by judicial order, nor when bankruptcy proceedings are opened since the latter automatically result in the dissolution of the foundation.
The supervisory authority (which is the government or – in the case of foundations that are not subject to government supervision – the judge) is also empowered to dissolve a foundation on application by participants (NLArt.552 §39 Para.5 PGR). The supervisory authority can revoke a resolution of dissolution by the Foundation Council if there is no reason why the foundation should be dissolved (NLArt.552 §39

In the event of **liquidation** of any assets belonging to a Panamanian foundation, the Foundation Council must perform the following actions in line with the wishes of the founder:

- Disburse the remaining assets to the beneficiaries (the founder defines the procedure for, and amounts of, disbursement.
- Sell specific or all assets.
- Return assets to the individual who provided the assets to the founder who, in turn, transferred them to the foundation, incl. any income derived from the same.
- Reinstate the foundation with a different purpose and different provisions and reorganize the administration and control of the same.
- Revoke the foundation and subsequently delete it from the Public Registry.

Prior to distribution of the foundation assets, any tax debts must, of course, first be paid, followed by the amounts owing to the Foundation Council members, other governing bodies and the local representative, etc.[340]

Once the foundation has been liquidated, it must be **deregistered**. The deregistration procedure is not defined in the law. As such, the provisions regulating joint stock corporations apply.[341] A foundation cannot be deregistered by an official body; a judicial order is needed for such deregistration.[342] Foundations that have not paid their annual fees after 2 years are, however, declared **invalid**[343] *ex officio* by the Register Office.

In Panama, the information about the foundation cannot be removed from the Public Registry, *i.e.* even if it is deregistered, the Public Registry still contains all

---

Para.5 PGR). In the case of foundations that are dissolved by judicial order, the supervisory authority can permit the foundation to continue if the reasons for the dissolution have been eliminated (NLArt.552 §39 Para.5 PGR).

340 In the sequence stipulated by bankruptcy law.

341 Following the amendments to Liechtenstein foundation law, the general provisions applying to associations are now applicable to the liquidation and deregistration of a registered foundation (Art.130 et seqq. PGR.) (Cf. NLArt.552 §40 PGR).

342 This is similar to Liechtenstein law: OLArt.569 PGR defined the right of legal action and deregistration. Accordingly, the supervisory authority as the representative of public law was entitled to file legal action, as was anyone with an interest. The action may be annotated in the Public Register before or during the proceedings, up to the time of final decision, upon application or *ex officio*. A hearing of the governing bodies of the foundations and any other participants had to take place prior to the ruling. The new law governing foundations in Liechtenstein adopted this regulation (Cf. NLArt.552 §40 Para.1 PGR).

343 (Fundación) "inválida".

of the information pertaining to the foundation, together with the remark "deregistered".

Deregistration must be notified to the Register in any case. The foundation is deregistered from the Public Registry on application by the Foundation Council and is published in Panama's official gazette. As such, the deregistration procedure comprises the following steps:

1. Resolution to dissolve the foundation. This resolution can be adopted by the Foundation Council, the founder himself, any other governing body defined in the Bylaws or regulations of the foundation, or by a third party who has been granted power of attorney to execute this task. It must be certified by a public notary.
2. The resolution to dissolve the foundation is entered in the Public Registry against presentation of the receipt documenting payment of the annual fee.
3. The resolution of dissolution and the subsequent deregistration are published in the official gazette.
4. The foundation is deregistered in the foundation register of the Public Registry.[344]

VII. Relocation of domicile

1. Foreign foundations in Panama

Pursuant to Art.28 LFIP, foundations that have been legally established abroad in compliance with foreign legislation can subject themselves voluntarily to the Panamanian law governing private foundations.

For example, if a Liechtenstein foundation wishes to move its domicile to Panama, it can do so pursuant to Art.234 Para.1 PGR and to the Decree of

---

344 In Liechtenstein, the dissolution must be notified to the Office of Land and Public Registration; deregistration is then performed by act of law. The foundation is deregistered in the foundation register in Liechtenstein as well (OLArt.569 Para.1 PGR, NLArt.552 §40 Abs.3 PGR).
Equally pursuant to the amended foundation law, the liquidation of non-registered foundations is restricted to the settlement of outstanding debts and the distribution of the surplus assets in line with the provisions of the Foundation Charter. Once the liquidation has been completed, the Foundation Council must notify the Office of Land and Public Registration that the liquidation has been completed and the foundation deregistered. Assets that subsequently emerge must be distributed in line with the provisions governing subsequent liquidation (Art 139 PGR) (new Art.552 §40 Para.5 PGR). This regulation is similar to §19 Paras.3 and 4 TrUG.

11.02.2003 governing the relocation of domicile of a native association to a foreign country (LGBl. 2003 N.68).

Art.234 Para.1 PGR regulates the relocation of domicile of a Liechtenstein foundation from Liechtenstein to another country: "The permission of the Office of Land and Public Registration must be obtained before a native association can subject itself to foreign legislation and, as such, relocate to a foreign country without prior dissolution."

The representative stipulated for all Liechtenstein associations in Art.239 Para.1 PGR applies to the Office of Land and Public Registration for permission to relocate the domicile to Panama and must present the following documentation:

a. Resolution adopted by the Foundation Council to relocate the domicile
b. Schedule of the foundation's assets
c. Confirmation of payment of due taxes by the tax authorities
d. Declaration by the Foundation Council that the foundation does not owe any debts to third parties
e. Confirmation that the foundation will continue to exist under Panamanian law.

a. Resolution adopted by the Foundation Council to relocate the domicile

The resolution by the Foundation Council can be worded as follows:

"The Foundation Council has adopted the following resolution based on the powers granted to it by law: The domicile of the Foundation shall be relocated to Panama without prior dissolution in the context of Art.234 PGR." (Date and signature of the Foundation Council).

b. Schedule of the foundation's assets

The schedule of assets is a simple balance sheet. It results from the applicability of Art.1045 PGR in conjunction with Art.945 and OLArt.557, NLArt.552 §26 PGR for deposited family foundations. Art.1045 PGR only stipulates the mandatory preparation of accounts for all legal entities that are subject to mandatory entry in the Public Register: "Whoever is under obligation to enter his company in the Public Register (Art.945 PGR) and who operates a commercial business enterprise (Art.107 PGR) is under obligation to prepare proper accounts."

This obligation to prepare accounts pursuant to Art.1045 does not affect family foundations that were established in accordance with old Liechtenstein foundation law since, pursuant to OLArt.557 Para.2 PGR, they came into existence without being entered in the Public Register: "Ecclesiastical foundations, pure mixed family foundations and foundations whose beneficiaries are defined or definable acquire legal character without being entered in the Public Registry."

NLArt.552 §26 PGR (accounting) is applicable to family foundations established in accordance with the new law governing foundations in Liechtenstein. A schedule of assets, which must be signed by the Foundation Council, could contain the following:

"Liechtenstein Foundation / Schedule of Assets: Assets, comprising bank balances/receivables/investments/reserves in a total amount of CHF 30,000 and liabilities, comprising the foundation capital in a total amount of CHF 30,000." (Date and signature of the Foundation Council).

c. Confirmation of payment of due taxes by the tax authorities

The confirmation issued by the Liechtenstein tax authorities that is required for a relocation of domicile is worded as follows:

"Liechtenstein Tax Authorities / Confirmation: We hereby confirm that the foundation domiciled in LI-9490 Vaduz and the corresponding tax reference number are registered with the Liechtenstein tax authorities and subject to Liechtenstein taxation. The association currently does not owe any taxes to the tax authorities." (Date, stamp and signature of the tax authorities)

d. Declaration by the Foundation Council that the foundation does not owe any debts to third parties

The Foundation Council must present this declaration in the form of a resolution adopted by the Foundation Council with the following wording:

"Resolution adopted by the Foundation Council / Confirmation: Based on the powers granted to it by law, the Foundation Council confirms that the foundation does not owe any debts to third parties." (Date and signature of the Foundation Council).

e. Confirmation that the foundation will continue to exist under Panamanian law.

This confirmation is needed for the authorization to relocate the domicile and must be written on the letterhead of a Panamanian lawyer and contain the following:

"To whom it may concern / I, Panamanian Lawyer, duly qualified to practice law in the Republic of Panama, hereby confirm the following: A Foundation incorporated under the laws of Liechtenstein which transfers its residence from

Liechtenstein to Panama, may continue (under the laws of Panama) as a Panamanian Foundation." (Date and signature of the Panamanian lawyer).

f. Application

The relocation application to the Office of Land and Public Registration must contain the following, in addition to the documents listed in a-e above:

"Legal representative / On behalf of the foundation and in our capacity as legal representative we apply, in application of Art.234 PGR, for permission to relocate the domicile of this foundation without prior dissolution." (Date, appendices a.-e., signature of the legal representative).

g. Disposition

The disposition of the Office of Land and Public Registration with regard to the application for relocation of domicile is worded as follows:

"Office of Land and Public Registration / Disposition: Based on Art.234 Para.1 PGR, LGBl.1926 No.4, as amended, and the VO dated 11.02.2003 governing the relocation of domicile of native associations to a foreign country, LGBl.2003 No.68, the following decree is passed with regard to the application by the representative for permission to relocate the domicile of the foundation to Panama, Republic of Panama:

1. Permission is granted to relocate the domicile of the foundation to a foreign country without prior dissolution.
2. The administrative fee is CHF 600. This fee will be invoiced by the court cashier.

Substantiation: The legal representative has applied in writing for permission to relocate the domicile of the foundation to Panama without prior dissolution. The following documentation was presented:

Resolution adopted by the Foundation Council to relocate the domicile, schedule of assets, confirmation from the tax authorities that all taxes owing in Liechtenstein have been paid, declaration by the Foundation Council that the foundation does not have any debts owing to third parties, confirmation by a Panamanian lawyer that the foundation may continue under Panamanian law.

The Office of Land and Public Registration has therefore studied the application and – after appropriate consideration of the documents – has reached the conclusion that there are no impediments to hinder the relocation of domicile of this particular foundation to a foreign country without prior dissolution pursuant to Art.234 Para.1 PGR.

The fee for this decision is based on Art.2 VO dated 11.02.2003, LGBl.2003 No.68 governing the relocation of domicile of a native association to a foreign country." (List of recipients, instruction on the right to appeal, date, stamp and signature of the Office of Land and Public Registration).

h. Publication

Based on the internal official list of recipients, the Office of Land and Public Registration's authorization to relocate the domicile is sent to the Liechtenstein tax authorities for information purposes, together with the additional remark on the latest excerpt from the Public Register as follows:

"Liechtenstein Public Register / Deregistration of Foundation: As a result of the relocation of its domicile to Panama, the foundation has been deleted from the Public Register *ex officio*." (Date, stamp and signature of the Office of Land and Public Registration and invoice for CHF 150).

2. Panamanian registration regulations for foreign foundations in Panama

Foundations established abroad under foreign legislation that wish to become subject to Panamanian law must submit the documentation pursuant to Art.29 and Art.30 LFIP to a Panamanian lawyer, together with a corresponding power of attorney. The documentation primarily includes a resolution adopted by the Foundation Council to relocate the domicile – a so-called "Declaration" – and a further resolution by the Foundation Council – the "Certificate" – with regard to the uninterrupted continuation of existence of the foundation in Panama, in each case together with the appendices defined in in Art.29 and Art.30 LFIP.

In practical terms, the sequence for preparation of the documents for Panamanian registration is recommended as follows:

a. Deed of Constitution / Foundation Charter

Art.30 Para.1 LFIP describes this generally as an official confirmation of constitution from the country of origin. It must be certified by a public notary and apostilled.

b. Official confirmation / Excerpt from the Public Register

Art.29 Para.2 LFIP describes this as the valid confirmation of registration from the country of origin. It must be recent and, pursuant to Art.29 Para.1 LFIP, contain the name and date of constitution of the foundation, and must be certified with apostille.

c. Bylaws of the foundation

Pursuant to Art.30 Para.1 LFIP, these must be presented in a valid version, certified by the responsible authority and apostilled.

d. Declaration

This resolution by the Foundation Council with apostille, which may be edited in English, should manifest the desire to relocate the domicile to Panama and the will to continue the foundation in Panama, pursuant to Art.29 Para.3 LFIP. It also confirms the intention to comply with all of the registration formalities demanded by law, pursuant to Art.5 LFIP. The resolution by the Foundation Council can be worded as follows:

"Resolution: The Board of the (Liechtenstein) Foundation, based on the legal and statutory powers granted to it, herewith resolves as follows:

1. To transfer the domicile and the registered office of the Foundation to Panama City, Panama.
2. To continue the legal existence of the Foundation under applicable Panamanian Law.
3. To comply in all respects with all provisions of Panamanian law, and in particular, Article 5 of the Panamanian law on Private Foundations."

(Date and signature of the Foundation Council).

e. Certificate

The certificate, which must be certified and apostilled, and again takes the form of a resolution by the Foundation Council that is issued by the Foundation Council as the responsible governing body in respect of the internal organization of the Foundation, must contain the documentation listed in a-d as appendices, pursuant to Art 29 and Art. 30. It can be worded as follows:

"Certificate of Continuation:

The undersigned Members of the Board of Foundation hereby certify that this Foundation was constituted under the laws of the Principality of Liechtenstein on the same day when the Foundation's Charter was deposited with the Public Registry of Liechtenstein.

In agreement with the provisions of Law no.25 of 1995 and Executive Degree no.417 of August 8, 1995 of the Republic of Panama, we hereby expressly declare that it is our wish to continue the legal existence of this Foundation as a Panamanian Foundation.

To such end and to comply with the requirements of the Panamanian Law on Private Foundations, we agree to amend and/or add the following articles to the Foundation Charter, so that they shall be as follows

The Domicile / Applicable Law: The new domicile of the Foundation will be that of the resident agent. By means of the Board resolution the domicile may at any time be transferred to another place in Panama or abroad. All legal relationships arising from the constitution and existence of the foundation are subject to the law in force at the domicile of the foundation. The competent courts of jurisdiction for the foundation are those of its domicile.

The Resident Agent: The resident agent of the foundation is the law firm..., Panama.

The Board: The Board of Foundation may consist of natural and/or legal (juridical) persons. The tenure of office of the Board of Foundation is unlimited. The Members of the Board of Foundation and their addresses are:... as President / Counsellor and Secretary, all with sole signatory right.

Vacancies: In case of vacancies or nomination of additional members, the Board of Foundation appoints the new members itself, by cooptation. The nomination of additional members requires unanimity. If there is no member of the Board left or if the remaining member of the Board is incapable to act, the Resident Agent shall be authorized to appoint the new members of the Board.

In witness whereof we sign the present Certificate of Continuation." (Date and signatures of the members of the Foundation Council).

The certificate of continuation and the documentation to be included with it pursuant to Art.29 and Art.30 are properly recorded and entered in the Public Registry to ensure the continuation of the legal existence of the private foundation in Panama.

f. Apostilled power of attorney extended to a Panamanian lawyer to carry out the necessary procedures to affect the continuation of the foundation in Panama.

The power of attorney, which must be certified and apostilled, is generally worded as follows in Panama:

"The undersigned Members of the Board of the (Liechtenstein) Foundation herewith authorize the (Panamanian) Law Office in Panama, to undertake all necessary steps in order to continue the legal existence of the above mentioned foundation under the laws of the Republic of Panama and appoint the same as Resident Agent of the continued foundation in Panama.

After final registration of the continued foundation at the Foundation Section of the Panamanian Public Registry, the foundation shall be deleted from the Liechtenstein Register."

(Date and signature of the Foundation Council)

3. Relocation of domicile of Panamanian foundations abroad

Pursuant to Art.32 LFIP, foundations constituted in accordance with Panamanian foundation law, as well as the assets which constitute their patrimony, may transfer or become subject to the laws and jurisdiction of another country, as may be provided by their Foundation Charter or their regulations.

Section 5 Summary

Private foundations were incorporated as legal entities on 12 June 1995 by means of Law No. 25, *La Ley de Fundaciones de Interés Privado* ("LFIP") as a **lex specialis** into Panama's **legal system**[345]. The law is virtually identical to Liechtenstein provisions governing family foundations, although new Articles were added. For the Liechtenstein foundation, in turn, served as a role model Switzerland.[346]

In light of the history of foundations as a legal form, **historical** interpretation[347] reveals the existence of legal norms dating as far back as ancient times which governed the material elements of a foundation – the founder's intention, and the purpose, assets and beneficiaries of the foundation. Every country which adopted the foundation law from another country invariably implemented considerable changes. As such, the (unfortunately frequent) conclusions by analogy for adopted legal formats are often inapplicable. The same applies to Panama, which is why the law governing foundations in Panama is much more flexible and, to a certain extent, more modern than the Liechtenstein original it was modelled on.

The law governing foundations in Panama is worded more simply than is the case in Liechtenstein and the legal norms are better arranged and more clearly defined than their Liechtenstein counterparts. The regulations for **registering**[348] a foundation in Panama demonstrate a better legal system than is the case with the Liechtenstein provisions. Since Liechtenstein provides for both deposited[349] and registered[350] foundations, a foreign legal practitioner is confronted with statutory regulations that are only understandable after in-depth and thorough study of Liechtenstein legislation.[351] In this respect, the Panamanian regulations[352] could act as a role model for Liechtenstein.[353]

345 Cf. above, §3 Systematic Interpretation.
346 *Santo-Passo*, 2002, p.46 et seqq.
347 Cf. above, §2 Historical Interpretation.
348 Cf. the clear enumeration pursuant to Art.5 LFIP.
349 Cf. Art.554 PGR.
350 Cf. Art.556 PGR.
351 Cf. the regulations governing execution of deposited and registered foundations in Section 9 "Foundation" Art.89 (Constitutional documents; Auditing) and Art.90 (Reg-

Panama does not require the classification of foundations into various **types**, *e.g.* ecclesiastical foundations, pure and mixed family foundations, foundations with defined and/or definable beneficiaries, charitable and common-benefit foundations, depending on their **purpose**, which is such a central element of Liechtenstein foundation law.[354] Panamanian foundation law does not impose any restrictions on,[355] or demand classification of, the foundation purpose. As such, the choice of foundation purpose does not result in any consequences whatsoever.[356] The totally liberal and free will of the founder is clearly paramount and does not have to adapt to any generalized, dogmatic pre-definition of purpose, since there is none. This is a clear benefit for foreign legal practitioners[357] and substantially simplifies legal counselling.[358]

---

istration) OeRegV. Although it was later amended and put into effect in June 2003, OeRegV does not distinguish between the requirements for registered and deposited foundations. Readers must themselves systematize these with the aid of references to OLArt.554 PGR (deposited foundations) resp. OLArt.556 PGR (registered foundations) in the text of the decree. The same applies to the new law governing foundations in Liechtenstein (Cf. NLArt.552 §16 in conjunction with §19 Para.3 resp. §20 Para.2 PGR), which is vague and confusing for non-legal practitioners. Although it is older, the Panamanian regulation (Art.5 LFIP) could act as a role model for Liechtenstein.

352 Because it is more recent with a recent editing of the wording. Cf. above, §2 Historical Interpretation and §3 Systematic Interpretation.

353 The boundaries between a foundation existing and not existing are fluid in Liechtenstein. The old PGR itself refers to judicial rulings on the coming into existence of foundations in cases of insufficient clarity as to the purpose for which the assets were being administered. Cf. OLArt.552 Para.3 PGR: "The judge shall decide in the individual case the extent to which separately administered assets (fund) shall be entitled to independence according to private law or to the character of trust property." The new law governing foundations in Liechtenstein adopted this regulation (Cf. NLArt.552 §14 Para.5 in conjunction with §20 and 21 PGR). Thanks to its stipulation of mandatory registration, Panamanian foundation law does not induce this legal uncertainty.

354 Cf. above, §4.II. Types of foundation, since the LFIP only regulates **private foundations**.

355 Cf. above, §3 Systematic Interpretation / The Incorporation of the LFIP into Panama's Legal System

356 Such as a consequence of state supervision or similar (Cf. OLArt.564 PGR, NLArt.552 §21 and §29 PGR).

357 A foreign legal practitioner who is counselling the founder can assume a general autonomy of the parties without having to worry about the tax consequences resp. to suffer restrictions and mandatory designations of beneficiaries in order to escape state supervision, etc. (unlike Liechtenstein regulations pursuant to OLArt.553 Para.2, OLArt.557 Para.2, OLArt.564 Para.1 PGR, and NLArt.552 §21 and §29 PGR).

358 As such, the founder does not need to worry about models and predefinitions of a foundation as a "family foundation", "company foundation", "foundation with

The Panamanian law governing foundations gives **founders** a level of freedom and benefits that he will not find in virtually any European jurisdiction. Panamanian law,[359] allows him to appoint himself as beneficiary,[360] to vote himself onto the Foundation Council,[361] to reserve the right to amend the purpose[362] or other Bylaws,[363] to determine the controlling[364] and executive governing bodies[365] together with their powers of authority[366] etc.[367]

The exclusion of claims by heirs whose rights to statutory shares are infringed[368] ensures that all appointments of **beneficiaries** are completely valid. This is not the case in Liechtenstein.[369]

The number of members on the Foundation Council is restricted to a minimum of 3 natural persons or one legal entity. All **members of the Foundation Council** can be from Panama or abroad; neither a professional qualification nor a domicile in Panama is required. The founder may belong to the Foundation Council. The law addresses the liability of the Foundation Council differently,

---

charitable characteristics", etc., that are so important in other countries since this predefinition of purpose does not induce any consequences whatsoever in Panama.

359 The principle of the extremely strong status of the founder, even after constitution of the foundation, dominates the entire LFIP since any rights that the founder may wish to reserve are prevalent throughout the wording of the law. (Cf. for example, Art.5 Para.11 LFIP on amending the Foundation Charter and bylaws: (and) ... "Any other lawful clauses which the founder may consider convenient."

360 Cf. Art.5 Para.7 in conjunction with Art.24 Para.2 No.9 LFIP.

361 Art.5 Para.3 in conjunction with Art.21 LFIP.

362 Art.5 Para.6 and 10 LFIP.

363 Art.5 Para.8 LFIP.

364 Art.19 in conjunction with Art.24 Para.1 and 2 LFIP.

365 Art.21 LFIP in conjunction with Art. 24 Para.2 Nos. 4,5,6 LFIP.

366 Art.17 LFIP and Art.24 LFIP.

367 The general clause in Art.5 Para.11 ("...any other lawful clauses which the founder may consider convenient.") allows the founder to include definitions of legal transactions in the bylaws which may seem problematic in other jurisdictions, such as borrowing money and granting loans, mandatory arbitration court responsibility with Panamanian judges to resolve all disputes, etc.

368 Art. 14 LFIP specifies that the inheritance laws that are applicable at the domicile of the founder or the beneficiaries do not have any influence on the validity of the foundation. The only governing elements are the provisions in the constitution document and the regulations. This means that a judge in Panama must solely and exclusively respect the wishes of the founder.

369 Liechtenstein law differs in this respect, as it does indeed observe entitlements to statutory shares.

depending on whether the Foundation Council is bound by instructions[370] or not.[371] This is an autonomous regulation in Panama-[372]

The appointment of the **Protector** is optional.[373]

Panamanian law only recognizes judicial supervision.[374] State control is not exercised, with the exception of the norm combating money laundering.[375] The regulations governing dissolution and liquidation are equally of a private nature.[376]

The absence of any form of proof of capital, the non-existence of a published schedule of assets, no control of any amendments to the Bylaws by the Public Registry, no requirement for a local member on the Foundation Council and the absence of state control make the constitution and administration of a Panamanian foundation a thoroughly liberal, discreet and practical affair that any liberally-minded lawyer will appreciate.[377]

---

[370] Art.19 LFIP.

[371] Art.20 LFIP.

[372] And is diametrically opposed to Liechtenstein law, where the Foundation Council is primarily liable irrespective of any engagement contract with a third party.

[373] His responsibilities as listed in Art.24 LFIP are therefore only meant as examples; his election and dismissal is not addressed by the law at all.

[374] Art.26 LFIP.

[375] Art.34 LFIP.

[376] No provision is made for *ex officio* deregistration. The procedure for dissolution, liquidation and deregistration is similar to that for joint stock corporations.

[377] By contrast, both Swiss and European experts ask themselves whether such a liberal solution is not open to potential misuse, which was the reason behind the recent amendment and reform of the law governing foundations in Liechtenstein (Cf. Section "Supervision and Control").

I. Published foundation documentation (CR excerpt)

A. Excerpt from the commercial register (original Spanish version)

REPUBLICA DE PANAMA
REGISTRO PUBLICO DE PANAMA

CERTIFICA
CON VISTA A LA SOLICIDUD NUMERO:
QUE LA FUNDACION:
se encuentra registrada la Ficha: Documento: desde el: en la Seccion de Fundaciones de Interés Privado.
QUE la Fundación se encuentra vigente.
QUE su(s) Fundador(es) es(son):
QUE sus miembros del consejo son:
QUE su agente residente es:
QUE su patrimonio es de 10'000.- dolares americanos
QUE su duración es perpetua
QUE su domicilio es Panamá
Expedido y firmado en la Provincia de Panama, el:
Nota: esta certificacion pago derechos por un valor de B. 30.-, Comprobante no:
no.certificado: Fund.Int.Priv. no:
Fecha: Certificador:
(Sello del Registro Público de Panamá – Departamento de Certificados / Firma del Certificador)

B. Excerpt from the commercial register (German translation)

PANAMAISCHE REPUBLIK
DAS PANAMAISCHE ÖFFENTLICHKEITSREGISTER

BESTÄTIGT AMTLICH
GEMÄSS GESUCH Nr.
DASS DIE STIFTUNG:
Registriert ist unter Microfilm-Fiche: Dokument:
seit dem Datum:
in der Abteilung für Private Stiftungen
DASS die Stiftung rechtsgültig besteht
DASS ihr(e) Stifter sind:
DASS ihre Stiftungsratsmitlgieder sind:
DASS ihr lokaler Resident-Agent ist:
DASS ihr Kapital aus 10'000.- US Dollar besteht.
DASS ihre Dauer unbeschränkt ist.
DASS ihr Sitz in Panama ist.

Herausgegeben und unterschrieben in der Provinz Panama am:
Bemerkung: Dieser Registerauszug trägt eine Stempelsteuer von B.30.- mit der Quittungsnummer:
Zertifikationsnummer:
Datiert: Urkundsperson:
(Stempel: Panamaisches Oeffentlichkeitsregister – Abteilung für Zertifikate / Unterschrift der Urkundsperson)

C. Excerpt from the commercial register (English translation)

REPUBLIC OF PANAMA
PUBLIC REGISTRY OF PANAMA
CERTIFIES:
PURSUANT TO THE REQUEST No:
THAT THE FOUNDATION:
Is recorded at Microjacket-Fiche: Document:
Since:
In the Section of Private Interest Foundations.
THAT the Foundation is in good standing.
THAT the Founder(s) is(are):

THAT the Members of the Foundation Council are:
THAT its Resident Agent is:
THAT its patrimony is 10’000.- American Dollars.
THAT its duration is perpetual.
THAT its domicile is in Panama.
Issued and signed in Panama province on:
Note: This certification has paid a stamp tax of B.30.- Voucher No:
Certificate Number:
Dated: Certifier:
(Seal of the Public Registry- Certifications Department / Signature of the Certifier)

II. Unpublished foundation documentation (Regulations)

A. Regulations (German version)

Beistatut der Stiftung

Der unterzeichnete Stiftungsrat erlässt, gestützt auf seine statutarischen Kompetenzen bezüglich der Begünstigten und der Begünstigungsrechte folgendes Beistatut:

1. Erstbegünstigter

Der Stiftungsrat bestellt als ersten und einzigen Begünstigten und Genussberechtigten:
–

Der Erstbegünstigte ist mit sofortiger Wirkung für die Dauer seines Lebens begünstigt auf die nach Abzug bestehender Verpflichtungen frei verfügbaren Erträgnisse und auf das Vermögen der Stiftung.

2. Zweitbegünstigter

Nach dem Ableben des Erstbegünstigten tritt:
–

mit gleichen Rechten und im gleichen Umfang an seine Stelle.

3. Drittbegünstigte

Nach dem Ableben des Erstbegünstigten und des Zweitbegünstigten werden zu Drittbegünstigten zu gleichen Teilen bestellt:

–

–

Im Falle des Vorversterbens oder Ablebens eines Drittbegünstigten treten seine direkten Nachkommen auf den Ueberrest zu gleichen Teilen nach Stämmen an seine Stelle.

4. Begünstigung Minderjähriger

Im Falle der Minderjährigkeit eines Begünstigten macht der Stiftungsrat an diesen nur in dem Umfang Ausschüttungen aus den Erträgnissen als es notwendig ist, um die Kosten für Unterhalt, Erziehung, und Ausbildung zu bestreiten. Der Stiftungsrat mach solche Zuwendungen nach seinem freien Ermessen.

5. Begünstigungsdauer

Das Begünstigungsrecht eines Begünstigten gilt lediglich für die Dauer des Lebens des jeweiligen Begünstigten. Eine testamentarische Verfügung über das Begünstigungsrecht ist ausgeschlossen.

Macht ein Begünstigter von seinem Bezugsrecht zeit seines Lebens nicht oder nicht im vollen Umfange Gebrauch, so fallt sein Recht den nachfolgenden Begünstigten gemäss diesem Beistatut zu.

6. Ausschüttungen

Der Stiftungsrat führt die Ausschüttungen an die Begünstigten durch. Der Zahlungsort wird von den Begünstigten selber festgelegt, jedoch hat der Stiftungsrat das Recht, die Auszahlung auf eine Konto bei einer Bank in der Schweiz vorzunehmen.

Sollte eine Zuwendung an die Begünstigten verhindert oder deren freie Verfügung mittelbar oder unmittelbar eingeschränkt werden, so soll der Stiftungsrat keine weiteren Zuwendungen vornehmen, solange der Hinderungsgrund besteht.

7. Aenderung des Beistatuts

Der Stiftungsrat wird das Beistatut nur auf Antrag und mit Zustimmung des Erstbegünstigten ändern. Nach dem Ableben des Erstbegünstigten wird dieses Beistatut unabänderlich.

Datum / Ort: Der Stiftungsrat:

B. Regulations (English version)

Regulations of the Foundation

The undersigned Members of the Board of Foundation resolve in accordance with the statutes and articles of incorporation to pass and implement these by-laws with regard to the beneficiaries and their beneficial interest in the foundation:

1. First beneficiary

As first beneficiary for his lifetime is appointed:

–

His beneficial interest includes the right to claim at any time all the net assets as well as the net proceeds of the foundation's assets.

2. Second beneficiary

After the death of the first beneficiary, second beneficiary in remainder to all the net assets and net proceeds of the foundation's assets shall be:

–

3. Third beneficiaries

After the death of the first and the second beneficiary third beneficiaries in equal parts in remainder to all the net assets and net proceeds of the foundation's assets shall be:

–

–

In case of either one of these beneficiaries being predeceased his/her descendants in equal parts per stirpes and, if there are none, the surviving beneficiaries in equal parts will take over his/her beneficial interest.

4. Minority beneficiaries

All beneficial rights are valid under the reservation that all the beneficiaries, until they reach the age of twenty five years, only receive such disbursements as is deemed necessary by the Board of Foundation to maintain an adequate standard of living and provide well for their good education and maintenance.

5. Transfer of beneficial rights

All beneficial rights are valid during the life time of the respective beneficiaries only. None of the beneficiaries shall have the right or title to assign, sell, transfer, charge or dispose by will of this beneficial interest.

If a beneficiary does not make use of, or claim his beneficial interest during his lifetime, the remaining undistributed assets as well as the accumulated proceeds hereof will accrue to the next following beneficiary or beneficiaries as designated by these bylaws.

6. Distributions

The Board of Foundation is responsible for distributions to the beneficiaries upon their rightful demand at such place and date and in such form as indicated by them unless the foundation itself or other beneficiaries are put into jeopardy by such distribution.

In such a case the Board of Foundation can at any time be discharged of its obligations towards the beneficiaries by consigning the assets corresponding to their part in a Swiss bank to be held at the free disposal of such beneficiaries.

The Board of Foundation will, however, follow the wishes of the beneficiaries, if these wishes are usual and reasonable and will do so at the sole risk of these beneficiaries.

7. Modification

These regulations are subject to amendment, modification or revocation upon the prior written consent of the first beneficiary. After his decease these regulations shall be irrevocable and non-amendable.

Date and Place: The Board of Foundation:

Section 7 Wording of Laws

I. LFIP, Law No. 25/95 dated 12 June 1995, which regulates private foundations

1. LFIP wording in Spanish (original version)

Ley 25 de 12 de Junio de 1995 por la cual se regulan las Fundaciones de interés privado

Artículo No. 1

Definición y constitución de las fundaciones de interés privado.

Podrán crear una fundación de interés privado de conformidad con las formalidades prescritas en la presente Ley, una o más personas naturales o jurídicas, por sí o por medio de terceros. Para ello, se requiere la constitución de un patrimonio destinado exclusivamente a los objetos o fines expresamente previstos en el acta fundacional. El patrimonio inicial podrá ser aumentado por el creador de la fundación, que se denominará el fundador, o por cualquier otra persona.

Artículo No. 2

Fundaciones de interés privado diferentes a fundaciones tradicionales humanitarias, caritativas o de interés público.

Las fundaciones de interés privado se regirán por el acta fundacional y sus reglamentos, así como por las disposiciones de esta Ley y demás disposiciones legales o reglamentarias que le sean aplicables. A estas fundaciones no se les aplicarán los preceptos del Título II del Libro I del Código Civil.

Artículo No. 3

Fundaciones de interés privado no deberán ser creadas para realizar negocios de manera usual o para fines comerciales o de lucro.

Las fundaciones de interés privado no podrán perseguir fines de lucro. No obstante, podrán llevar a cabo actividades mercantiles en forma no habitual, o ejercer los derechos provenientes de los títulos representativos del capital de sociedades mercantiles que integren el patrimonio da la fundación, siempre que el resultado o producto económico de tales actividades sea dedicado exclusivamente a los fines de la fundación.

Artículo No. 4

Fundaciones de interés privado podrán ser creadas intervivos o mortis causa. Formalidades para la creación de testamento no serán aplicables a las fundaciones mortis causa.

Las fundaciones de interés privado podrán constituirse para que surtan sus efectos, desde el momento de su creación o después de la muerte de su fundador, por cualesquiera de los siguientes métodos:

Mediante documento privado suscrito por el fundador, cuya firma deberá estar autenticada por notario público del lugar de su constitución.

Directamente ante notario público del lugar de su constitución.

Sea cual fuere el método de la constitución, deberán cumplirse las formalidades que para la creación de las fundaciones se establecen en la presente Ley.

En caso de que la fundación sea creada, ya sea por documento público o privado, para que surta efecto después de la muerte del fundador, no se requerirán las formalidades previstas para el otorgamiento del testamento.

Artículo No. 5

Información o formalidades que deberán contener las fundaciones de interés privado.

El acta fundacional deberá contener:

El nombre de la fundación, expresando en cualquier lengua con caracteristicas del alfabeto latino, el que no será igual o similar al de otra fundación preexistente en la República de Panamá, a objeto de que no se preste a confusión. El nombre deberá incluir la palabra fundación para distinguirlo de otras personas naturales o jurídicas de otra naturaleza.

El patrimonio inicial de la fundación, expresado en cualquier moneda de curso legal, que en ningún caso será inferior a una suma equivalente a diez mil balboas (B/. 10'000.00).

La designación, en forma completa y clara, incluyendo la dirección del miembro o de los miembros del Consejo de Fundación, al que podrá pertenecer el fundador.

El domicilio de la fundación.

El nombre y domicilio del agente residente de la fundación en la República de Panamá, que deberá ser abogado, o una firma de abogados, quien deberá refrendar al acta fundacional, antes de su inscripción en el Registro Público.

Los fines de la fundación.

La forma de designar a los beneficiarios de la fundación, entre los cuales puede incluirse al fundador.

La reserva del derecho a modificar el acta fundacional cuando se considere conveniente.

La duración de la fundación.

El destino que se le dará a los bienes de la fundación, y la forma de la liquidación de su patrimonio, en caso de disolución.

Cualquier otra cláusula lícita que el fundador considere conveniente.

Artículo No. 6

Observancia de las regulaciones con el registro de los actos y títulos en el Registro Público.

El Acta Fundacional, lo mismo que cualquier modificación se le haga a ésta, deberá redactarse en cualquier lengua con caracteres del alfabeto latino y cumplir con las normas de inscripción de actos y títulos en el Registro Público, para lo cual ha de ser previamente protocolizado en una notaría de la República.

Si el Acta Fundacional o sus modificaciones no estuvieren redactadas en idioma español, deberán ser protocolizadas, junto con su traducción por un intérprete público autorizado de la República de Panamá.

Artículo No. 7

Modificaciones al acta fundacional.

Las modificaciones al acta fundacional, cuando sean permitidas, han de efectuarse y firmarse de acuerdo con lo que en ella se establece. El respectivo acuerdo, resolución o acto de modificación, deberá contener la fecha en que se realizó, el nombre claramente identificable de la persona o de las personas que lo suscriben y las firmas, que deberán ser autenticadas por notario público del lugar donde se firme el documento.

Artículo No. 8

Derecho de inscripción y tasa anual de las fundaciones de interés privado similares a los establecidos para las sociedades anónimas.

Toda fundación de interés privado deberá pagar derecho registral y una tasa única anual equivalente a lo que se establecen para las sociedades anónimas en los artículos 318 y 318A del Código Fiscal.

El procedimiento y la forma de pago, el recargo por mora, las consecuencias por la falta de pago y todas las otras disposiciones complementarias de los preceptos lelgales antes citados, le serán aplicadas a las fundaciones de interés privado.

Artículo No. 9

Inscripción de fundaciones de interés privado en el Registro Público le otorgará personería jurídica.

La inscripción del acta fundacional en el Registro Público le otorgará a la fundación personalidad jurídica sin necesidad de ninguna otra autorización legal o administrativa. La inscripción en el Registro Público constituye, además, medio de publicidad frente a terceros.

En consequencia, la fundación podrá adquirir y poseer bienes de toda clase, contraer obligaciones y ser parte en procesos administrativos y judiciales de todo orden, con areglo a lo que establecen las disposiciones que resulten aplicables.

Artículo No. 10

Obligaciones del fundador o terceras partes en contribuir bienes para la fundación.

Una vez que la fundación ha adquirido personalidad jurídica, el fundador o los terceros que se han obligado a aportar bienes a la fundación, por sí mismos, o a petición de cualqier persona con interés en la fundación, deberán formalizar la transferencia a la fundación, de los bienes a que se obligaron.

Cuando la fundación sea constituida para surtir efectos a partir de fallecimiento del fundador, se considerará que ha existido con anterioridad a su muerte, con respecto a las donaciones que éste le haya hecho a la fundación.

Artículo No. 11

Bienes de la fundación constituyen un patrimonio separado y aparte del patrimonio del fundador.

Para todos los efectos legales, los bienes de la fundación constituirán un patrimonio separado de los bienes personales del fundador.

Por tanto no podrán ser secuestrados, embargados, ni objeto de acción o medida cautelar, excepto por obligaciones incurridas o danos, causados con ocasión de la ejecución de los fines u objetivos de la fundación, o por derechos legítimos de sus beneficiarios.

En ningún caso responderán por obligaciones personales del fundador o de los beneficiarios.

Artículo No. 12

Revocación de las fundaciones.

Las fundaciones serán irrevocables, salvo en los siguientes casos:

Cuando el Acta Fundacional no ha sido registrada en el Registró Público.

Cuando se establezca expresamente lo contrario en el Acta Fundacional.

Por cualquier de las causales de revocación de las donaciones.

Las transferencias que se hagan a las fundaciones serán irrevocables por quien haya hecho la transferencia, salvo que se establezca expresamente lo contrario en el acto de transferencia.

Artículo No. 13

Fundaciones creadas por disposiciones testamentarias, derechos para revocar las mismas.

En adición a lo dispuesto en el artículo anterior cuando la fundación ha sido creada para que surta efectos después de la muerte del fundador, éste tendrá, en forma excluyente e ilimitada, el derecho de revocarla.

Los herederos del fundador no tendrán derecho a revocar la creación o las transferencias, aún en el caso de que la fundación no haya sido inscrita en el Registro Público antes del fallecimiento del fundador.

Artículo No. 14

Reglas de herencia forzosa del domicilio del fundador o de los beneficiarios no afectarán a la fundación o su validez.

La existencia de disposiciones legales en materia hereditaria en el domicilio del fundador o de los beneficiarios, no será oponible a la fundación, ni afectará su validez, ni impedirá la realización de sus objetivos, en la forma prevista en el acta fundacional o sus reglamentos.

Artículo No. 15

Los aportes en favor de la fundación, fraude de acreedores del fundador.

Tendrán derecho a impugnar los aportes o las transferencias de bienes en favor de una fundación, los acreedores del fundador, o de un tercero, cuando la transferencia constituya acto en fraude de acreedores.

Los derechos y acciones de dichos acreedores prescribirán a los tres (3) anos, contados a partir del aporte o la transferencia de los bienes a la fundación.

Artículo No. 16

Las normas sobre transmisión de bienes en favor de la fundación

El patrimonio de la Fundación puede originarse en cualquier negocio jurídico lícito y podrá estar constituido sobre bienes de cualquier naturaleza, presentes o futuros.

También podrán incorporarse al patrimonio sumas periódicas de dinero u otros bienes por parte del fundador o de terceros.

La transferencia de bienes al patrimonio de la fundación puede realizarse por documento público o privado. No obstante, si se trataré de bienes inmuebles, la transferencia se ajustará a las normas sobre transmisión de bienes inmuebles.

Artículo No. 17

Consejo de Fundación

La fundación deberá tener un Consejo de Fundación, cuyas atribuciones o responsabilidades serán establecidas en el acta fundacional o en sus reglamentos.

Salvo que fuese una persona jurídica, el número de miembros del Consejo de Fundación no será menor de (3) tres.

Artículo No. 18

Responsabilidades del Consejo de Fundación

El Consejo de Fundación tendrá a su cargo el cumplimiento de los fines u objetivos de la fundación.

Salvo que se exprese otro señalamiento en el acta fundacional o en sus reglamentos, el Consejo de Fundación tendrá las siguientes obligaciones y deberes generales:

Administrar los bienes de la fundación, de acuerdo con el acta fundacional o sus reglamentos.

Celebrar actos, contratos o negocios jurídicos que resulten convenientes o necesarios para cumplir el objeto de la fundación, e incluir en los contratos, convenios y demás instrumentos u obligaciones, cláusulas y condiciones necesarias y convenientes, que se ajusten a los fines de la fundación y que no sean contrarios a la ley, la moral, las buenas costumbres o al orden público.

Informar a los beneficiarios de la fundación de la situación patrimonial de ésta, según lo establezca el acta fundacional o sus reglamentos.

Entregar a los beneficiarios de la fundación los bienes o recursos que a su favor haya establecido el acta fundacional o sus reglamentos.

Realizar los actos que esta Ley y demás disposiciones legales o reglamentarias que sean aplicables, le permiten a la fundación.

Artículo No. 19

Facultades del Protector

El acta fundacional o sus reglamentos podrán disponer que los miembros del Consejo de Fundación sólo puedan ejercer sus facultades con la autorización previa de un protector, comité o cualquier otro órgano de fiscalización, designado por el fundador o por la mayoría de los fundadores.

Los miembros del Consejo de Fundación no serán responsables por la pérdida o deterioro de los bienes de la fundación, ni por los daños o perjuicios causados, cuando la mencionada autorización haya sido debidamente obtenida.

Artículo No. 20

Cuentas anuales

Salvo que se disponga otra cosa en el acta fundacional o en sus reglamentos, el Consejo de Fundación deberá rendir cuentas de su gestión a los beneficiarios y, en su caso, al órgano de fiscalización.

Si el acta fundacional o en sus reglamentos nada establecieren sobre el particular, la rencidión de cuentas deberá hacerse anualmente.

Si la cuenta presentada no se objetaré dentro del término previsto en el acta fundacional o en sus reglamentos, en su defecto, se considerará que ha sido aprobada, dentro de (90) noventa días, contado a partir del día en que si recibió, para lo cual se dejará constancia de este plazo en el informe de rendición de cuentas.

Transcurrido dicho período o aprobada la cuenta, los miembros del Consejo de Fundación quedarán exonerados de responsabilidad por su gestión, salvo que no hubiesen actuado con la diligencia de un buen padre de familia.

Tal aprobación no los exonera frente a los beneficiarios o terceros que tengan interés en la fundación, por los daños causados por culpa grave o dolo en la administración de la fundación.

Artículo No. 21

Derecho de remover, designar o adicionar nuevos miembros del Consejo de Fundación

En el acta fundacional, el fundador podrá reservarse para sí mismo, o para otras personas, el derecho de remover a los miembros del Consejo de Fundación, lo mismo que designar o adicionar nuevos miembros.

Artículo No. 22

Derecho de remover judicialmente los miembros del Consejo de Fundación

Cuando el acta fundacional o los reglamentos nada estableciesen sobre el derecho y las causas de remoción de los miembros del Consejo de Fundación, estos podrán ser removidos judicialmente, mediante los trámites del proceso sumario, por las siguientes causas:

Cuando sus intereses fuesen incompatibles con los intereses de los beneficiarios o del fundador.

Si administraren los bienes de la fundaci?on sin la diligencia de un buen padre de familia.

Si fueren condenados por delito contra la propiedad o la fe pública. En este caso, mientras se tramita el proceso penal, se podrá decretar la suspención temporal del miembro procesado.

Por incapacidad o imposibilidad para ejecutar los objetivos de la fundación, desde que tales causales se configuren.

Por insolvencia, quiebra o concurso.

Artículo No. 23

Petición por la remoción de los miembros del Consejo de Fundación

Pueden pedir la remoción de los miembros de Consejo de Fundación, el fundador y el beneficiario o los beneficiarios.

Si los beneficiarios fuesen incapacitados o menores de edad, éstos podrán ser representados por quienes ejerzan sobre ellos la patria potestad o la tutela, en su caso.

Artículo No. 24

Órganos de fiscalización

El acta fundacional o sus reglamentos podrán prever la constitución de órganos de ficalización, que podrán estar constituidos por personas naturales o jurídicas, tales como auditores, protectores de la fundación u otros similares.

Las atribuciones de los órganos de fiscalización se establecerán en el acta fundacional o en sus reglamentos y podrán incluir, entre otras, las siguientes:

Velar porque se cumplan los fines de la fundación por parte de Consejo de Fundación y por los derechos e intereses de los beneficiarios.

Exigir rendición de cuentas al Consejo de Fundación.

Modificar los fines y objetivos de la fundación, cuando éstos resultasen de imposible o gravosa realización.

Designar nuevos miembros en el Consejo de Fundacón, por ausencia temporal, definitiva o por extinción del período de alguno de ellos.

Nombrar nuevos miembros del Consejo de Fundación en casos de ausencia temporal o accidental de alguno de ellos.

Aumentar el número de los miembros del Consejo de Fundación.

Refrendar los actos adoptados por el Consejo de Fundación, indicados en el acta fundacional o sus reglamentos.

Custodiar los bienes de la fundación y procurar que se cumpla su aplicación a los usos o finalidades enunciadas en el acta fundacional.

Excluir a beneficiarios de acta fundacional o sus reglamentos.

Artículo No. 25

Disolución de la fundación

La fundación se disolverá por:

La llegada del día indicado en que deba terminar la fundación de acuerdo con el acta fundacional.

El cumplimiento de los fines para los cuales fue constituida o por hacerse imposible su realización.

Encontrarse en estado de insolvencia, cesación de pagos o haberse declarado judicialmente el concurso de acreedores.

La pérdida o extinción total de los bienes de la fundación.

Su revocación.

Cualquier otra causa establecida en el acta fundacional o en la presente Ley.

Artículo No. 26

Derechos de los beneficiarios

Todo beneficiario de la fundación podrá impugnar los actos de la fundación que lesionen los derechos que ésta le confiere, denunciando dicha circunstancia al protector o a otros órganos de fiscalización si los hubiere, o en su defecto, promoviendo directamente la reclamación judicial correspondiente, ante el juzgado competente del domicilio de la fundación.

Artículo No. 27

Impuestos

Estarán exentos de todo impuesto, contribución, tasa, gravamen o tributo de cualquier clase o denominación, los actos de constitución, modificación o extinción de la fundación, así como los actos de transferencia, transmisión o gravamen de los bienes de la fundación y la renta proveniente de dichos bienes o cualquier otro acto sobre ellos, siempre que tales bienes constituyan:

1. Bienes situados en el extranjero.
2. Dinero depositado por personas naturales o jurídicas cuya renta no sea de fuente panameña o no sea gravable en Panama por cualquier causa.
3. Acciones o valores de cualquier clase, emitidos por sociedades cuya renta no sea de fuente panamena, o cuando su renta no sea gravable por cualquier causa, aún cuando tales acciones o valores estén depositados en la República de Panamá.

También estarán exentos de todo impuesto, los actos de transferencia de bienes inmuebles, títulos, certificaciones de depósitos, valores, dinero o acciones efectuadas por razón del cumplimiento de los fines u objetivos o por la extinción de la fundación, a favor de los parientes dentro del primer grado de consanguinidad y del cónyuge del fundador.

Artículo No. 28

Fundaciones extranjeras

las fundaciones constituidas de conformidad con una ley extranjera, podrán acogerse a las disposiciones de esta Ley.

Artículo No. 29

Certificado de continuación

Las fundaciones a que se refiere el artículo anterior, que opten por acogerse a las disposiciones de esta Ley, presentarán un certificado de continuación, expedido por los órganos que con arreglo a su régimen interno les corresponda, el cual deberá contener:

1. El nombre de la fundación y la fecha de su constitución.
2. Los datos de su inscripción o el depósito registral en su país de origen.
3. La declaración expresa de su deseo de continuar su existencia legal como una fundación panameña.
4. Los requisitos que para la constitución de fundaciones de interés privado estipula el artículo 5 de esta Ley.

Artículo No. 30

Acta original de constitución, Poder para la continuación de la fundación en Panamá

A la certificación contentiva de la resolución de continuación y lo demám requisitos mencionados en el artículo anterior, deberán adjuntarse los siguientes documentos:

1. La copia del acta original de constitución de la fundación que exprese su deseo de continuar en Panamá, junto con cualquier modificación posterior.
2. El poder otorgado a un abogado panameño para que lleve a cabo los trámites para hacer efectiva la continuación de la fundación en Panamá.

Artículo No. 31

Consequencias del cambio de domicilio y legislación

En los casos previstos en el artículo 26, las responsabilidades, deberes y derechos de la fundación, adquiridos con anterioridad al cambio de domicilio o de legislación, continuarán vigentes, así como los procesos que se hubieren instaurado en su contra, o los que la fundación hubiere promovido, sin que resulten afectados tales derechos y obligaciones con el cambio autorizado por las citadas disposiciones legales.

Artículo No. 32

Continuación de fundaciones panameñas en extranjero

Las fundaciones constituidas de conformidad con la presente Ley, así como bienes que integran su patrimonio, podrán trasladarse o someterse a las leyes y jurisdicción de otro país, según lo disponga el acta fundacional o sus reglamentos.

Artículo No. 33

Inscripciones en el Registro Público

Las inscripciones relacionadas con las fundaciones de interés privado se efectuarán en el Registro Público, en la sección especial, que se denominará „Sección de Fundaciones de Interés Privado".

El Órgano Ejecutivo, por conducto de Ministerio de Gobierno y Justicia, expedirá el reglamento aplicable a esta sección.

Artículo No. 34

Uso indebido de las fundaciones, el lavado de dinero procedente del narcotráfico
Para evitar el uso indebido de las fundaciones de interés privado se aplicarán, para su funcionamiento, todas la sdisposiciones legales contenidas en el Decreto Ejecutivo no.468 de 1994 y cualquier otra norma vigente, destinada a combatir el lavado de dinero procedente del narcotráfico.

Artículo No. 35

Confidencialidad

Los miembros del Consejo de Fundación y de los órganos de fiscalización, si los hubiere, así como los servidores públicos o privados que tuviesen conocimiento de las actividades, transacciones u operaciones de las fundaciones, deberán mantener reserva y confidencialidad al respecto, en todo momento.

Las infracciones a este deber serán sancionadas con prisión de 6 (seis) meses y multa de cincuenta mil balboas (B/.50'000.-), sin perjuicio de la responsabilidad civil correspondiente.

Lo dispuesto en este artículo se aplicará sin perjuicio de las informaciones que deberán revelarse a las autoridades oficiales y de las inspecciones que éstas deban efectuar en la forma establecida por la Ley.

Artículo No. 36

Controversias

Todas controversia que no tenga señalada en esta Ley un procedimiento especial, será resuelta por los trámites del juicio sumario.

Podrá establecerse en el acta fundacional o en los reglamentos de la fundación, que qualquier controversia que surja sobre la fundación, será resuelta por árbitros o arbitradores, así como el procedimiento, a que ellos deban sujetarse.

En caso de que no se hubiere establecido tal procedimiento, se aplicarán las normas que al respecto contenga el Código Judicial.

Artículo No. 37

Vigor

Esta Ley comenzará a regir a partir de su promulgación.

2. LFIP wording in English (translation)

Article No. 1

Definition and constitution of a Private Foundation

One or more natural or juridical persons, acting in their own name or through another, may constitute a private foundation in accordance with the procedures provided in this law. For such purpose, it shall be required the endowment of a patrimony for the purposes expressly provided in the foundation charter. The original endowment may be increased by the creator of the foundation, hereinafter referred to as the founder, or by any other person.

Article No. 2

Private foundations different from traditional foundations (for charitable purposes)

Private foundations shall be governed by the foundation charter and its regulations, as well as by the provisions of this law and other applicable legal and regulatory provisions. The provisions of Title II of Book I of the Civil Code shall not apply to private foundations.

Article No. 3

Private foundation shall not be created to carry out business on a habitual manner, commercial or profit oriented activities

Private foundations shall not be profit oriented. They may nevertheless engage in commercial activities in a non-habitual manner or exercise rights deriving from titles representing the capital of business companies held as part of a foundation's assets, provided that the economic result or proceed from such activities are used exclusively towards the foundation's objectives.

Article No. 4

Private foundations can be created inter-vivos or mortis causa. Formalities for the creation of wills shall not apply to foundations mortis causa

Private foundations may be constituted to become effective at the time of constitution or after death of their founder, in either of the following manners:

1. By private document subscribed by the founder whose signature shall be authenticated by a public notary at the place of constitution.
2. Directly before a public notary at the place of constitution.

In either case, the constitution of the foundation shall comply with the formalities established in the present law for the creation of foundations.

In case of a foundation being created to become effective after the death of the founder, whether by public or private document, the formalities required for the execution of wills shall not apply.

Article No. 5

Information or formalities which the private foundation charter shall contain

The foundation charter shall contain:

- The name of the foundation in any language with characters of the Latin alphabet, and which shall not be identical or similar to that of any other foundation previously existing in the Republic of Panama, to avoid confusion. The name shall include the word foundation to distinguish it from a natural person or from a different kind of juridical person.
- The initial capital of the foundation, expressed in any currency of legal tender, and which shall in no case be less than an amount equivalent to $ 10’000.00.
- A complete and clear designation of the member or members of the Foundation Council, to which the founder may belong, including their addresses.
- The domicile of the foundation.
- The name and domicile of the resident agent of the foundation in the Republic of Panama, who must be an attorney or law firm. The resident agent must countersign the foundation charter prior to its registration at the Public Registry.
- The purposes or objects of the foundation.
- The manner of appointing the beneficiaries of the foundation, which may include the founder.
- The reservation of the right to modify the foundation charter when deemed convenient.
- The duration of the foundation.
- The destination to be given to the estate of the foundation and the manner of liquidation such estate in the event of dissolution.
- Any other lawful clauses which the founder may consider convenient.

Article No. 6

Compliance with regulations regarding registration of acts and titles at the Public Registry

The foundation charter, as well as any amendment thereto, may be drafted in any language with characters of the Latin alphabet, and must comply with the regulations regarding registration of acts and titles at the Public Registry, for which purpose it must be protocolized by a public notary of the Republic of Panama.

If the foundation charter or its amendments are not written in Spanish, the same shall be protocolized together with its Spanish translation made by a certified public translator of the Republic of Panama.

Article No. 7

Amendment to the foundation charter, formalities to follow

Any amendment to the foundation charter, when permitted, shall be executed and signed in accordance to the provisions of the foundation charter itself. The relevant agreement, resolution or act of amendment shall contain the date in which it was carried out, and a clear indication of the name of the person or persons executing such amendments, whose signatures shall likewise be authenticated by a notary public at the place of execution of the document.

Article No. 8

Registration and annual taxes of private foundations similar to those established for Panamanian corporations

Every private foundation shall pay registration fees and annual taxes equivalent to those established for corporations in articles 318 and 318A of the Fiscal Code. The procedure and form of payment, the surcharge for late payment, the consequences of non-payment, as well as all the complementary dispositions of the legal precepts previously cited, will also be applicable to private foundations.

Article No. 9

Registration of foundations at the Public Registry shall grant juridical personality

The registration of the foundation charter of a private foundation at the Public Registry shall confer upon it juridical personality without the need for any other legal or administrative authorization. Registration at the Public Registry shall in addition constitute a means of publicity with regard to third parties.

Consequently, a foundation may acquire and own assets of all kinds, incur obligations and be a party to administrative and judicial proceedings of any order, in accordance with any applicable legal provisions.

Article No. 10

Obligations of founder or third parties to contribute assets to the foundation

Once a foundation has acquired juridical personality, the founder or any third party who has acquired an obligation to contribute assets to the foundation, either by himself/herself or at the request of another person with interest in the foundation, shall formalize the transfer to the foundation of the assets which they agreed to transfer. When the foundation is constituted to be effective at the time of death of its founder, it shall be deemed to have existed prior to the death of the founder with respect to the donations which he/she may have made to the foundation.

Article No. 11

Assets of the foundation to constitute an estate separate and apart from that of the founder

The assets of the foundation shall constitute an estate separate from the founder's personal assets for all legal purposes, and may not be seized or attached or be subject to any precautionary action or measure, except in the case of obligations incurred, or damages caused by virtue of actions taken fulfilling the purposes or objectives of the foundation, or of legitimate rights of the beneficiaries of the foundation.

In no case shall such assets be affected or used to respond for the personal obligations of the founder or of the beneficiaries.

Article No. 12

Revocation of foundations

Foundations shall be irrevocable except in the following cases:
If the foundation charter has not been entered in the Public Registry.
If the foundation charter provides otherwise.
For any of the causes of revocation applicable to donations.

The transfers of assets made to foundations shall be irrevocable by the person who made the transfer, unless it is expressly stated otherwise in the act of transfer of such assets.

Article No. 13

Foundations created by testamentary dispositions, rights to revoke the same

In addition to the foregoing provisions, if a foundation has been created to be effective at the time of death of its founder, he / she shall have the exclusive and unlimited right to revoke it.

The heirs of the founder, after his / her death, shall have no right to revoke the creation or transfer of assets to the foundation, even when it has not been registered at the Public Registry before the death of the founder.

Article No. 14

Forced heirship rules of the domicile of the founder or beneficiaries shall not affect foundation or its validity

The existence of legal provisions regarding inheritance, at the place of domicile of the founder or the beneficiaries shall not affect the foundation or its purposes in the manner provided in the foundation charter or its regulations.

Article No. 15

Transfer of assets to the foundations with intent to defraud creditors. Statute of limitations

The creditors of the founder or of a third party shall have the right to contest the contribution or transfer constitutes an act in fraud of the creditors.

The rights and actions of such creditors shall lapse at the expiration of three (3) years, counted from the dated of the contribution or transfer of the assets to the foundation.

Article No. 16

Assets of the foundation may originate from any lawful business, but transfer must follow appropriate formalities

The patrimony of the foundation may originate from any lawful business and may consist of assets of any kind, present or future. Other sums of money or assets may periodically be incorporated to the estate by the founder or third parties. The transfer of assets to the estate of the foundation may be effected by public or private document, provided however that, in the case of immovable property, the transfer shall comply with the rules for the transfer of such property.

Article No. 17

Foundation Council

The foundation shall have a Foundation Council whose powers or responsibilities shall be established in the foundation charter or in its regulation.

Unless the Council is a juridical person, the number of members of the Foundation Council shall be no less than three (3).

Article No. 18

Responsibilities of Foundation Council

The Foundation Council shall be responsible for carrying out the purposes or objectives of the foundation. Unless the foundation charter or its regulations provide otherwise, the Foundation Council shall have the following general obligations and duties:

- To administer the assets of the foundation in accordance with the foundation charter or its regulations.
- To carry out acts, contracts or lawful business which are convenient or necessary
- To advance the purposes of the foundation, and to include in such contracts, agreements and other instruments or obligations such clauses and conditions as are necessary or convenient and not contrary to the law, to bonos mores, or to public order and which are in accordance with the purposes of the foundation.

- To inform the beneficiaries of the foundation or the economic situation of the same as provided by the foundation charter or its regulations.
- To deliver to the beneficiaries of the foundation the assets, properties or resources designated for them by the foundation charter or its regulations.
- To carry out all such acts or contracts which are permitted to the foundation by the present law and by other applicable legal or regulatory provisions.

Article No. 19

Responsibilities of members of the Foundation Council when prior authorization of protector or third party is necessary to exercise their powers

The foundation charter or its regulations may provide that, in order to exercise their powers, the members of the Foundation Council must obtain the previous authorization of a protector, committee or the majority of the founders.

The members of the Foundation Council shall not be held liable for the loss or deterioration of the assets of the foundation or for the damages caused by their decisions, provided that the above mentioned authorization has been duly obtained.

Article No. 20

Rendering of accounts of its administration by foundation Council

Unless the foundation charter or its regulations provide otherwise, the Foundation Council must render accounts of its administration to the beneficiaries and, where applicable, to the supervisory entity.

If the foundation charter or its regulations contain no provision in this regard, the rendering of accounts must be done annually.

If the accounts so rendered are not objected within the time specified in the foundation charter or its regulations, or, if the charter does not regulate the matter, within ninety (90) days from the date the accounts were received, they shall be deemed to have been approved, for which purpose the above mentioned period of ninety (90) days must be indicated in the report rendering the accounts.

On the lapse of such period or upon the approval of the accounts, the members of the Foundation Council shall be free of liability for their administration, unless they had failed to act with the diligence of a bonus paterfamilias.

The above mentioned approval does not exonerate the members of the Foundation Council vis-à-vis the beneficiaries or third parties having an interest in the foundation with respect to damages caused by gross negligence or fraud in the administration of the foundation.

Article No. 21

Reservation of right to remove members of Foundation Council by founder or by another person

The Founder may reserve for himself/herself or for other persons, in the foundation charter, the right to remove the members of the Foundation Council as well as the right to designate or add new members.

Article No. 22

Right to remove members of Foundation Council by judicial proceeding

If the foundation charter or its regulations contain no provision regarding the right and causes for removal of the members of the Foundation Council, said members may be removed by means of summary judicial proceedings for the following causes:

- When their interests are incompatible with the interests of the beneficiaries or of the founder.
- If they do not administer the assets of the foundation with the diligence of a bonus pater familias.
- If they are convicted of a crime against private property or public faith. In such case, while the criminal proceedings are taking place, the temporary suspension of the member on trial may be decreed.
- For incapacity or impossibility to carry out the objectives of the foundation, from the time such causes arise.
- For insolvency or bankruptcy proceedings.

Article No. 23

Founders and beneficiaries are the only parties authorized to petition for judicial removal of members of Foundation Council

The judicial removal of the members of the Foundation Council may be requested by the founder and the beneficiary or beneficiaries. If the beneficiaries were disabled or minors, they may be represented by whoever exercises patriae potestas or legal guardianship over them, as the case may be.

The judgment of the court decreeing the removal shall also appoint new members to replace the former, who must be persons with sufficient capacity, qualifications and recognized moral standing to administer the assets of the foundation in accordance with the purposes established by the founder.

Article No. 24

Supervisory body or similar entities, possible authority

The foundation charter or its regulations may provide for the constitution of supervisory bodies, which may be composed of natural or juridical persons, such as auditing companies, protectors of the foundation, or other similar entities.

The powers of the supervisory entities shall be established in the foundation charter or its regulations, and may include, among others, the following:

- To ensure the fulfilment of the foundation's purposes, by the Foundation Council and to protect the rights and interests of the beneficiaries.
- To require the Foundation Council to render accounts.
- To modify the objects and purposes of the foundation when their fulfilment becomes impossible or too burdensome.
- To appoint new members of the Foundation Council by reason of temporary or permanent absence, or for the expiration of the period for which they were appointed.
- To appoint new members of the Foundation Council in replacement of existing members in the event of temporary or accidental absence of any of them.
- To increase or reduce the number of members of the Foundation Council.
- To approve the acts done by the Foundation Council pursuant to the foundation charter or its regulations.

- To act as custodian of the assets of the foundation and to oversee the application thereof to the objects or purposes contained in the foundation charter.
- To remove beneficiaries of the foundation and to add new beneficiaries in accordance with the provisions of the foundation charter or its regulations.

Article No. 25

Dissolutions of Foundations

The foundation shall be dissolved:

- On the date in which the foundation must come to an end in accordance with the foundation charter.
- On the accomplishment of the ends or purposes for which it was created or if their fulfilment becomes impossible.
- If it becomes insolvent, incapable of making payments, or it has been judicially declared to be subject to bankruptcy proceedings.
- On the loss or total extinction of the assets of the foundation.
- On its revocation.
- For any other reason established in the foundation charter or in the present law.

Article No. 26

Beneficiaries of the Foundation may object acts of the foundation which damage their rights or interests

Any beneficiary of the foundation may object acts of the foundation which damage his or her rights or interests by denouncing such circumstance to the protector or other supervisory body, if any, or if there are none, by directly instituting the corresponding judicial action before the appropriate court of the domicile of the foundation.

Article No. 27

Exemption of certain taxes for private foundations

The acts of constitution, amendment or extinction of the foundation, as well as the act of transfer, transmittal or encumbrance of assets of the foundation and the income arising therefrom, or any other act in connection therewith, shall be exempt from all taxes, contributions, duties, liens or assessments of any kind, provided they relate to assets located abroad.

Money deposited by natural or juridical persons whose income does not derive from a Panamanian source or is not taxable in Panama for any reason.

Shares or securities of any kind issued by corporations which income is not derived from a Panamanian source, or which are not taxable for any reason, even when such shares or securities are deposited in the Republic of Panama.

The transfer of immovable property, titles, certificates of deposit, assets, funds, securities or shares carried out by reason of the fulfilment of the objectives of the foundation or the termination of the same, in favour of relatives within the first degree of consanguinity or the spouse of the founder shall be exempted from all taxes.

Article No. 28

Foreign Foundations

Foundations organized in accordance with a foreign law may become subject to the provisions of this law.

Article No. 29

Requirements for foreign foundations to continue as Panamanian private foundations

Foundations referred to in the preceding article that elect to become subject to the provisions of this law shall present a certificate of continuation, issued by the corresponding body or organ of the foundation which according to its own internal organization shall issue the same, and which shall contain:

- The name of the foundation and the date of its constitution.
- Data about the registration or deposit of the instrument at the registry of the country of origin.
- An express declaration of its desire to continue its legal existence as a Panamanian foundation.
- The requirements of article 5 of this law for the constitution of Panamanian private foundations.

Article No. 30

Additional requirements of foreign foundations to continue as Panamanian private foundations

The certification containing the resolution of continuation and the other requirements mentioned in the preceding article shall have the following documents attached to it:

- Copy of the original act of constitution of the foundation which desires to continue as a Panamanian foundation, together with any subsequent amendment.
- Power of attorney extended to a Panamanian lawyer to carry out the necessary procedures to affect the continuation of the foundation in Panama.

Article No. 31

Continuation of foreign foundations to continue as Panamanian private foundations, obligations and responsibilities shall continue in effect

In the cases provided for in article 28, the responsibilities, duties and rights acquired prior to the change of jurisdiction of the foundation, as well as proceedings brought against it or those brought by the foundation, shall continue in effect, and such rights and obligations shall not be affected by the change of jurisdiction authorized by the aforementioned legal provisions.

Article No. 32

Panamanian Private Foundations can migrate or become subject to the laws of other countries

Foundations constituted in accordance with this law, as well as the assets which constitute their patrimony, may transfer or become subject to the laws and jurisdiction of another country, as may be provided by their foundation charter or their regulations.

Article No. 33

Registration of private foundations shall be made at special section of Public Registry

Registration in connection with private foundations shall be made at the Public Registry in a especial section to be known as „Section of Private Foundations".

The Executive Branch of Government, acting through the Ministry of Government and Justice, shall issue the regulations applicable to such section.

Article No. 34

All pertinent legal precepts shall apply to Panamanian private foundations to avoid their use for money laundering activities form the drug-traffic business

To avoid the undue use of private foundations, all the provisions in Executive Decree No. 468 of 1994 and any other legal disposition in force aimed at combating money laundering arising from drug trafficking shall be applied to their operations.

Article No. 35

The need to maintain secrecy on information about private foundations by attorneys, public employees or third parties handling the information.

All members of the Foundation Council and of the supervisory bodies, if any, as well as public or private employees, who have any knowledge of the activities, transactions or operations of the foundations, must at all times hold the same in secret and confidentiality. Breaches of this duty shall be sanctioned with imprisonment of six months and a fine of $50,000.00, without prejudice to the corresponding civil liability.

The provisions of this article are applicable without prejudice to the information which must be disclosed to official authorities and the inspections the latter must carry out in the manner established by the law.

Article No. 36

Controversies shall be resolved by summary proceedings but foundational documents might establish obligation to submit to arbitration.

Any controversy for which no special procedure is specified in the present law shall be resolved by summary proceedings. The foundation charter or its regulations may establish that any controversy arising in connection with the foundation shall be resolved by an arbitrator or arbitrators, as well as the procedure to be followed thereby. In the event no such procedure has been established, the statutes ruling such matters as contained in the Judicial Code shall apply.

Article No. 37

Date of entering into effect of law

This law shall enter into force after its promulgation.

3. LFIP wording in German (translation)

Artikel Nr. 1

Definition und Umschreibung der Privatstiftung

Eine oder mehrere natürliche oder juristische Personen können im eigenen Namen oder im Namen von anderen Dritten eine Stiftung gemäss den Bestimmungen dieses Gesetzes errichten.

Zur Errichtung einer Stiftung bedarf es der Widmung eines Vermögens für einen bestimmt bezeichneten, in der Stiftungsurkunde ausdrücklich festgelegten Zweck.

Das ursprünglich gewidmete Stiftungsvermögen kann durch den Gründer der Stiftung, weiter Stifter genannt, oder durch jede andere Person erhöht werden.

Artikel Nr. 2

Abgrenzung der Privatstiftung gegenüber den traditionellen wohltätigen und charitativen Stiftungen sowie gegenüber den öffentlichrechtlichen Stiftungen

Die Privatstiftungen werden sowohl durch die Stiftungsurkunde und deren Beistatuten als auch durch die Bestimmungen dieses Gesetzes und anderen zuständigen gesetzlichen und regulierenden Vorschriften geregelt.

Die Vorschriften und Bestimmungen des Titels II, Buch I, Zivilgesetzbuch sind für Privatstiftungen nicht anwendbar.

Artikel Nr. 3

Verbot der gewinnbringenden kommerziellen oder gewinnorientierten Geschäftstätigkeit einer Privatstiftung

Private Stiftungen dürfen keine gewinnorientierte Zwecke verfolgen.

Dennoch können sie ausnahmsweise eine nach kaufmännischer Art geführte kommerzielle Tätigkeit betreiben oder aufgrund von kommerziellen Beteiligungen im Stiftungsvermögen eine solche kommerzielle Geschäftstätigkeit ausüben, unter der Bedingung, dass der wirtschaftliche Erlös ausschließlich der Verfolgung ihres nichtwirtschaftlichen Stiftungszweckes zugute kommt.

Artikel Nr. 4

Gründung inter-vivos oder mortis-causa. Nichtanwendbarkeit der Formvorschriften für Testamente und letztwillige Verfügungen

Private Stiftungen können auf die Art und Weise gegründet werden, dass sie ihre Wirkung ab dem Zeitpunkt ihrer Gründung oder aber erst nach dem Tode des Stifters entfalten, nämlich:

mittels eines vom Stifter unterschriebenen, privaten Dokumentes, wobei die Unterschrift notariell, am Ort der Gründung beglaubigt werden muss,

mittels einer vor dem Notar, am Ort der Gründung, unterzeichneten, beglaubigten Stiftungsurkunde.

In beiden Fällen müssen die Anforderungen, welche für die Gründung einer Stiftung in diesem Gesetz verlangt werden, erfüllt werden.

Im Falle dass die Stiftung, sei es durch ein privates oder öffentliches Dokument so gegründet wird, dass sie ihre Wirkung nach dem Tode des Stifters entfalten soll, finden die ansonsten für letzwillige Verfügungen und Testamente gültigen Formvorschriften keine Anwendung.

Artikel Nr. 5

Stiftungsurkunde

Die Stiftungsurkunde hat zu enthalten:

1. Den Namen der Stiftung, in jeder beliebigen Sprache ausgedruckt, jedoch geschrieben in lateinischen Buchstaben, welcher gegenüber den bereits in Panama existenden Stiftungen weder identisch noch ähnlich ist. Der Stiftungsname soll den Begriff Stiftung beinhalten um die Stiftung von anderen natürlichen oder juristischen Personen zu unterscheiden.
2. Das Stiftungsvermögen, bewertet in einer beliebigen gesetzlichen Währung, jedoch nicht minder als (zehn Tausend US Dollar) USD 10'000.-.
3. Die vollständige und klare Bezeichnung aller Mitglieder des Stiftungsrates, inklusive Wohnort-Anschriften, zu welchen auch der Stifter gehören darf.
4. Den Sitz der Stiftung.
5. Den Namen und die Adresse des lokalen, residenten Agenten der Stiftung in der panamaischen Republik, welcher entweder ein Rechtsanwalt oder eine Rechtsanwaltskanzlei sein muss und welcher die Stiftungsurkunde vor der Eintragung in das Oeffentlichkeitsregister gegenzeichnen muss.
6. Den Zweck der Stiftung.
7. Die Art und Weise der Bezeichnung der Begünstigten, zu welchen auch der Stifter gehören darf.
8. Den Aenderungsvorbehalt der Stiftungsurkunde, falls nötig.
9. Die Dauer der Stiftung.
10. Die Bestimmung über die Vewendung des Stiftungsvermögens im Falle der Auflösung der Stiftung.
11. Andere Vorschriften, welche der Stifter als massgebend erachtet.

Artikel Nr. 6

Eintragung der Stiftungsurkunde ins Stiftungsregister

Die Stiftungsurkunde, sowie alle Aenderungen der Stiftungsurkunde, können in einer beliebigen Sprache, jedoch unter Verwendung der lateinischen Buchstaben, verfasst werden, und müssen für ihre Registrierung den Vorschriften des panamaischen Oeffentlichkeitsregisters entsprechen, und zu diesem Zwecke vor einem Notaren der panamaischen Republik beurkundet werden.

Falls die Stiftungsurkunde oder ihre Abänderung in einer anderen als der spanischen Sprache verfasst ist, muss sie zusammen mit einer amtlichen spanischen Uebersetzung vor einem Notaren der panamaischen Republik beurkundet werden.

Artikel Nr. 7

Aenderungen der Stiftungsurkunde

Jede Aenderung der Stiftungsurkunde, falls in der Stiftungsurkunde vorgesehen und erlaubt, muss den diesbezüglichen Vorschriften der Stiftungsurkunde selbst entsprechen.

Die Aenderung hat in beglaubigter Form eines unterzeichneten Beschlusses, eines Rechtsaktes oder einer Vereinbarung zu erfolgen, beinhaltend das entsprechende Aenderungsdatum, den Ausübungsort und den Namen der Personen, welche bei der Aenderung mitgewirkt und dieselbe vor einem Notaren unterschrieben haben.

Artikel Nr. 8

Gründungs- und Jahressteuer

Die Entrichtung der Gründungs- und Jahressteuer einer Privatstiftung entspricht den gleichen für die Gesellschaften relevanten Abgaben gemäss Art.318 und Art.318A des Steuergesetzes.

Die Bestimmungen über die Art und Form der Steuerbezahlung, sowie die Anwendung der Bussen für eine verspätete Steuerbezahlung, wie sie in den vorerwähnten Bestimmungen des Steuergesetzes vorgesehen sind, sind ebenfalls für die Privatstiftungen anwendbar.

Artikel Nr. 9

Entstehung

Die Stiftung entsteht mit der Eintragung der Stiftungsurkunde ins Oeffentlichkeitsregister und die Stiftung erlangt mit dieser Eintragung das Recht der Persönlichkeit, ohne Erfordernis von weiteren rechtlichen oder administrativen Massnahmen.

Die Eintragung ins Oeffentlichkeitsregister ist zudem gegenüber dritten Parteien bindend.

Folglich kann die Stiftung Güter aller Art erwerben und halten sowie Verbindlichkeiten eingehen und als aktiv und passiv legitimierte Partei in Verwaltungs- und Rechtsprozessen, wie sie im allgemeinen für die Oeffentlichkeit gelten, auftreten.

Artikel Nr. 10

Vermögenszuwendung

Ist die Stiftung entstanden und erlang sie das Recht der Persönlichkeit, so ist der Stifter oder ein Dritter, aufgrund eines Schuldverhältnisses, auf das Verlangen des Stifters oder von einem Stiftungs-Interessenten, verpflichtet, das der Stiftung zugesicherte Vermögen auf die Stiftung formell zu übertragen.

Wird die Stiftung erst mit dem Tode des Stifters wirksam, so gilt sie für die Zuwendungen des Stifters als schon vor dem Tode des Stifters entstanden.

Artikel Nr. 11

Stiftungsvermögen als Sondervermögen

Das Stiftungsvermögen stellt ein vom übrigen Vermögen des Stifters abgesondertes, separates Sondervermögen, dar.

Folglich darf das Stiftungsvermögen nicht Gegenstand von gegen den Stifter gerichteten Vermögensmassnahmen sein, ausgenommen solche, welche im Zusammenhang mit der Verfolgung des Stiftungszweckes oder im Zusammenhang mit der Verfolgung legitimer Rechte der Begünstigten stehen.

Auf keinen Fall haftet das Stiftungsvermögen für persönliche Verbindlichkeiten des Stifters oder der Begünstigten.

Artikel Nr. 12

Widerruf der Stiftung

Stiftungen sind unwiderruflich, außer in den folgenden Fällen:
Wenn die Stiftungsurkunde nicht im Öffentlichkeitsregister registriert wurde.

Wenn der Widerruf ausdrücklich in der Stiftungsurkunde vorgesehen ist.

Wenn einer der Gründe des Widerrufs von Schenkung eintrifft.

Überweisungen von Vermögen an die Stiftung sind unwiderruflich für und durch die Person, die sie gemacht hat, ausser das Gegenteil wurde ausdrücklich im Überweisungsdokument der Verrmögenszuwendung festgelegt.

Artikel Nr. 13

Widerruf von Stiftungen gegründet durch testamentarische Anordnungen

Zusätzlich zu den Anordnungen des vorangehenden Artikels, wenn die Stiftung so gegründet wurde, dass sie ihre Wirkung nach dem Tode des Stifters tun soll, hat dieser das ausschließliche und unbeschränkte Recht, die Stiftung zu widerrufen.

Die Erben des Stifters, nach dem Tode desselben, haben kein Recht die Gründung der Stiftung oder die Vermögensüberweisungen an sie zu widerrufen, auch wenn die Stiftung während Lebzeiten des Stifters nicht ins Öffentlichkeitsregister eingetragen wurde.

Artikel Nr. 14

Pflichtteilsrechte

Rechtsvorschriften, welche die Erbschaft des Stifters oder der Begünstigten an ihrem Wohnort regeln, haben keine Wirkung auf die Stiftung oder auf ihre Gültigkeit oder auf die Verfolgung des Zwecks der Stiftung, so wie er in der Stiftungsurkunde oder in Beistatuten der Stiftung vorgesehen und geregelt ist.

Artikel Nr. 15

Gläubigerschutz

Die Vermögenszuwendungen zu Gunsten der Stiftung können von den Gläubigern des Stifters oder von Dritten angefochten werden, falls diese Vermögenszuwendungen auf betrügerische Art und Weise erfolgten.

Die Anfechtungsfrist der Gläubiger beträgt drei (3) Jahre ab dem Datum der Vermögenszuwendung.

Artikel Nr. 16

Vermögensarten

Das Stiftungsvermögen darf verschiedener Herkunft sein, vorausgesetzt es stammt aus legalen, bereits erfolgten oder künftigen Rechtsgeschäften.

Ebenfalls können, seitens des Stifters oder von Dritten, periodische Zuwendungen dem Stiftungsvermögen zugefügt werden.

Die Vermögenszuwendung kann in einem privaten oder öffentlichen Dokument verbrieft werden.

Falls es sich bei der Vermögenszuwendung um Immobilien handelt sind die entsprechenden formellen Uebertragungsvorschriften zu beachten.

Artikel Nr. 17

Stiftungsrat

Die Stiftung verfügt über einen Stiftungsrat, dessen Kompetenzen und Pflichten in der Stiftungsurkunde bestimmt sind.

Die Zahl der Stiftungsratsmitglieder beträgt mindestens (3) drei, es sei denn, eine juristische Person amtet als Stiftungsratsmitglied.

Artikel Nr. 18

Rechte und Pflichten des Stiftungsrates

Der Stiftungsrat ist verantwortlich für die Verfolgung und Durchführung des Stiftungszweckes.

Falls die Stiftungsurkunde nicht anderweitig bestimmt, obliegen dem Stiftungsrat folgende Rechte und Pflichten:

1. Verwaltung des Stiftungsvermögens gemäss den Bestimmungen der Stiftungsurkunde.
2. Durchführung von Rechtshandlungen, Rechtsgeschäften und Ausführungshandlungen, welche der Erfüllung des Stiftungszweckes dienen, mittels Abschluss von Verträgen, Uebernahme von Verpflichtungen und Bedingungen, vorausgesetzt dass diese Handlungen nicht gegen das Gesetz, die öffentliche Moral und Ordnung verstossen.
3. Information an die Begünstigten über die Wirtschaftslage der Stiftung, auf die Art und Weise wie in der Stiftungsurkunde oder in den Beistatuten vorgesehen.
4. Ausschüttungen an die Begünstigten aus dem Stiftungsvermögen und Erträgnissen, gemäss Bestimmungen der Stiftungsurkunde sowie der Beistatuten.
5. Durchführung von Massnahmen und Anwendung von Rechtsvorschriften, welche dieses Gesetz für die Verwaltung der Stiftung vorsieht.

Artikel Nr. 19

Protektor

Die Stiftungsurkunde kann bestimmen, dass die Stiftungsratsmitglieder Handlungen nur nach vorheriger Genehmigung des Protektors oder eines anderen Aufsichtsorgans, bestimmt vom Stiftungsgründer oder von der Mehrheit der Stiftungsgründer, ausführen dürfen.

Die Stiftungsratsmitglieder sind nicht haftbar für Handlungen, welche sie aufgrund der obenerwähnten Genehmigung ausführten, selbst wenn diese Verluste am Stiftungsvermögen, Vermögensschaden und sonstige Verminderung des Stiftungsvermögens nach sich ziehen.

Artikel Nr. 20

Buchführung

Falls die Stiftungsurkunde oder die Beistatuten nicht anderweitig bestimmen, muss der Stiftungsrat einen Jahresabschluss an die Begünstigten und, falls vorgesehen, auch an das Aufsichtsorgan abliefern.

Falls die Stiftungsurkunde und die Beistatuten keine solche Bestimmung kennen, muss der Jahresabschluss alljährlich erfolgen.

Falls der Jahresabschluss nicht innerhalb der in der Stiftungsurkunde oder in den Beistatuten vorgesehenen Frist beanstandet wird, oder falls die Stiftungsurkunde die Buchführung nicht regelt, gilt der Jahresabschluss als genehmigt, sollte er nicht innerhalb von (90) neunzig Tagen seit Erhalt beanstandet werden, wobei zu diesem Zwecke die Frist von (90) neunzig Tagen im Jahresbericht anzumerken ist.
Nach Fristablauf oder nach erfolgter Genehmigung sind die Stiftungsratsmitglieder von jeglicher Haftung hinsichtlich der Verwaltung befreit, es sei denn, sie handelten gegen den Grundsatz ‚bonus pater familias'.

Die obenerwähnte Genehmigung hat keine Wirkung gegenüber den Begünstigten und Dritten, welche Rechte im Zusammenhang mit der Stiftung besitzen, sowie keine Wirkung im Falle einer schweren Schuld hinsichtlich der Verwaltung der Stiftung.

Artikel Nr. 21

Abwahl und Zuwahl von Stiftungsratsmitgliedern durch den Stifter

Mittels Stiftungsurkunde kann sich der Stifter selbst, oder anderen Personen, das Recht vorbehalten, Stiftungsratsmitglieder abzuwählen sowie neue Stiftungsratsmitglieder zu bestimmen und neue zu wählen.

Artikel Nr. 22

Abwahl und Zuwahl von Stiftungsratsmitgliedern mittels Verfahren

Falls die Stiftungsurkunde oder die Beistatuten keine Abwahlregelung der Stiftungsratsmitglieder vorsehen, kann die Abwahl der Stiftungsratsmitglieder durch ein summarisches Verfahren prozessualrechtlich in folgenden Fällen erfolgen:

1. Falls ihre Interessen mit denjenigen des Stifters oder der Begünstigten nicht übereistimmen.
2. Falls sie das Stiftungsvermögen nicht mit der Sorgfalt eines ‚bonus pater familias' verwalten.
3. Falls sie verurteilt wurden für Vermögensdelikte oder Delikte gegen öffentliche Ordnung. In einem solchen Falle, solange als das Verfahren pendent ist, kann ein Stiftungsratsmitglied auf dem Verordnungswege ad interim seines Amtes enthoben werden.
4. Aufgrund der Unfähigkeit den Stiftungszweck zu verfolgen, und dies seit dem Kausalzusammenhang der Unmöglichkeit.

5. Aufgrund des Konkurses oder der Zahlungsunfähigkeit.

Artikel Nr. 23

Aktivlegitimation für die Abwahl und Zuwahl von Stiftungsratsmitgliedern
Das juristische Verfahren einer Abwahl von Stiftungsratsmitgliedern kann vom Stifter oder von den Begünstigten beantragt werden.

Im Falle der Minderjährigkeit oder der Bevormundung der Begünstigten kann den Antrag auf Abwahl der Stiftungsratsmitglieder ihr gesetzlicher Vertreter oder ein solcher Vertreter, welcher die ‚patriae potestas' ausübt, stellen.

Das Abwahl-Urteil wird gleichzeitig das neue Ersatzmitglied des Stiftungsrates bestellen, wobei dieses neue Stiftungsratsmitglied die Anforderungen hinsichtlich der entsprechenden Qualifikation für die Verwaltung des Stiftungsvermögens sowie hinsichtlich einer anerkannten moralischen Höhe, aufgestellt durch den Stifter, erfüllen muss.

Artikel Nr. 24

Aufsichtsorgane

Die Stiftungsurkunde oder die Beistatuten können die Errichtung von Aufsichtsorganen vorsehen, welche sich aus natürlichen oder juristischen Personen zusammensetzen können, wie zum Beispiel Revisionsgesellschaften, Protektoren oder ähnliche Personen.

Ihre Kompetenzen und Befugnisse der Aufsichtsorgane sind in der Stiftungsurkunde oder in den Beistatuten vorzusehen und können, unter anderem, folgende Befugnisse beinhalten:

1. Die Ueberwachung der Erfüllung des Stiftungszweckes durch den Stiftungsrat sowie die Verteidigung der Rechte und der Interessen der Begünstigten.
2. Die Entgegennahme der Berichterstattung des Stiftungsrates.
3. Die Aenderung des Stiftungszweckes falls ein solcher Zweck unmöglich oder allzu schwer erreichbar ist.
4. Die Zuwahl von neuen Stiftungsratsmitgliedern, falls vakant aufgrund von Ablauf der Amtszeit eines gewählten Stiftungsratsmitglieds.
5. Die generelle Zuwahl und Ersatzwahl von neuen Stiftungsratsmitgliedern.
6. Die zahlenmässige Erhöhung oder Reduktion der Stiftungsratsmitgliedern.

7. Die Prüfung der Geschäftstätigkeit des Stiftungsrates gemäss der Stiftungsurkunde oder der Beistatuten.
8. Die Aufbewahrung des Stiftungsvermögens sowie die Ueberwachung der Verwendung des Stiftungsvermögens im Sinne des Stiftungszweckes, in Uebereinstimmung mit der Stiftungsurkunde.
9. Die Abwahl und Zuwahl von Begünstigten, in Uebereinstimmung mit der Stiftungsurkunde oder mit den Beistatuten.

Artikel Nr. 25

Auflösung

Die Stiftung wird aufgelöst:

1. Wenn die Zeitdauer gemäss der Stiftungsurkunde abgelaufen ist.
2. Sobald der Stiftungszweck erfüllt oder sobald der Stiftungszweck unerreichbar geworden ist.
3. Wenn die Stiftung insolvent und nicht in der Lage ist, Zahlungen zu leisten oder sie befindet sich im Konkursverfahren.
4. Mangels genügenden Vermögens.
5. Infolge Widerrufs.
6. Aufgrund einer in diesem Gesetz bestimmten gesetzlichen Regelung oder aufgrund einer in der Stiftungsurkunde vorgesehenen Bestimmung.

Artikel Nr. 26

Begünstigte

Jeder Begünstigte kann beim Aufsichtsorgan oder beim Protektor die Verwaltungstätigkeit, welche seine Rechte verletzt, beanstanden, und im Falle Nichtvorhandenseins des Aufsichtsorgans, sich an den Richter am Sitz der Stiftung wenden.

Artikel Nr. 27

Steuerprivileg

Steuerfreiheit sowie Steuerbefreiung von allen Steuern, Abgaben, Gebühren usw. jeglicher Art, geniessen die Verwaltungsakte bezüglich der Stiftungsgründung, Stiftungsabänderung, Vermögenszuwendung, Vermögensbelastung, Vermögens-ausschüttung, sei es Kapital- oder Erträgniss-Auschüttung aus dem Stiftungsvermögen, vorausgesetzt, folgende Bedingungen hinsichtlich des Vermögens zutreffen:

1. Das Stiftungsvermögen liegt im Ausland.
2. Das Stiftungsvermögen sowie dessen Erträgnisse, welches nicht panamaischer Herkunft ist, egal ob von einer natürlichen oder juristischen Person aufbewahrt, ist von jeglicher Besteuerung in Panama befreit.
3. Aktien und Wertpapiere aller Art, herausgegeben von Gesellschaften, welche ihr Einkommen nicht aus panamaischen Quelle beziehen, oder welche Steuerfreiheit, aus welchem Grunde auch immer, geniessen, unabhängig, ob solche Aktien und Wertpapiere in Panama aufbewahrt werden oder nicht.

Die Vermögenszuwendungen von beweglichen Sachen, Titeln, Aufbewahrungszertifikaten, Wertsachen, Geld, Aktien und Obligationen, ausgeführt im Sinne der Erfüllung des Stiftungszweckes oder im Sinne ihrer Beendigung und Stiftungsauflösung, zu Gunsten der Blutsverwandten ersten Grades des Stifters oder seiner Gemahlin, sind von allen Steuern befreit.

Artikel Nr. 28

Ausländische Stiftungen

Die im Ausland gemäss ausländischem Recht rechtmässig gegründete Stiftungen können sich freiwillig diesem Gesetz unterstellen.

Artikel Nr. 29

Formvorschriften für ausländische Stiftungen in Panama

Die im Ausland gemäss ausländischem Recht gegründete Stiftungen, welche sich diesem Gesetz unterstellen wollen, haben ein Zertifikat bezüglich der ununterbrochenen Kontinuität des Stiftungsbestehens, ausgestellt vom zuständigen Stiftungsorgan im Sinne der internen Stiftungsorganisation, welches zu enthalten hat:

1. Name und Gründungsdatum der Stiftung.
2. Gründungsamtsbestätigung und Registerbestätigung aus dem Ursprungsland.
3. Ausdrückliche Deklaration über die gewünschte rechtliche Weiterexistenz der Stiftung als panamaische Stiftung.

4. Uebrige Erfordernisse für die Stiftungsgründung gemäss Art.5 dieses Gesetzes.

Artikel Nr. 30

Zusätzliche Beilagen für die Unterstellung unter das panamaische Stiftungsgesetz

Das Zertifikat, wie im vorstehenden Artikel beschrieben, ist mit folgenden Beilagen zu versehen:

1. Kopie der ursprünglichen Stiftungsgründungsurkunde zusammen mit allen allfälligen Aenderungen.
2. Vollmacht zugunsten eines panamaischen Anwaltes mit der entpsrechenden Ermächtigung das Verfahren der ununterbrochenen Kontinuität der Stiftung in Panama durchzuführen.

Das Zertifikat bezüglich der Kontinuität sowie die diesem Zertifikat gemäss diesem Artikel erwähnte, beigelegte Dokumentation wird im Oeffentlichkeitsregister ordentlich protokolliert und eingetragen, um die Kontinuität des Rechtsexistenz der Privatstiftung in Panama zu gewährleisten.

Artikel Nr. 31

Rechtsfolgen der Unterstellung unter das panamaische Stiftungsgesetz

In Fällen gemäss Art.28, bleiben in Kraft sämtliche, vor der Aenderung der Jurisdiktion geltenden Verantwortlichkeiten, Rechte und Pflichten, sowie die gegen diese Stiftungen gerichtete Gerichtsverfahren oder die seitens der Stiftungen initiierten, pendenten Gerichtsverfahren. Die Gültigkeit solcher Rechte und Pflichten wird durch die Aenderung Jurisdiktion nicht berührt.

Artikel Nr. 32

Panamaische Stiftungen im Ausland

In Anwendung der Bestimmungen der Stiftungsurkunde oder der Beistatuten können sowohl die unter diesem Gesetz gegründeten Stiftungen als auch ihre Vermögenswerte ins Ausland transferiert werden oder sich der ausländischen Jurisdiktion unterstellen.

Artikel Nr. 33

Oeffentlichkeitsregister

Die Registrierung der Privatstiftungen erfolgt in einer Spezialabteilung des Oeffentlichkeitsregisters, genannt als „Sektion der Privatstiftungen“. Die entsprechende Verordnung für das Registrationsverfahren erlässt die Exekutivabteilung des Justizministeriums.

Artikel Nr. 34

Missbrauchbekämpfung, Massnahmen gegen die Geldwäscherei

Zwecks Missbrauchbekämpfung sind für die Privatstiftungen alle Rechtsvorschriften der Verwaltungsverordnung Nr.468 aus dem Jahre 1994, sowie sämtliche anderen Rechtsnormen, welche die Bekämpfung der Geldwäscherei, resultierend aus dem Drogenhandel regeln, anwendbar.

Artikel Nr. 35

Geheimhaltungspflicht

Alle Stiftungsratsmitglieder und allfällige Mitglieder der Aufsichtsorgane, sowie private Angestellte und Beamte, welche Kenntnis über die Tätigkeit, Transaktionen und Operationen einer Stiftung erlangen, müssen dies gegenüber jedermann dauernd geheim halten.

Verletzungen der Geheimhaltungspflicht werden mit Gefängnis bis 6 (sechs) Monaten und einer Busse von USD 50’000.- bestraft. Vorbehalten bleiben die zivilrechtlichen Ansprüche.

Artikel Nr. 36

Streitigkeiten

Alle Streitigkeiten und Kontroversen welche durch dieses Gesetz nicht im einzelnen geregelt sind unterliegen dem summarischen Verfahren.

Die Stiftungsurkunde kann Vorschriften aufsetzen, die alle Streitigkeiten, welche im Zusammenhang mit der Stiftung entstehen können, einem oder mehreren Richtern zur Entscheidung, im Rahmen eines besonderen Verfahrens, anvertraut. Sollten keine Verfahrensnormen in der Stiftungsurkunde vorgesehen werden, gelten die allgemeinen Verfahrensnormen.

Artikel Nr. 37

Inkraftsetzung

Dieses Gesetz tritt am Tage der Kundmachung in Kraft.

II. PGR, Persons and Companies Act dated 26 January 1926, Section 2: Legal Entities, Title 5: Establishments and Foundations, Section 2: Foundations (Art. 552 - 570)

1. Former law, valid until 1 April 2009 (original wording)

DIE STIFTUNGEN

A. Umschreibung und Abgrenzung

Art. 552

I. Im Allgemeinen

1) Zur Errichtung einer Stiftung durch Einzelpersonen oder Verbandspersonen oder Firmen bedarf es der Widmung eines Vermögens (Stiftungsgut) für einen bestimmt bezeichneten Zweck. Als Zwecke fallen insbesondere in Betracht: kirchliche, Familien- und gemeinnützige Zwecke. Die Stiftung darf ein nach kaufmännischer Art geführtes Gewerbe nur betreiben, wenn es der Erreichung ihres nichtwirtschaftlichen Zweckes dient oder Art und Umfang der Haltung von Beteiligten einen kaufmännischen Betrieb erfordern.

2) Vermögenswidmungen ohne Persönlichkeit (unselbständige Stiftungen, Zustiftungen) oder Zuwendungen mit Auflage einer besonderen Verwaltung unter besonderem Namen und der Verwendung für einen besonderen Zweck und dergleichen an schon bestehende Verbandspersonen oder Einzelpersonen oder Gesellschaften stehen unter den besonderen hierauf anwendbaren Vorschriften,

wie über Schenkung oder über das Erbrecht und ergänzend unter den Vorschriften über das stillschweigende Treuhandverhältnis.

3) Inwieweit einem abgesondert verwalteten Vermögen (Fonds) privatrechtliche Selbständigkeit oder die Eigenschaft eines Treuhandgutes zukommt, ist vom Richter im Einzelfalle zu beurteilen.

4) Die Vorschriften über das Treuunternehmen mit Persönlichkeit finden auf Stiftungen, insbesondere hinsichtlich der Stiftungsbeteiligten (Stifter, Stiftungsvorstand, Stiftungsgeniesser) entsprechende Anwendung, wenn und soweit sich aus den nachfolgenden Bestimmungen oder den Stiftungsstatuten oder aus den Vorschriften über die Anmeldungspflicht der Treuunternehmen nicht Abweichungen ergeben.

Art. 553

II. Kirchliche und Familienstiftung

1) Kirchliche Stiftungen im Sinne dieses Abschnittes sind zu kirchlichen Zwecken errichtete Stiftungen.

2) Eine Familienstiftung ist eine reine, wenn das Stiftungsvermögen dauernd zum Zwecke der Bestreitung der Kosten der Erziehung und Bildung, der Ausstattung oder Unterstützung von Angehörigen einer oder mehrerer bestimmter Familien, oder zu ähnlichen Zwecken verbunden ist.

3) Sie ist eine gemischte, wenn ein derart gewidmetes Vermögen ausserdem oder ergänzend auch ausserhalb der Familie liegenden, kirchlichen oder sonstigen Zwecken dienen soll.

Art. 554

III. Hinterlegung

Zur Ueberwachung der Eintragungspflicht und Verhütung von Stiftungen mit widerrechtlichem oder unsittlichem Zwecke sowie zur Vermeidung von Umgehungen einer allfälligen Aufsicht ist bei Errichtung einer Stiftung die Stiftungsurkunde bzw. eine beglaubigte Abschrift der letztwilligen Verfügung oder des Erbvertrages und bei Abänderung des Stiftungszweckes die diesbezügliche Urkunde durch den Stiftungsvorstand oder Repräsentanten bzw. durch das

Verlassenschaftsgericht beim Grundbuch- und Oeffentlichkeitsregisteramt zu hinterlegen, sofern nicht sonst eine Anmeldung zur Eintragung ins Oeffentlichkeitsregister erfolgt.

B. Errichtung

Art. 555

I. Stiftungsurkunde

1) Die Errichtung der Stiftung erfolgt in der Form einer Urkunde, auf der die Untersschriften der Stifter beglaubigt sind, durch letztwillige Verfügung oder durch Erbvertrag.

2) Die Stiftungsurkunde (der Stiftsbrief) oder das Statut sollen enthalten die Bezeichnung und den Sitz der Stiftung, ihren Zweck oder Gegenstand, die Bezeichnung des Stiftungsvorstandes und die Art und Weise, wie ein anderer Vorstand bestellt wird, sowie die Bestimmung über die Verwendung des Vermögens im Falle der Auflösung der Stiftung.

Art. 556

II. Eintragung ins Stiftungsregister

1) Die Anmeldung der Stiftung zum Stiftungsregister ist unter Beilage einer beglaubigten Abschrift der Stiftungsurkunde von sämtlichen Mitgliedern der Verwaltung persönlich zu Protokoll zu erklären oder schriftlich in beglaubigter Form einzureichen.

2) Die Eintragung und Veröffentlichung, welche durch Anschlag an der Gerichtstafel erfolgen kann, haben zu enthalten: Namen (Firma), Sitz, Zweck der Stiftung, das Datum der Errichtungsurkunde, die Organisation und Vertretung, wobei Namen und Wohnort beziehungsweise Firma und Sitz der Mitglieder des Vorstandes beziehungsweise sonstiger Vertreter anzugeben sind.

3) Die Eintragung und Veröffentlichung kann nötigenfalls auf Grund der Stiftungsurkunde auch auf Anordnung der Regierung als Aufsichtsbehörde, allenfalls von der Registerbehörde von Amtes wegen auf Anzeige der Verlassenschaftsbehörde oder auf Antrag von Bedachten erfolgen.

Art. 557

III. Entstehung

1) Die Stiftung entsteht erst mit der Eintragung ins Oeffentlichkeitsregister als Stiftungsregister.

2) Kirchliche Stiftungen, reine und gemischte Familienstiftungen sowie Stiftungen, deren Genussberechtigte bestimmt oder bestimmbar sind, erlangen ohne Eintragung ins Oeffentlichkeitsregister das Recht der Persönlichkeit.

3) Stiftungen, die ein nach kaufmännischer Art geführtes Gewerbe betreiben, sind zur Eintragung verpflichtet und erlangen erst mit der Eintragung das Recht der Persönlichkeit.

4) Die Eintragung einer durch letztwillige Verfügung errichteten Stiftung hat erst nach dem Tode des Stifters und beim Erbvertrage, wenn dieser es nicht anders bestimmt, eines der Stifter zu erfolgen.

Art. 558

IV. Vermögenszuwendung

1) Ist die Stiftung entstanden, so ist der Stifter oder der Dritte auf Verlangen der Aufsichtsbehörde, des Vertreters des öffentlichen Rechts oder von Interessenten verpflichtet, das in der Stiftungsurkunde zugesicherte Vermögen auf die Stiftung zu übertragen.

2) Rechte, zu deren Uebertragung eine Abtretungserklärung genügt, gehen mit der Entstehung kraft Gesetzes auf die Stiftung über.

3) Wird die Stiftung erst mit dem Tode des Stifters oder nach Beendigung einer Firma oder Verbandsperson wirksam, so gilt sie für die Zuwendungen des Stifters oder Dritter als schon vor dem Tode beziehungsweise Beendigung des Stifters entstanden.

4) Die Widmung eines Vermögens kann insbesondere auch durch Begründung eines Schuldverhältnisses gegenüber dem Stifter oder Dritten, wie namentlich derart erfolgen, dass der Stifter oder ein Dritter sich verfplcihtet, jährlich oder

sonst in bestimmten Zeitabschnitten einen festen oder veränderlichen Betrag oder sonst Vermögenswerte zu leisten (Widmung von Renten).

5) Im Zweifel hat die Vermögenslage nach den Vorschriften über treuhandsichere Anlagen zu erfolgen.

Art. 559

V. Widerruf

1) Ein Widerruf der Stiftung ist nur zulässig:

1. wenn die Stiftung noch nicht ins Oeffentlichkeitsregister eingetragen ist, falls eine Eintragung zum Entstehen erforderlich ist;

2. falls eine Eintragung der Stiftung nicht erforderlich ist und diese noch zu Lebzeiten des Stifters rechtswirksam werden soll, bis zum Abschluss der Beurkundung;

3. bei den durch letztwillige Verfügung oder Erbvertrag errichteten Stiftungen nach den hierfür geltenden erbrechtlichen Vorschriften.

2) Bei letztwilligen Verfügungen hat der Stifter selbst ein unbeschränktes Widerrufsrecht, nicht dagegen die Erben nach dessen Tode, auch wenn die Stiftung noch nicht ins Oeffentlichkeitsregister eingetragen ist.

3) Ebenso haben die Erben kein Widerrufsrecht, wenn der Stifter bei der Stiftung unter Lebenden die Urkunde zwar errichtete, jedoch vor der Eintragung der Stiftung ins Oeffentlichkeitsregister gestorben ist.

4) Der nach Inhalt der Stiftungsurkunde ausdrücklich vorbehaltene Widerruf oder die vorbehaltene Abänderung der Urkunde oder des Statuts ist jederzeit zulässig.

Art. 560

VI. Anfechtung

1) Eine Stiftung kann von den Erben oder den Gläubigern gleich einer Schenkung angefochten werden.

2) Der Stifter und seine Erben können die Stiftung gegen Willensmängeln gleich den Vorschriften über Mängel des Vertragsabschlusses auch nach der Eintragung anfechten.

C. Organisation

Art. 561

I. Im Allgemeinen

1) Die Organe der Stiftung, wie Stiftungsvorstand, Revisionsstelle und dergleichen, sowie die Art der Geschäftsführung und Vertretung und dergleichen werden durch die Stiftungsurkunde oder durch ein vom Stifter mittels Urkunde, letztwilliger Verfügung oder Erbvertrages aufgesetztes Stiftungsstatut festgestellt.

2) Die Verleihung des Stiftungsgenusses kann unabhängig von der Stiftungsverwaltung einem besonderen Organe (Kollatoren) übertragen werden.

3) Auf die Befugnisse und Pflichten der in dieser Art bestellten Organe finden die Vorschriften über die bezüglichen Organe bei der Anstalt unter Vorbehalt folgender Bestimmungen entsprechende Anwendung.

Art. 562

II. Anordnung der Aufsichtsbehörde

1) Ist keine Organisation vorgesehen oder die vorgesehene ungenügend, so hat die Aufsichtsbehörde im Verwaltungswege unter entsprechender Berücksichtigung der Vorschriften über die Organisation der Anstalt die nötigen Verfügungen zu treffen und erforderlichernfalls ins Oeffentlichkeitsregister eintragen zu lassen.

2) Können diese nicht zweckdienlich getroffen werden, wie etwa bei zu geringem Vermögen, so hat die Aufsichtsbehörde, sofern der Stifter keine Einspruch erhebt oder nicht eine Bestimmung der Stiftungsurkunde oder des Stiftungsstatuts ausdrücklich entgegensteht, das Vermögen einer anderen Stiftung mit möglichst gleichartigem Zwecke zu treuen Händen zuzuwenden.

Art. 563

D. Haftung und Ausschluss der Vollstreckung usw.

1) Für die Schulden der Stiftung haftet den Gläubigern nur das Stiftungsvermögen.

2) Von der weitergehenden Bestimmung bei Familienstiftungen abgesehen, dürfen Einkünfte, welche jemand aus einer Stiftung unentgeltlich bezieht, auf dem Wege des Sicherungsverfahrens, der Zwangsvollstreckung oder des Konkurses nur insoweit entzogen werden, als sie nicht zur Bestreitung des notwendigen Unterhalts des Bedachten für sich, seinen Ehegatten und seine noch unversorgten Kinder erforderlich sind.

3) Unbekannte Stiftungsgeniesser können bei den der Aufischt unterstehenden Stiftungen durch die Regierung, sonst aber auf Antrag durch den Richter im Aufgebotsverfahren ermittelt werden.

E. Aufsicht

Art. 564

I. Im Allgemeinen

1) Mit Ausnahme der kirchlichen, der reinen und gemischten Familienstiftungen oder solcher Stiftungen, als deren Genussberechtigte bestimmte oder bestimmbare natürliche oder juristische Personen, Firmen oder deren Rechtsnachfolger bezeichnet sind oder die nur Vermögen verwalten und seine Erträgnisse verteilen, Beteiligung oder dergleichen bezwecken, stehen die Stiftungen unter der Aufsicht der Regierung, der die Registerbehörde von jeder eintragungspflichtigen Stiftung Mitteilung zu machen hat.

2) Die Stiftungsurkunde kann auch andere Stiftungen der Aufsicht der Regierung unterstellen.

3) Die Aufsichtsbehörde hat dafür zu sorgen, dass das Stiftungsvermögen seinen Zwecken gemäss verwaltet und verwendet wird; sie kann zu diesem Zwecke die gebotenen Anordnungen, wie Kontrolle und Abberufung der Stiftungsorgane treffen.

4) Gegen eine dem Stiftungszwecke widersprechende Verwaltung und Verwendung des Vermögens durch die Stiftungsorgane kann jeder, der an einer bestimmungsmässigen Verwaltung und Verwendung des Vermögens, seines Ertrages oder Gebrauchs ein Interesse hat, und der Vertreter des öffentlichen Rechts bei der Aufsichtsbehörde Beschwerde führen.

5) Vor Fällung eines Entscheides der Aufsichtsbehörde oder des Verwaltungsgerichtshofes sind die Beteiligten zu hören.

II. Aenderung

Art. 565

1. Der Organisation

1) Die Regierung darf auf Antrag eines Beteiligten oder von Amtes wegen nach Anhörung des obersten Stiftungsorganes und jener Personen, deren Rechte berührt werden, die Organisation der Stiftung im Verwaltungswege abändern, wenn die Erhaltung des Vermögens oder die Wahrung des Zweckes der Stiftung die Abänderung dringend erheischt und sofern die Stiftungsurkunde oder das Statut nicht ein anderes Organ oder einen Dritten mit der Aenderung der Organisation betraut hat.

2) Als Stiftungsorgan kann von der Aufsichtsbehörde insbesondere die Landesbank bezeichnet werden.

3) Gegen solche Abänderungsanordnungen können die Beteiligten die Verwaltungsbeschwerde an den Verwaltungsgerichtshof ergreifen.

Art. 566

2. Des Zweckes

1) Die Regierung darf auf Antrag von Beteiligten oder von Amtes wegen und nach Anhörung des obersten Stiftungsorganes und jener Personen, deren Rechte berührt werden, den Zweck der Stiftung im Verwaltungswege abändern, wenn ihr ursprünglicher Zweck eine ganz andere Bedeutung oder Wirkung erhalten hat, so dass die Stiftung dem Willen des Stifters offenbar entfremdet ist.

2) Die Stiftungsurkunde oder das Statut können auch vorsehen, dass ein Stiftungsorgan oder ein Dritter die Aenderung des Zweckes vornehmen können, wie beispielsweise, wenn der Zweck unerreichbar, unerlaubt oder vernunftwidrig ist.

3) Unter gleichen Voraussetzungen können Auflagen oder Bedingungen, die den Stiftungszeck beeinträchtigen, aufgehoben oder abgeändert werden.

4) Der letzte Absatz des vorhergehenden Artikels findet entsprechende Anwendung.

Art. 567

F. Familienstiftung, Kirchliche Stiftung und dergleichen

1) Die dauernde oder zeitweilige richterliche Aufsicht in bezug auf Anordnung und Organisation und des Zweckes über die der Aufsicht nicht unterstehenden Stiftungen, soweit es nicht kirchliche sind, und ihre Umwandlung kann auf Antrag von Beteiligten vom Richter im Rechtsfürsorgeverfahren ausgesprochen und, wenn hinreichende Gründe vorliegen, wieder aufgehoben werden; in diesem Falle kann der Richter gleich der Regierung als Aufsichtsbehörde die entsprechenden Anordnungen treffen.

2) Ueber sonstige Anstände privatrechtlicher Natur, wie über die Frage der Genussberechtigung (Anrecht und Vorrecht), ihren Umfang und dergleichen entscheidet in allen Fällen der Richter im Streitverfahren soweit nicht freies Ermessen der Stiftungsorgane vorgesehen ist.

3) Bei Familienstiftungen kann der Stifter zugleich bestimmen, dass die Gläubiger der bestimmt bezeichneten Drittbedachten (Destinatäre) diesen ihren unentgeltlich erlangten Stiftungsgenuss auf dem Wege des Sicherungsverfahrens, der Zwangsvollstreckung oder Konkurses nicht entziehen dürfen.

4) Es können auch Treuhandzertifikate an die Genussberechtigten ausgegeben werden.

G. Aufhebung

Art. 568

I. Von Gesetzes wegen

Die Aufhebung einer Stiftung erfolgt von Gesetzes wegen, sobald ihr Zweck unerreichbar geworden ist, insbesondere wenn der Stiftungszweck nicht mehr verwirklicht werden kann, wenn sie mangels genügenden Vermögens ihre Aufgaben nicht mehr erfüllen kann oder die in der Stiftungsurkunde oder dem Statut vorgesehene Zeitdauer abgelaufen ist.

Art. 569

II. Klagerecht und Löschung im Register

1) Zur Klage berechtigt ist die Aufsichtsbehörde, der Vertreter des öffentlichen Rechts, sowie jedermann, der ein Interesse hat.

2) Die Aufhebung ist dem Grundbuch- und Oeffentlichkeitsregisteramt von Amtes wegen behufs Löschung anzuzeigen.

3) Die Klage kann vor oder während des Verfahrens bis zum endgültigen Entscheid auf Antrag oder von Amtes wegen im Oeffentlichkeitsregister angemerkt werden und vor dem Entscheide sind die Stiftungsorgane und sonstige Beteiligte anzuhören.

Art. 570

III. Umwandlung

Eine Stiftung kann ohne Liquidation vom Stiftungsrat oder durch einen von ihm ermächtigten Dritten, wenn die Umwandlung ausdrücklich vorbehalten ist und sonst die erfolrderlichen Voraussetzungen, wie Statut oder Organe, geschaffen werden, in eine Anstalt oder ein Treuunternehmen mittels formrichtiger Urkunde umgewandelt werden.

2. Former law, valid until 1 April 2009 (in English)

Second Section

THE FOUNDATIONS

A. Definition and delimitation

Art. 552

I. In general

1) For a foundation to be formed by natural persons or legal entities or firms, it is necessary for assets to be endowed (foundation property) for a certain specific purpose. Ecclesiastical, family and non-profit making purposes may be given particular consideration. Commercial activities may be undertaken by a foundation only provided such activity serves its non-commercial purpose or the type and scope of the participations held require the facilities of a commercial business.

2) Asset donations without legal personality (dependent foundations) or donations tied to the condition of a special administration under a special name and of application for a special purpose and similar conditions to already existing legal entities or natural persons or companies are subject to special regulations such as those applying to gifts or concerning the law of succession and, supplementary, to the regulations concerning the implied trust relationship.

3) The judge shall decide in the individual case the extent to which separately administered assets (fund) shall be entitled to independence according to private law or to the character of trust property.

4) The regulations concerning the trust enterprise with legal personality shall be applied to foundations accordingly, particularly with regard to foundation participants (founder, foundation council, beneficiaries), where and insofar as the following provisions of the foundation articles or the regulations concerning the obligation of trust enterprises to register do not determine to the contrary.

Art. 553

II. Ecclesiastical and family foundations

1) Ecclesiastical foundations within the intendment of this section are foundations formed for ecclesiastical purposes.

2) A family foundation is a pure family foundation where the foundation assets are continuously connected with the purpose of defraying the expenses for the upbringing and education, outfitting or support of the relatives of one or several designated families, or with similar purposes.

3) It is a mixed foundation where assets so donated serve ecclesiastical or other purposes outside the family in addition or supplementary.

Art. 554

III. Deposition

To ensure observance of the obligation to register, to prevent foundations with unlawful or immoral purposes and to avoid circumvention of possible supervision, the foundation deed including all amendments of the foundation's articles and/or certified copy of the testamentary disposition or the deed of inheritance must be deposited by the foundation council or the legal representative and/or the probate court with the Register Office at the time a foundation is formed, insofar as an application for entry does not ensue otherwise.

B. Formation

Art. 555

I. Foundation Deed

1) The formation of a foundation ensues in the form of a deed on which the signatures of the founders are certified, by testamentary disposition or by deed of inheritance.

2) The foundation deed or the articles must contain the name and domicile of the foundation, its purpose or object, the designation of the foundation council members and the method for appointing another foundation council as well as a provi-

sion concerning the application of the assets in the event of the dissolution of the foundation.

Art. 556

II. Entry in the Foundation Register

1) The foundation's application to register in the Foundation Register must be recorded by all the members of the foundation council personally or submitted in writing in certified form, whereby the application must be accompanied by a certified copy of the foundation deed.

2) The entry and publication, which may ensue by announcement on the court notice board, must contain: the name (name of the firm), address and purpose of the foundation, the date of the formation deed, the names and addresses and/or the name and domicile of the firm of the foundation council members and/or of other representatives.

3) If necessary, entry and publication may also be undertaken by order of the Government as supervising authority by virtue of the foundation deed, possibly by the Register Authority ex officio upon notification by the Probate Authority or upon petition of the Beneficiaries.

Art. 557

III. Existence

1) The foundation only comes into existence when entered in the Public Register as Foundation Register.

2) Ecclesiastical foundations, pure and mixed family foundations and foundations whose entitled beneficiaries are specifically designated or definable, acquire legal personality without being entered in the Public Register.
3) Foundations which engage in commercial activities are under the obligation to register and acquire legal personality only when entered in the Public Register.

4) The registration of a foundation formed by testamentary disposition shall ensue only after the death of the founder, and, in the case of a deed of inheritance, provided that this does not determine otherwise, only after the death of one of the founders.

Art. 558

IV. Donation of assets

1) When the foundation has come into existence, the founder or the third party, upon demand of the Supervising Authority, the representative of public law or of interested parties, is required to transfer to the foundation the assets mentioned in the deed of foundation.

2) Rights, for whose transfer a declaration of assignment is sufficient, devolve by operation of the law upon the foundation on coming into existence.

3) Where the foundation only becomes effective on the death of the founder or after the termination of a firm or legal entity, the said foundation shall be deemed to have been in existence already before the death or termination of the founder for the donations of the founder or third party.

4) The donation of assets may also be effected, in particular, by the establishment of a contractual relationship to the founder or third party according to which the founder or third party undertakes to donate annually or at certain intervals a fixed or variable sum or other assets (donation of periodical payments).

5) In case of doubt, the investment of assets shall ensue pursuant to the regulations concerning trust investments.

Art. 559

V. Revocation

1) Revocation of the foundation is admissible only:

1. if a foundation has not yet been entered in the Public Register, in as much as existence ensues only in the event of such entry;

2. in the event that registration of the foundation is not necessary and the foundation should become effective in law during the founder's lifetime, up to the time of conclusion of registration;

3. in the case of foundations formed by testamentary disposition or deed of inheritance, pursuant to the regulations of the laws of succession applicable to these circumstances.

2) In the case of testamentary dispositions, the founder personally has an unrestricted right of revocation but not, on the other hand, the heirs after the founder's death, not even if the foundation is not yet entered in the Public Register.

3) Likewise, the heirs do not have a right of revocation where in the case of the foundation inter vivos the founder certainly drew up the deed but died before the foundation was entered in the Public Register.

4) Revocation expressly reserved in the foundation deed or the reserved amendment of the deed or of the articles is admissible at any time.

Art. 560

VI. Contestation

1) The validity of a foundation may be disputed by the heirs or the creditors in the same way as gift.

2) Also after it has been registered, the founder and his heirs may dispute the validity of the foundation on grounds of deficiency of intention in the manner admissible pursuant to the provisions of contract law.

C. Governing Bodies

Art. 561

I. In general

1) The foundation's governing bodies, such as the foundation council, the audit authority and similar bodies, as well as the type of administration and representation, etc., are determined in the deed of foundation or in the foundation's articles, drawn up by the founder in a document, a will or a deed of inheritance.

2) The conferment of beneficial interest in the foundation may be entrusted to a special body (collators), independently of the foundation council.

3) The regulations concerning the governing bodies in question in the case of establishments shall be applied accordingly to the powers and duties of the bodies appointed in this manner, with reservation of the following provisions.

Art. 562

II. Order of the Supervisory Authority

1) Where no governing bodies have been provided for or where those provided are inadequate, the Supervisory Authority shall take the necessary steps with appropriate observance of the regulations concerning the establishment's governing bodies, and, if required, the Supervisory Authority shall arrange for an entry in the Public Register.

2) In the event that such steps cannot be taken expediently, if, for instance, there are inadequate assets, the Supervisory Authority, provided the founder does not object or a provision of the foundation deed or the foundation articles is not expressly opposed to this, shall donate the assets on trust to another foundation having as far as possible the same kind of purpose.

Art. 563

D. Liability and exclusion of enforcement etc.

1) Only the foundation's assets shall be liable for the foundation's debts to the creditors.

2) Except for the extensive provisions in the case of family foundations, income which a person receives from a foundation without valuable consideration may be withdrawn by injunction, levy of execution and writ or bankruptcy proceedings only, when said income is not required for the defrayal of the essential living expenses of the beneficiary, his spouse and his children without means.
3) In the case of foundations subject to supervision, unknown beneficiaries of the foundation may be traced by the Government or, otherwise, upon application by the judge in public citation proceedings.

E. Supervision

Art. 564

I. In general

1) With exception of ecclesiastical foundations, pure and mixed family foundations or such foundations as those whose entitled beneficiaries are specifically designated or definable natural persons or legal entities, firms or their successors in title, or those foundations whose purpose is solely to administer the assets and distribute the income, participation or similar, the foundations are subject to supervision by the Government, which shall be notified by the Register Authority of every foundation under obligation to register.

2) The foundation deed may also subject other foundation to Government supervision.

3) It shall be incumbent upon the Supervising Authority to ensure that the foundation assets are administered and applied pursuant to their purposes; this Supervising Authority may give the necessary orders regarding, for example, auditing and the dismissal of the foundations' governing bodies.

4) Any person who has an interest in the administration and application of the assets, their yield or use and the representative of public law may lodge a complaint with the Supervisory Authority concerning an administration and application of the assets by the foundations' bodies, which is in conflict with the purpose of the foundation.

5) The participants shall be heard before a decision is pronounced by the Supervising Authority of the Administrative Court of Justice.

II. Amendment

Art. 565

1. Concerning governing bodies

1) After hearing the foundation's supreme authority and those persons, whose rights are affected, the Government, upon application of one of the participants or ex officio, may change the foundation's organization by administrative action,

if this is required urgently, in order to preserve the assets or safeguard the foundation's purpose and insofar as the foundation deed or the articles has/have not entrusted another body or a third party with the changing of the organization.

2) The Landesbank in particular may be designated as foundation governing body by the Supervisory Authority.

3) In opposition to such amendment orders, the participants may lodge an appeal with the Administrative court.

Art. 566

2. Concerning the purpose

1) After hearing the foundation's supreme body and those persons whose rights are affected, the Government, upon application by participants or ex officio, may amend the foundation deed by administrative action, if its original purpose has acquired a completely different meaning or effect and as a result of this the foundation is obviously estranged from the intentions of the founder.

2) The foundation deed or the articles may also provide for a foundation governing body or a third party to be empowered to effect amendment of the purpose if it is incapable of achievement, inadmissible or unreasonable.

3) Charges and conditions which impair the foundation's purpose may be cancelled or amended under the same preconditions.

4) The last paragraph of the preceding article shall be applied accordingly.

Art. 567

F. Family foundations, ecclesiastical foundations and similar

1) Permanent or temporary judicial supervision with respect to the regulation of the governing bodies and the purpose of foundations not subject to supervision, insofar as ecclesiastical foundations are not concerned, and their conversion may, upon application of participants, be pronounced by the judge in extrajudicial proceedings and, if adequate reason exists, be cancelled again; in this case, the judge, like the Government as Supervising Authority, may give the necessary instructions.

2) If provision has not been made for the absolute discretion of the foundation's governing bodies, the judge shall in all cases decide in contentious proceedings concerning other difficulties of a private law nature, such as, for example, the question of beneficial interest (entitlement or privilege), its scope and so forth.

3) In the case of family foundations, the founder may determine at the same time that the creditors of the specifically designated third-party beneficiaries shall not withdraw from these their beneficial interest, acquired without valuable consideration by way of injunction, levy of execution and writ or bankruptcy proceedings.

4) Trust certificates may also be issued to the entitled beneficiaries.

G. Cancellation

Art. 568

I. By operation of law

The cancellation of a foundation ensues by operation of the law as soon as the purpose cannot be achieved, particularly when the foundation purpose can no longer be realized, when, owing to lack of adequate assets, the duties of the foundation can no longer be fulfilled or the duration specified in the foundation deed has expired.

Art. 569

II. Right of action and deregistration

1) The Supervising Authority, the Representative of Public Law and any interested party is entitled to take action.

2) The cancellation shall be reported to the Registrar ex officio in order that the cancellation may ensue.

3) The action may be annotated in the Public Register before or during the proceedings, up to the time of final decision, upon application or ex officio, whereby the governing bodies of the foundation and other participants shall be heard before the decision is made.

Art. 570

III. Conversion

Where conversion is expressly provided for and also the necessary prerequisites, such as articles or governing bodies are provided, the foundation, without being wound up, may be converted by the foundation council into an establishment or a trust enterprise by means of a document which must be correct with respect to the form.

3. New law, valid from 1 April 2009 (original wording)

216.0 (Systematische Sammlung)

Liechtensteinisches Landesgesetzblatt Jahrgang 2008 Nr. 220 ausgegeben am 26. August 2008 Gesetz vom 26. Juni 2008 über die Abänderung des Personen- und Gesellschaftsrechts

Dem nachstehenden vom Landtag gefassten Beschluss erteile Ich Meine Zustimmung:

I. Abänderung bisherigen Rechts

Das Personen-und Gesellschaftsrecht vom 20. Januar 1926, LGBl. 1926 Nr. 4, in der geltenden Fassung, wird wie folgt abgeändert:

Art. 106 Abs. 2 Ziff. 3

Aufgehoben

Art. 107 Abs. 4a

Wo das Gesetz von gemeinnützigen oder wohltätigen Zwecken spricht, sind darunter solche Zwecke zu verstehen, durch deren Erfüllung die Allgemeinheit gefördert wird. Eine Förderung der Allgemeinheit liegt insbesondere vor, wenn die Tätigkeit dem Gemeinwohl auf karitativem, religiösem, humanitärem, wissenschaftlichem, kulturellem, sittlichem, sozialem, sportlichem oder ökologischem Gebiet nützt, auch wenn durch die Tätigkeit nur ein bestimmter Personenkreis gefördert wird.

Art. 182 Abs. 2

Sie hat das Unternehmen der Verbandsperson mit Sorgfalt zu leiten und zu fördern und haftet für die Beobachtung der Grundsätze einer sorgfältigen Geschäftsführung und Vertretung. Ein Mitglied der Verwaltung handelt im Einklang mit diesen Grundsätzen, wenn es sich bei seiner unternehmerischen Entscheidung nicht von sachfremden Interessen leiten liess und vernünftigerweise annehmen durfte, auf der Grundlage angemessener Information zum Wohle der Verbandsperson zu handeln.

Art. 259 Abs. 2

Aufgehoben

Überschrift vor Art. 552

2. Abschnitt

Die Stiftungen

Art. 552

Für die Stiftung gelten nachfolgende Vorschriften:

A. Im Allgemeinen

I. Begriff und Zweck

§ 1

1. Umschreibung und Abgrenzung

1) Eine Stiftung im Sinne dieses Abschnittes ist ein rechtlich und wirtschaftlich verselbständigtes Zweckvermögen, welches als Verbandsperson (juristische Person) durch die einseitige Willenserklärung des Stifters errichtet wird. Der Stifter widmet das bestimmt bezeichnete Stiftungsvermögen und legt den unmittelbar nach aussen gerichteten, bestimmt bezeichneten Stiftungszweck sowie Begünstigte fest.

2) Eine Stiftung darf ein nach kaufmännischer Art geführtes Gewerbe nur dann ausüben, wenn es der Erreichung ihres gemeinnützigen Zwecks unmittelbar dient oder aufgrund einer spezialgesetzlichen Grundlage zulässig ist. Soweit es die ordnungsgemässe Anlage und Verwaltung des Stiftungsvermögens erfordert, ist die Einrichtung eines kaufmännischen Betriebes auch bei privatnützigen Stiftungen zulässig.

3) Liegt kein Fall des Abs. 2 Satz 1 vor, so darf die Stiftung auch nicht unbeschränkt haftende Gesellschafterin einer personenrechtlichen Gemeinschaft sein, die ein nach kaufmännischer Art geführtes Gewerbe betreibt.

§ 2

2. Stiftungszwecke

1) Als Stiftungszwecke kommen gemeinnützige oder privatnützige Zwecke in Betracht.

2) Eine gemeinnützige Stiftung im Sinne dieses Abschnitts ist eine solche, deren Tätigkeit nach der Stiftungserklärung ganz oder überwiegend gemeinnützigen Zwecken nach Art. 107 Abs. 4a zu dienen bestimmt ist, wenn es sich nicht um eine Familienstiftung handelt.

3) Eine privatnützige Stiftung im Sinne dieses Abschnitts ist eine solche, die nach der Stiftungserklärung ganz oder überwiegend privaten oder eigennützigen Zwecken zu dienen bestimmt ist. Das Überwiegen ist nach dem Verhältnis der den privatnützigen Zwecken zu den den gemeinnützigen Zwecken dienenden Leistungen zu beurteilen. Steht nicht fest, dass die Stiftung in einem bestimmten Zeitpunkt ganz oder überwiegend privatnützigen Zwecken zu dienen bestimmt ist, so ist sie als gemeinnützige Stiftung anzusehen.

4) Als privatnützige Stiftungen kommen insbesondere in Betracht:

1. reine Familienstiftungen; dies sind Stiftungen, deren Stiftungsvermögen ausschliesslich der Bestreitung der Kosten der Erziehung oder Bildung, der Ausstattung oder Unterstützung von Angehörigen einer oder mehrerer Familien oder ähnlichen Familieninteressen dienen;

2. gemischte Familienstiftungen; dies sind Stiftungen, die überwiegend den Zweck einer reinen Familienstiftung verfolgen, ergänzend hierzu aber auch gemeinnützigen oder anderen privatnützigen Zwecken dienen.

II. Stiftungsbeteiligte

§ 3

1. Begriff

Als Beteiligte der Stiftung gelten:

1. der Stifter;
2. die Begünstigungsberechtigten;
3. die Anwartschaftsberechtigten;
4. die Ermessensbegünstigten;
5. die Letztbegünstigten;
6. die Organe der Stiftung gemäss den §§ 11, 24, 27 und 28 sowie die Mitglieder dieser Organe.

§ 4

2. Stifter

1) Stifter können eine oder mehrere natürliche oder juristische Personen sein. Eine durch letztwillige Verfügung errichtete Stiftung kann nur einen Stifter haben.

2) Hat eine Stiftung mehrere Stifter, so können die dem Stifter zustehenden oder vorbehaltenen Rechte nur von allen Stiftern gemeinsam ausgeübt werden, es sei denn, die Stiftungserklärung sieht etwas anderes vor. Fällt einer der Stifter weg, so erlöschen im Zweifel die vorgenannten Rechte.

3) Wird die Stiftung durch einen indirekten Stellvertreter errichtet, so gilt der Geschäftsherr (Machtgeber) als Stifter. Handelt auch dieser als indirekter Stellvertreter für einen Dritten, so gilt dessen Geschäftsherr (Machtgeber) als Stifter. In jedem Fall ist der indirekte Stellvertreter verpflichtet, dem Stiftungsrat die Person des Stifters bekannt zu geben.

§ 5

3. Begünstigter

1) Als Begünstigter gilt diejenige natürliche oder juristische Person, die mit oder ohne Gegenleistung tatsächlich, unbedingt oder unter bestimmten Voraussetzungen oder Auflagen, befristet oder unbefristet, beschränkt oder unbeschränkt, widerruflich oder unwiderruflich, zu irgendeinem Zeitpunkt während des Rechtsbestands der Stiftung oder bei ihrer Beendigung in den Genuss eines wirtschaftlichen Vorteils aus der Stiftung (Begünstigung) kommt oder kommen kann.

2) Begünstigte im Sinne von Abs. 1 sind:

1. die Begünstigungsberechtigten (§ 6 Abs. 1);
2. die Anwartschaftsberechtigten (§ 6 Abs. 2);
3. die Ermessensbegünstigten (§ 7); und
4. die Letztbegünstigten (§ 8).

§ 6

4. Begünstigte mit Rechtsanspruch

1) Begünstigungsberechtigt ist derjenige, der einen sich auf die Stiftungsurkunde, die Stiftungszusatzurkunde oder Reglemente gründenden rechtlichen Anspruch auf einen auch der Höhe nach bestimmten oder bestimmbaren Vorteil aus dem Stiftungsvermögen oder den Stiftungserträgnissen hat.

2) Anwartschaftsberechtigt ist derjenige, der nach Eintritt einer aufschiebenden Bedingung oder bei Erreichung eines Termins, insbesondere nach dem Wegfall eines im Rang vorgehenden Begünstigten, einen rechtlichen Anspruch hat, aufgrund der Stiftungsurkunde, der Stiftungszusatzurkunde oder eines Reglements eine Begünstigungsberechtigung zu erlangen.

§ 7

5. Ermessensbegünstigter (Begünstigter ohne Rechtsanspruch)

1) Ermessensbegünstigt ist derjenige, der dem durch den Stifter benannten Begünstigtenkreis angehört und dessen mögliche Begünstigung in das Ermessen des Stiftungsrats oder einer anderen dazu berufenen Stelle gestellt ist. Wer nur

eine Anwartschaft auf eine solche künftige Begünstigung hat, zählt nicht zu den Ermessensbegünstigten.

2) Ein rechtlicher Anspruch des Ermessensbegünstigten auf einen bestimmten Vorteil aus dem Stiftungsvermögen oder den Stiftungserträgnissen entsteht in jedem Fall erst mit gültiger Beschlussfassung des Stiftungsrats oder des sonst dafür zuständigen Organs (§ 28) über eine tatsächliche Ausschüttung an den entsprechenden Ermessensbegünstigten und erlischt mit Empfang derselben.

§ 8

6. Letztbegünstigter

1) Letztbegünstigt ist derjenige, dem gemäss Stiftungsurkunde oder Stiftungszusatzurkunde ein nach Durchführung der Liquidation der Stiftung verbleibendes Vermögen zukommen soll.

2) Mangels Bestimmung eines Letztbegünstigten oder Vorhandensein des Letztbegünstigten fällt das nach Durchführung der Liquidation verbleibende Vermögen an das Land.

3) Mangels einer Bestimmung über die Vermögensverwendung im Falle eines Widerrufs gemäss § 30 Abs. 1 gilt der Stifter selbst als Letztbegünstigter, unabhängig davon, ob er vorgängig eine Begünstigtenstellung innehatte.

III. Informations- und Auskunftsrechte der Begünstigten

§ 9

1. Im Allgemeinen

1) Der Begünstigte hat, soweit es seine Rechte betrifft, Anspruch auf Einsichtnahme in die Stiftungsurkunde, die Stiftungszusatzurkunde und allfällige Reglemente.

2) Er hat ferner, soweit es seine Rechte betrifft, Anspruch auf Auskunftserteilung, Berichterstattung und Rechnungslegung. Zu diesem Zweck hat er das Recht, Einsicht in alle Geschäftsbücher und Papiere zu nehmen und Abschriften herzustellen sowie alle Tatsachen und Verhältnisse, insbesondere das Rechnungswesen, persönlich oder durch einen Vertreter zu prüfen und zu untersuchen. Das

Recht darf jedoch nicht in unlauterer Absicht, in missbräuchlicher oder nicht in einer den Interessen der Stiftung oder anderer Begünstigten widerstreitenden Weise ausgeübt werden. Ausnahmsweise kann das Recht auch aus wichtigen Gründen zum Schutz des Begünstigten verweigert werden.

3) Dem Letztbegünstigten stehen diese Rechte erst nach der Auflösung der Stiftung zu.

4) Die Rechte des Begünstigten sind im Rechtsfürsorgeverfahren geltend zu machen.

5) Vorbehalten bleiben die Ausnahmen gemäss §§ 10 bis 12.

§ 10

2. Bei Widerrufsrecht des Stifters

1) Hat sich der Stifter in der Stiftungserklärung das Recht vorbehalten, die Stiftung zu widerrufen (§ 30), und ist er selbst Letztbegünstigter, so stehen dem Begünstigten die Rechte gemäss § 9 nicht zu.

2) Wurde die Stiftung von mehreren Stiftern errichtet, so können diese Rechte von jedem einzelnen Stifter, der sich das Widerrufsrecht vorbehalten hat, ausgeübt werden.

§ 11

3. Bei Einrichtung eines Kontrollorgans

1) Hat der Stifter in der Stiftungserklärung ein Kontrollorgan für die Stiftung eingerichtet, so kann der Begünstigte nur über Zweck und Organisation der Stiftung sowie über seine eigenen Rechte gegenüber der Stiftung Auskunft verlangen und deren Richtigkeit durch Einsichtnahme in die Stiftungsurkunde, die Stiftungszusatzurkunde und die Reglemente überprüfen.

2) Als Kontrollorgan kann eingerichtet werden:

1. eine Revisionsstelle, auf die § 27 sinngemäss anzuwenden ist;

2. eine oder mehrere vom Stifter namentlich genannte natürliche Personen, welche über ausreichende Fachkenntnisse auf dem Gebiet des Rechts und der Wirtschaft verfügen, um ihre Aufgaben erfüllen zu können; oder
3. der Stifter.

3) Das Kontrollorgan muss von der Stiftung unabhängig sein. § 27 Abs. 2 gilt sinngemäss.

4) Das Kontrollorgan ist verpflichtet, einmal jährlich zu überprüfen, ob das Stiftungsvermögen seinen Zwecken gemäss verwaltet und verwendet wird. Über das Ergebnis dieser Prüfung hat es dem Stiftungsrat einen Bericht vorzulegen. Besteht kein Grund zur Beanstandung, so genügt eine Bestätigung, wonach eine Verwaltung und Verwendung des Stiftungsvermögens entsprechend dem Stiftungszweck und im Einklang mit den Bestimmungen des Gesetzes und der Stiftungsdokumente durchgeführt wurde. Ist dies nicht der Fall oder stellt das Kontrollorgan bei Wahrnehmung seiner Aufgaben Tatsachen fest, die den Bestand der Stiftung gefährden, so hat es den Begünstigten, soweit diese ihm bekannt sind, und dem Gericht Mitteilung zu machen. Das Gericht geht erforderlichenfalls gemäss § 35 vor.

5) Ist ein Kontrollorgan eingerichtet, so kann der Begünstigte von der Stiftung und von dem Kontrollorgan die Übermittlung der Berichte gemäss Abs. 4 verlangen.

6) Macht der Begünstigte seine Rechte gemäss § 9 geltend, so obliegt der Stiftung der Beweis, dass ein Kontrollorgan vorhanden ist, das den Anforderungen nach Abs. 2 iVm Abs. 3 entspricht.

§ 12

4. Bei beaufsichtigten Stiftungen

Die Rechte gemäss § 9 stehen dem Begünstigten nicht zu, wenn die Stiftung unter der Aufsicht der Stiftungsaufsichtsbehörde (§ 29) steht.

§ 13

IV. Stiftungsvermögen

1) Das Mindestkapital der Stiftung beträgt 30 000 Franken. Es kann auch durch Euro oder US-Dollar aufgebracht werden und beträgt dann 30 000 Euro oder 30 000 US-Dollar.

2) Erfolgt eine weitere Vermögenszuwendung an die Stiftung nach ihrer rechtsgültigen Entstehung durch den Stifter, handelt es sich um eine Nachstiftung.

3) Erfolgt eine Vermögenszuwendung an die Stiftung durch einen Dritten, handelt es sich um eine Zustiftung. Der Zustifter erlangt dadurch nicht die Stellung eines Stifters.

4) Wird die Stiftung erst mit dem Ableben des Stifters oder nach Beendigung einer Verbandsperson wirksam, so gilt sie für die Zuwendungen des Stifters als schon vor dessen Tod bzw. deren Beendigung entstanden.

B. Errichtung und Entstehung

I. Im Allgemeinen

§ 14

1. Stiftung unter Lebenden

1) Die Errichtung der Stiftung erfolgt durch eine Stiftungserklärung. Sie bedarf der Schriftform und der Beglaubigung der Unterschriften der Stifter.

2) Im Falle einer direkten Stellvertretung oder einer indirekten Stellvertretung gemäss § 4 Abs. 3 ist auf der Stiftungsurkunde die Unterschrift des Stellvertreters zu beglaubigen.

3) Bei direkter Stellvertretung bedarf der Vertreter einer besonderen auf dieses Geschäft lautenden Vollmacht des Stifters.

4) Gemeinnützige Stiftungen und privatnützige Stiftungen, die auf spezialgesetzlicher Grundlage ein nach kaufmännischer Art geführtes Gewerbe betreiben, sind

in das Öffentlichkeitsregister einzutragen und erlangen durch die Eintragung das Recht der Persönlichkeit.

5) Andere privatnützige Stiftungen können in das Öffentlichkeitsregister eingetragen werden. Eine Rechtspflicht besteht jedoch nicht.

§ 15

2. Stiftung von Todes wegen

1) Die Stiftung kann auch durch letztwillige Verfügung oder durch Erbvertrag entsprechend den hierfür geltenden Formvorschriften errichtet werden.

2) Die Eintragung oder die Hinterlegung einer Gründungsanzeige einer durch letztwillige Verfügung errichteten Stiftung kann erst nach dem Tode des Stifters und beim Erbvertrag, wenn dieser es nicht anders bestimmt, eines der Stifter erfolgen.

3) § 14 Abs. 4 und 5 finden entsprechende Anwendung.

II. Stiftungsdokumente

§ 16

1. Stiftungsurkunde (Statut)

1) Die Stiftungsurkunde hat jedenfalls zu enthalten:

1. den Willen des Stifters, die Stiftung errichten zu wollen;
2. Name bzw. Firma und Sitz der Stiftung;
3. die Widmung eines bestimmten Vermögens, das zumindest dem gesetzlichen Mindestkapital entsprechen muss;
4. Zweck der Stiftung, einschliesslich der Bezeichnung der konkreten oder nach objektiven Merkmalen individualisierbaren Begünstigten oder des Begünstigtenkreises, sofern es sich nicht um eine gemeinnützige Stiftung handelt oder die Begünstigten sich sonst aus dem Stiftungszweck ergeben oder sofern nicht stattdessen ausdrücklich auf eine Stiftungszusatzurkunde verwiesen wird, welche dies regelt;
5. Datum der Errichtung der Stiftung;
6. Dauer der Stiftung, falls diese begrenzt ist;

7. Regelungen über die Bestellung, Abberufung, Funktionsdauer sowie Art der Geschäftsführung (Beschlussfassung) und Vertretungsbefugnis (Zeichnungsrecht) des Stiftungsrats;
8. eine Bestimmung über die Verwendung des Vermögens im Falle der Auflösung der Stiftung in sinngemässer Anwendung von Ziff. 4;
9. den Namen, Vornamen und Wohnsitz bzw. Firma und Sitz des Stifters bzw. bei indirekter Stellvertretung (§ 4 Abs. 3) den Namen, Vornamen und Wohnsitz bzw. Firma und Sitz des Stellvertreters. Auf das Tätigwerden als indirekter Stellvertreter ist dabei ausdrücklich hinzuweisen.

2) Sofern nachstehende Inhalte geregelt werden, sind diese ebenfalls in die Stiftungsurkunde aufzunehmen:

1. der Hinweis, dass eine Stiftungszusatzurkunde errichtet ist oder errichtet werden kann;
2. der Hinweis, dass Reglemente erlassen sind oder erlassen werden können;
3. der Hinweis, dass andere Organe errichtet sind oder errichtet werden können; nähere Angaben über die Zusammensetzung, Bestellung, Abberufung, Funktionsdauer sowie Aufgaben können in der Stiftungszusatzurkunde oder in Reglementen gemacht werden;
4. der Vorbehalt des Widerrufs der Stiftung oder zur Änderung der Stiftungsdokumente durch den Stifter;
5. der Vorbehalt der Änderung der Stiftungsurkunde oder Stiftungszusatzurkunde durch den Stiftungsrat oder durch ein anderes Organ gemäss §§ 31 bis 34;
6. der Ausschluss der Vollstreckung gemäss § 36 Abs. 1;
7. der Vorbehalt der Umwandlung (§ 41);
8. die Bestimmung, dass die Stiftung, obwohl sie privatnützig ist, der Aufsicht untersteht (§ 29 Abs. 1 Satz 2).

3) Als wesentlich im Sinne des Vernichtbarkeitsverfahrens gelten die Bestimmungen nach Abs. 1 Ziff. 1, 3 und 4.

§ 17

2. Stiftungszusatzurkunde (Beistatut)

Der Stifter kann eine Stiftungszusatzurkunde errichten, wenn er sich dies vorbehalten hat (§ 16 Abs. 2 Ziff. 1). Sie kann solche Bestandteile der Stiftungserklärung enthalten, die nicht in die Stiftungsurkunde aufgenommen werden müssen.

§ 18

3. Reglemente

Zur weiteren Ausführung der Stiftungsurkunde oder der Stiftungszusatzurkunde kann der Stifter, der Stiftungsrat oder ein anderes Stiftungsorgan interne Anordnungen in Form von Reglementen erlassen, wenn dies in der Stiftungsurkunde vorbehalten wurde (§ 16 Abs. 2 Ziff. 2). Vom Stifter erlassene Reglemente gehen jenen des Stiftungsrats oder eines anderen Stiftungsorgans vor.

III. Eintragung ins Öffentlichkeitsregister

§ 19

1) Unterliegt die Stiftung der Eintragungspflicht, so ist jedes Mitglied des Stiftungsrats unabhängig von seiner Vertretungsbefugnis verpflichtet, die Stiftung zur Eintragung ins Öffentlichkeitsregister anzumelden. Die Anmeldung ist unter Beilage des Originals oder einer beglaubigten Abschrift der Stiftungsurkunde schriftlich einzureichen. Der Stiftungsrat hat zu bestätigen, dass sich das gesetzliche Mindestkapital in der freien Verfügung der Stiftung befindet. Die Befugnis zur Anmeldung steht auch dem Repräsentanten zu.

2) Erfolgt die Eintragung ohne Bestehen einer Eintragungspflicht (§ 14 Abs. 5), so muss der Stiftungsrat überdies bestätigen, dass die Bezeichnung der konkreten oder nach objektiven Merkmalen individualisierbaren Begünstigten oder des Begünstigtenkreises durch den Stifter erfolgt ist, sofern sich dies nicht aus dem angezeigten Stiftungszweck ergibt.

3) Die Eintragung hat folgende Angaben zu enthalten:

1. Name bzw. Firma der Stiftung;
2. Sitz der Stiftung;
3. Zweck der Stiftung;
4. Datum der Errichtung der Stiftung;
5. Dauer der Stiftung, falls diese begrenzt ist;
6. Organisation und Vertretung, wobei Name, Vorname, Geburtsdatum, Staatsbürgerschaft und Wohnsitz oder Kanzleisitz bzw. Firma und Sitz der Mitglieder des Stiftungsrats sowie die Art der Zeichnung anzugeben sind;
7. Name, Vorname, Geburtsdatum, Staatsbürgerschaft und Wohnsitz oder Kanzleisitz bzw. Firma und Sitz der Revisionsstelle;

8. Name, Vorname, Geburtsdatum, Staatsbürgerschaft und Wohnsitz oder Kanzleisitz bzw. Firma und Sitz des Repräsentanten.

4) Die Eintragung kann nötigenfalls auf Grund der Stiftungsurkunde auch auf Anordnung des Richters im Rechtsfürsorgeverfahren erfolgen:

a) auf Antrag von Stiftungsbeteiligten;
b) auf Anzeige des Grundbuch- und Öffentlichkeitsregisteramts oder der Verlassenschaftsbehörde; oder
c) von Amts wegen.

5) Ändert sich der Zweck einer nicht in das Öffentlichkeitsregister eingetragenen Stiftung in der Weise, dass eine Eintragungspflicht entsteht, so sind die Mitglieder des Stiftungsrats verpflichtet, die Stiftunginnerhalb von 30 Tagen zur Eintragung ins Öffentlichkeitsregister nach Abs. 1 und 3 anzumelden. Abs. 4 findet sinngemäss Anwendung.

6) Die Bekanntmachung der Eintragung erfolgt im Sinne von Art. 957 Abs. 1 Ziff. 1.

IV. Gründungsanzeige

1. Hinterlegung der Gründungsanzeige

§ 20

1) Unterliegt die Stiftung keiner Eintragungspflicht, so ist zur Überwachung der Eintragungspflicht und Verhütung von Stiftungen mit gesetz- oder sittenwidrigem Zweck sowie zur Vermeidung von Umgehungen einer allfälligen Aufsicht jedes Mitglied des Stiftungsrats verpflichtet, innerhalb von 30 Tagen ab Errichtung eine Gründungsanzeige beim Grundbuch- und Öffentlichkeitsregisteramt zu hinterlegen. Die Befugnis zur Hinterlegung steht auch dem Repräsentanten zu. Ein in Liechtenstein zugelassener Rechtsanwalt, Treuhänder oder Träger einer Berechtigung nach Art. 180a hat die Richtigkeit der Angaben gemäss Abs. 2 schriftlich zu bestätigen.

2) Die Gründungsanzeige hat folgende Angaben zu enthalten:

1. Name der Stiftung;
2. Sitz der Stiftung;

3. Zweck der Stiftung;
4. Datum der Errichtung der Stiftung;
5. Dauer der Stiftung, falls diese begrenzt ist;
6. Name, Vorname, Geburtsdatum, Staatsbürgerschaft und Wohnsitz oder Kanzleisitz bzw. Firma und Sitz der Mitglieder des Stiftungsrats sowie die Art der Zeichnung;
7. Name, Vorname, Geburtsdatum, Staatsbürgerschaft und Wohnsitz oder Kanzleisitz bzw. Firma und Sitz des gesetzlichen Repräsentanten;
8. die Bestätigung, dass die Bezeichnung der konkreten oder nach objektiven Merkmalen individualisierbaren Begünstigten oder des Begünstigtenkreises durch den Stifter erfolgt ist, sofern sich dies nicht aus dem angezeigten Stiftungszweck ergibt;
9. die Bestätigung, dass die Stiftung nicht ganz oder überwiegend gemeinnützigen Zwecken zu dienen bestimmt ist;
10. die Angabe, ob die Stiftung gemäss einer Bestimmung der Stiftungsurkunde der Aufsicht unterstellt ist; sowie
11. die Bestätigung, dass sich das gesetzliche Mindestkapital in der freien Verfügung der Stiftung befindet.

3) Bei jeder Änderung einer in der Gründungsanzeige enthaltenen Tatsache sowie bei Vorliegen eines Auflösungsgrundes gemäss § 39 Abs. 1, sind die Mitglieder des Stiftungsrats verpflichtet, innerhalb von 30 Tagen eine Änderungsanzeige beim Grundbuch- und Öffentlichkeitsregisteramt zu hinterlegen. Die Befugnis zur Hinterlegung steht auch dem Repräsentanten zu. Ein in Liechtenstein zugelassener Rechtsanwalt, Treuhänder oder Träger einer Berechtigung nach Art. 180a hat die Richtigkeit derAngaben in der Änderungsanzeige schriftlich zu bestätigen.

4) Das Grundbuch- und Öffentlichkeitsregisteramt stellt auf Antrag der Stiftung nach jeder gesetzmässig ausgeführten Anzeige eine Amtsbestätigung über die Hinterlegung der Gründungsanzeige aus. Es stellt keine Amtsbestätigung aus, wenn:

1. der angezeigte Zweck gesetz- oder sittenwidrig ist; oder
2. sich aus der Anzeige eine Eintragungspflicht für die Stiftung ergibt.

2. Prüfbefugnis und Massnahmen

§ 21

1) Das Grundbuch- und Öffentlichkeitsregisteramt ist als Stiftungsaufsichtsbehörde berechtigt, die Richtigkeit der hinterlegten Gründungs- und Änderungsanzeigen zu überprüfen. Zu diesem Zweck kann es von der Stiftung Auskünfte verlangen und im Wege des Kontrollorgans oder, wenn ein solches nicht eingerichtet ist, im Wege eines beauftragten Dritten in die Stiftungsdokumente Einsicht nehmen, soweit dies zur Überprüfung erforderlich ist.

2) Kopien und Abschriften dürfen nur erstellt werden, wenn die Überprüfung Anhaltspunkte dafür gibt, dass die Gründungs- oder Änderungsanzeige unrichtig ist.

3) Ergibt die Überprüfung, dass die Stiftung einen gesetz- oder sittenwidrigen Zweck verfolgt, ist sie unter Anwendung der allgemeinen Vorschriften über die Verbandspersonen aufzulösen. Die Bestimmungen über die Änderung des Zwecks, der nachträglich unerlaubt geworden ist, bleiben vorbehalten (§§ 31 und 33). Stellt sich heraus, dass die Stiftung einer Eintragungspflicht unterliegt, so ist die Eintragung vom Grundbuch- und Öffentlichkeitsregisteramt unter Anwendung von § 19 Abs. 4vorzunehmen. Ergibt die Überprüfung, dass die Stiftung der Aufsicht gemäss § 29 unterliegt, hat die Stiftungsaufsichtsbehörde erforderlichenfalls die entsprechenden Massnahmen zu treffen.

4) Erlangen Gerichte, die Staatsanwaltschaft oder eine Verwaltungsbehörde Kenntnis davon, dass die Abgabe der Gründungs- oder Änderungsanzeige unterblieben oder die abgegebene Gründungs- oder Änderungsanzeige inhaltlich unrichtig ist, so ist ein Bericht zu erstellen und der Stiftungsaufsichtsbehörde zu übermitteln.

5) Die Regierung kann mit Verordnung nähere Bestimmungen über die Ausübung der Prüfbefugnis sowie die Festsetzung und Erhebung von Gebühren durch die Stiftungsaufsichtsbehörde erlassen.

C. Widerruf der Stiftungserklärung

§ 22

I. Durch den Stifter

Ein Widerruf der Stiftungserklärung ist nur zulässig:

1. wenn die Stiftung noch nicht ins Öffentlichkeitsregister eingetragen ist, falls die Eintragung zur Entstehung erforderlich ist;
2. falls eine Eintragung der Stiftung nicht erforderlich ist und diese noch zu Lebzeiten des Stifters rechtswirksam werden soll, bis zur Beglaubigung seiner Unterschrift in der Stiftungsurkunde;
3. bei den durch letztwillige Verfügung oder Erbvertrag errichteten Stiftungen nach den hierfür geltenden erbrechtlichen Vorschriften.

§ 23

II. Ausschluss der Erben

1) Bei den durch letztwillige Verfügung oder Erbvertrag errichteten Stiftungen kommt den Erben nach dem Tod des Erblassers und Stifters selbst dann kein Recht zum Widerruf der Stiftungserklärung zu, wenn die Stiftung noch nicht ins Öffentlichkeitsregister eingetragen ist.

2) Ebenso haben die Erben kein Recht zum Widerruf, wenn der Stifter bei der Stiftung unter Lebenden die Stiftungsurkunde zwar errichtete, jedoch vor der Eintragung ins Öffentlichkeitsregister verstorben ist.

D. Organisation

I. Stiftungsrat

§ 24

1. Im Allgemeinen

1) Der Stiftungsrat führt die Geschäfte der Stiftung und vertritt diese. Er ist unter Beachtung der Bestimmungen in den Stiftungsdokumenten für die Erfüllung des Stiftungszwecks verantwortlich.

2) Der Stiftungsrat hat sich aus mindestens zwei Mitgliedern zusammenzusetzen. Juristische Personen können Mitglied des Stiftungsrats sein.

3) Ist in der Stiftungsurkunde nichts anderes vorgesehen, gilt die Bestellung des Stiftungsrats für eine Amtszeit von drei Jahren, wobei eine Wiederbestellung zulässig ist und die Mitglieder ihre Tätigkeit entgeltlich oder unentgeltlich ausüben können.

4) Die für die Mitglieder des Stiftungsrats aufgestellten Bestimmungen gelten auch für allfällige Stellvertreter.

5) Die Mitglieder des Stiftungsrats haben in der Weise zu zeichnen, dass sie dem Namen der Stiftung ihre Unterschrift beifügen.

6) Werden Mitglieder des Stiftungsrats unentgeltlich tätig, so kann die Haftung für leichte Fahrlässigkeit in der Stiftungserklärung ausgeschlossen werden, soweit dadurch die Gläubiger der Stiftung nicht geschädigt werden.

2. Besondere Pflichten

§ 25

a) Vermögensverwaltung

1) Der Stiftungsrat verwaltet das Stiftungsvermögen unter Beachtung des Stifterwillens entsprechend dem Zweck der Stiftung nach den Grundsätzen einer guten Geschäftsführung.

2) Der Stifter kann in der Stiftungsurkunde, der Stiftungszusatzurkunde oder einem Reglement konkrete und verbindliche Verwaltungskriterien festlegen.

§ 26

b) Rechnungswesen

Stiftungen, die ein nach kaufmännischer Art geführtes Gewerbe ausüben, unterliegen den allgemeinen Vorschriften zur Rechnungslegung. Bei allen anderen Stiftungen hat der Stiftungsrat über die Verwaltung und Verwendung des Stiftungsvermögens unter Berücksichtigung der Grundsätze einer ordentlichen Buchführung den Vermögensverhältnissen der Stiftung angemessene Aufzeichnungen zu führen und Belege aufzubewahren, aus denen der Geschäftsverlauf und die Entwicklung des Stiftungsvermögens nachvollzogen werden können. Ferner hat der Stiftungsrat ein Vermögensverzeichnis zu führen, aus dem der Stand und die Anlage des Stiftungsvermögens ersichtlich sind. Art. 1059 ist sinngemäss anzuwenden.

II. Revisionsstelle

§ 27

1) Für jede gemäss § 29 der Aufsicht der Stiftungsaufsichtsbehörde unterstehende Stiftung bestellt das Gericht im Rechtsfürsorgeverfahren eine Revisionsstelle nach Art. 191a Abs. 1. Die Stiftungsaufsichtsbehörde hat in diesem Verfahren Parteistellung.

2) Die Revisionsstelle muss von der Stiftung unabhängig sein. Sie ist verpflichtet, dem Gericht und der Stiftungsaufsichtsbehörde die Gründe, die ihre Unabhängigkeit ausschliessen, bekannt zu geben. Die Stiftungsaufsichtsbehörde kann von der Revisionsstelle die zur Beurteilung der Unabhängigkeit erforderlichen Bescheinigungen und Nachweise verlangen. Als Revisionsstelle ist insbesondere ausgeschlossen, wer:

1. einem anderen Stiftungsorgan angehört;
2. in einem Arbeitsverhältnis zur Stiftung steht;
3. enge verwandtschaftliche Beziehungen zu Mitgliedern von Stiftungsorganen hat; oder
4. Begünstigter der Stiftung ist.

3) Der Stifter kann zwei Vorschläge für die Revisionsstelle unter Mitteilung seiner Präferenz unterbreiten. Hat der Stifter von diesem Recht nicht Gebrauch gemacht, so kann der Stiftungsrat beim Gericht einen solchen Vorschlag erstatten. Das Gericht bestellt, vorbehaltlich Abs. 2, in der Regel die vorzugsweise vorgeschlagene Revisionsstelle.

4) Die Revisionsstelle ist als Organ der Stiftung verpflichtet, einmal jährlich zu überprüfen, ob das Stiftungsvermögen seinen Zwecken gemäss verwaltet und verwendet wird. Über das Ergebnis dieser Prüfung hat sie dem Stiftungsrat und der Stiftungsaufsichtsbehörde einen Bericht vorzulegen. Besteht kein Grund zur Beanstandung, so genügt eine Bestätigung, wonach eine Verwaltung und Verwendung des Stiftungsvermögens entsprechend dem Stiftungszweck und im

Einklang mit den Bestimmungen des Gesetzes und der Stiftungsdokumente durchgeführt wurde. Stellt die Revisionsstelle bei Wahrnehmung ihrer Aufgaben Tatsachen fest, die den Bestand der Stiftung gefährden, so hat sie auch hierüber zu berichten. Die Stiftungsaufsichtsbehörde kann von der Revisionsstelle Auskunft über alle ihr im Zuge der Prüfung bekannt gewordenen Tatsachen verlangen.

5) Bei gemeinnützigen Stiftungen kann die Stiftungsaufsichtsbehörde auf Antrag von der Bestellung einer Revisionsstelle absehen, wenn die Stiftung nur geringes Vermögen verwaltet oder dies aus anderen Gründen zweckmässig erscheint. Die Regierung legt die Voraussetzungen für die Befreiung von der Pflicht, eine Revisionsstelle zu bestellen, mit Verordnung fest.

III. Weitere Organe

§ 28

1) Der Stifter kann weitere Organe, insbesondere zur Feststellung eines Begünstigten aus dem Begünstigtenkreis, zur Feststellung von Zeitpunkt, Höhe und Bedingung einer Ausschüttung, zur Verwaltung des Vermögens, zur Beratung und Unterstützung des Stiftungsrats, zur Überwachung der Stiftungsverwaltung zur Wahrung des Stiftungszwecks, zum Vorbehalt von Zustimmungen oder zur Erteilung von Weisungen sowie zur Interessenswahrung Stiftungsbeteiligter, vorsehen. Vertretungsbefugnis steht diesen Organen nicht zu.

2) § 24 Abs. 6 ist sinngemäss anzuwenden.

E. Aufsicht

§ 29

1) Gemeinnützige Stiftungen stehen unter der Aufsicht der Stiftungsaufsichtsbehörde. Dasselbe gilt für privatnützige Stiftungen, die durch eine Bestimmung der Stiftungsurkunde der Aufsicht unterstellt sind.

2) Stiftungsaufsichtsbehörde ist das Grundbuch- und Öffentlichkeitsregisteramt.

3) Die Stiftungsaufsichtsbehörde hat von Amts wegen dafür zu sorgen, dass das Stiftungsvermögen seinen Zwecken gemäss verwaltet und verwendet wird. Sie hat zu diesem Zweck das Recht, von der Stiftung Auskünfte zu verlangen und im

Wege der Revisionsstelle in die Bücher und Schriften der Stiftung Einsicht zu nehmen. Wurde von der Bestellung einer Revisionsstelle gemäss § 27 Abs. 5 abgesehen, so übt die Stiftungsaufsichtsbehörde das Recht auf Einsichtnahme in der Regel selbst aus. Ferner kann sie Auskünfte anderer Verwaltungsbehörden und der Gerichte einholen und die gebotenen Anordnungen, wie Kontrolle und Abberufung der Stiftungsorgane, Durchführung von Sonderprüfungen oder Aufhebung von Beschlüssen der Stiftungsorgane, beim Richter im Rechtsfürsorgeverfahren beantragen.

4) Gegen eine dem Stiftungszweck widersprechende Verwaltung und Verwendung des Vermögens durch die Stiftungsorgane kann überdies jeder Stiftungsbeteiligte beim Richter im Rechtsfürsorgeverfahren die Anordnung der gebotenen Massnahmen nach Abs. 3 beantragen. Besteht ein dringender Verdacht einer strafbaren Handlung durch ein Stiftungsorgan, so kann der Richter auch von Amts wegen, insbesondere aufgrund einer Mitteilung der Staatsanwaltschaft, tätig werden. Die Stiftungsaufsichtsbehörde hat in einem solchen Verfahren Parteistellung.

5) Unbekannte Begünstigte werden auf Antrag der Stiftungsaufsichtsbehörde im Aufgebotsverfahren ermittelt.

6) Die Regierung kann mit Verordnung nähere Bestimmungen über die Tätigkeit der Stiftungsaufsichtsbehörde sowie die Festsetzung und Erhebung von Gebühren durch die Stiftungsaufsichtsbehörde erlassen.

F. Änderung

§ 30

I. Rechte des Stifters

1) Der Stifter kann sich das Recht zum Widerruf der Stiftung oder zur Änderung der Stiftungserklärung in der Stiftungsurkunde vorbehalten. Diese Rechte können nicht abgetreten oder vererbt werden. Soll eines dieser Rechte durch einen direkten Stellvertreter ausgeübt werden, so bedarf dieser einer besonderen auf dieses Geschäft lautenden Vollmacht.

2) Ist der Stifter eine juristische Person, so kann er sich die Rechte nach Abs. 1 nicht vorbehalten.

3) Werden die Rechte nach Abs. 1 durch einen indirekten Stellvertreter (§ 4 Abs. 3) ausgeübt, so treten die Rechtswirkungen unmittelbar beim Stifter ein.

II. Rechte der Stiftungsorgane

§ 31

1. Änderung des Zwecks

1) Eine Änderung des Stiftungszwecks durch den Stiftungsrat oder ein anderes Stiftungsorgan ist nur zulässig, wenn der Zweck unerreichbar, unerlaubt oder vernunftwidrig geworden ist oder sich die Verhältnisse so geändert haben, dass der Zweck eine ganz andere Bedeutung oder Wirkung erhalten hat, so dass die Stiftung dem Willen des Stifters entfremdet ist.

2) Die Änderung muss dem mutmasslichen Willen des Stifters entsprechen und die Befugnis zur Änderung dem Stiftungsrat oder dem anderen Stiftungsorgan in der Stiftungsurkunde ausdrücklich vorbehalten sein.

§ 32

2. Änderung anderer Inhalte

Eine Änderung anderer Inhalte der Stiftungsurkunde oder der Stiftungszusatzurkunde, wie insbesondere der Organisation der Stiftung, ist durch den Stiftungsrat oder ein anderes Organ zulässig, wenn und soweit die Änderungsbefugnis dem Stiftungsrat oder dem anderen Stiftungsorgan in der Stiftungsurkunde ausdrücklich vorbehalten ist. Der Stiftungsrat übt das Recht zur Änderung unter Wahrung des Stiftungszwecks aus, wenn ein sachlich gerechtfertigter Grund vorliegt.

III. Rechte des Richters

1. Beaufsichtigte Stiftungen

§ 33

a) Änderung des Zwecks

1) Untersteht eine Stiftung der Aufsicht der Stiftungsaufsichtsbehörde, so kann diese beim Richter im Rechtsfürsorgeverfahren die Änderung des Zwecks der Stiftung beantragen, wenn:

1. der Zweck unerreichbar, unerlaubt oder vernunftwidrig geworden ist oder sich die Verhältnisse so geändert haben, dass der Zweck eine ganz andere Bedeutung oder Wirkung erhalten hat, so dass die Stiftung dem Willen des Stifters entfremdet ist; und
2. die Stiftungsurkunde nicht den Stiftungsrat oder ein anderes Stiftungsorgan mit der Änderung des Zwecks betraut hat.

2) Die Änderung muss dem mutmasslichen Willen des Stifters entsprechen.

3) Das Recht zur Antragstellung steht auch den Stiftungsbeteiligten zu; die Stiftungsaufsichtsbehörde hat in diesem Fall Parteistellung.

§ 34

b) Änderung anderer Inhalte

1) Untersteht eine Stiftung der Aufsicht der Stiftungsaufsichtsbehörde, so kann diese beim Richter im Rechtsfürsorgeverfahren die Änderung anderer Inhalte der Stiftungsurkunde bzw. der Stiftungszusatzurkunde, wie insbesondere der Organisation der Stiftung, beantragen, wenn:

1. dies zur Wahrung des Stiftungszwecks, insbesondere zur Sicherung des Fortbestands der Stiftung und zur Sicherung des Stiftungsvermögens, zweckmässig ist; und
2. die Stiftungsurkunde nicht den Stiftungsrat oder ein anderes Stiftungsorgan mit der Änderung der anderen Inhalte betraut hat.

2) Das Recht zur Antragstellung steht auch den Stiftungsbeteiligten zu; die Stiftungsaufsichtsbehörde hat in diesem Fall Parteistellung.

§ 35

2. Andere Stiftungen

1) Bei den nicht der Aufsicht der Stiftungsaufsichtsbehörde unterstehenden Stiftungen kann der Richter auf Antrag eines Stiftungsbeteiligten sowie in dringenden Fällen, gegebenenfalls aufgrund einer Mitteilung der Stiftungsaufsichtsbehörde (§ 21 Abs. 3) oder der Staatsanwaltschaft, auch von Amts wegen im Rechtsfürsorgeverfahren die Befugnisse gemäss §§ 33 und 34 ausüben sowie die gemäss § 29 Abs. 3 gebotenen Anordnungen treffen. Ein dringender Fall liegt insbesondere vor, wenn ein dringender Verdacht einer strafbaren Handlung durch ein Stiftungsorgan besteht.

2) Unbekannte Begünstigte können auf Antrag durch den Richter im Aufgebotsverfahren ermittelt werden.

G. Vollstreckungsrechtliche Bestimmungen

§ 36

1) Bei Familienstiftungen kann der Stifter bestimmen, dass die Gläubiger von Begünstigten diesen ihre unentgeltlich erlangte Begünstigungsberechtigung oder Anwartschaftsberechtigung, bzw. einzelne Ansprüche daraus, auf dem Wege des Sicherungsverfahrens, der Zwangsvollstreckung oder des Konkurses nicht entziehen dürfen. Bei gemischten Familienstiftungen kann eine solche Anordnung nur insoweit getroffen werden, als die jeweilige Berechtigung den Zwecken der Familienstiftung dient.

2) Kann ein Gläubiger der Stiftung aus dem Stiftungsvermögen keine Befriedigung erlangen, und hat der Stifter das gewidmete Vermögen noch nicht vollständig geleistet, so ist der Stiftungsrat verpflichtet, dem Gläubiger die zu seiner Rechtsverfolgung erforderlichen Auskünfte zu erteilen. Dies gilt im Konkurs der Stiftung sinngemäss gegenüber dem Masseverwalter.

H. Haftung

§ 37

1) Für die Schulden der Stiftung haftet den Gläubigern gegenüber nur das Stiftungsvermögen. Es besteht keine Nachschusspflicht.

2) Der Stiftungsrat darf Leistungen an Begünstigte zur Erfüllung des Stiftungszwecks nur vornehmen, wenn dadurch Ansprüche von Gläubigern der Stiftung nicht geschmälert werden.

I. Anfechtung

§ 38

1) Die Vermögenszuwendung an die Stiftung kann von den Erben oder den Gläubigern gleich einer Schenkung angefochten werden.

2) Der Stifter und seine Erben können die Stiftung wegen Willensmängeln gleich den Vorschriften über Mängel des Vertragsabschlusses auch nach der Eintragung anfechten.

K. Auflösung und Beendigung

§ 39

I. Auflösungsgründe

1) Die Stiftung wird aufgelöst, wenn:

1. über das Vermögen der Stiftung der Konkurs eröffnet worden ist;
2. der Beschluss, durch den die Eröffnung des Konkurses mangels eines zur Deckung der Kosten des Konkursverfahrens voraussichtlich hinreichenden Vermögens abgelehnt wird, Rechtskraft erlangt;
3. das Gericht die Auflösung beschlossen hat;
4. der Stiftungsrat einen rechtsgültigen Auflösungsbeschluss gefasst hat.

2) Der Stiftungsrat hat einen Auflösungsbeschluss zu fassen, sobald:

1. ihm ein zulässiger Widerruf des Stifters zugegangen ist;
2. der Stiftungszweck erreicht oder nicht mehr erreichbar ist;
3. die in der Stiftungsurkunde vorgesehene Dauer abgelaufen ist;
4. andere in der Stiftungsurkunde dafür genannte Gründe gegeben sind.

3) Der Auflösungsbeschluss nach Abs. 2 ist einstimmig zu fassen, sofern in der Stiftungsurkunde nichts anderes bestimmt ist. Bei den der Aufsicht der Stiftungsaufsichtsbehörde unterstehenden Stiftungen hat der Stiftungsrat dieser über den Auflösungsbeschluss Mitteilung zu machen.

4) Kommt ein Beschluss nach Abs. 2 trotz Vorliegens eines Auflösungsgrundes nicht zustande, so hat bei den nicht der Aufsicht der Stiftungsaufsichtsbehörde unterstehenden Stiftungen der Richter auf Antrag von Stiftungsbeteiligten im Rechtsfürsorgeverfahren die Stiftung aufzulösen; bei den übrigen Stiftungen kann die Auflösung auch von der Stiftungsaufsichtsbehörde beantragt werden.

5) Kommt ein Auflösungsbeschluss nach Abs. 2 zustande, obwohl kein Auflösungsgrund vorliegt, so hat bei den nicht der Aufsicht der Stiftungsaufsichtsbehörde unterstehenden Stiftungen der Richter auf Antrag von Stiftungsbeteiligten im Rechtsfürsorgeverfahren den Auflösungsbeschluss des Stiftungsrats aufzuheben; bei den übrigen Stiftungen steht das Antragsrecht auch der Stiftungsaufsichtsbehörde zu.

6) Betreibt die Stiftung ohne die Voraussetzungen gemäss § 1 Abs. 2 ein nach kaufmännischer Art geführtes Gewerbe, so hat der Richter auf Antrag eines Stiftungsbeteiligten oder von Amts wegen die Auflösung der Stiftung zu beschliessen, wenn die Stiftung einer rechtskräftigen Unterlassungsanordnung nicht innerhalb angemessener Frist nachgekommen ist.

§ 40

II. Liquidation und Beendigung

1) Auf die Liquidation und Beendigung der Stiftung finden die allgemeinen Vorschriften über die Verbandspersonen Anwendung.

2) Auf im Öffentlichkeitsregister nicht eingetragene Stiftungen finden die Bestimmungen betreffend den Gläubigeraufruf keine Anwendung.

3) Über die Beendigung einer Stiftung stellt das Grundbuch- und Öffentlichkeitsregisteramt eine Löschungsbestätigung in Form eines Registerauszugs bei eingetragenen Stiftungen oder einer Amtsbestätigung bei nicht eingetragenen Stiftungen aus.

4) Untersteht die Stiftung der Aufsicht der Stiftungsaufsichtsbehörde, so hat der Stiftungsrat der Stiftungsaufsichtsbehörde Mitteilung über die Beendigung der Stiftung zu machen. Ist die Stiftung im Öffentlichkeitsregister eingetragen, so ist auch ein Registerauszug vorzulegen. Die Befugnis zur Mitteilung steht auch dem gesetzlichen Repräsentanten zu.

5) Nachträglich hervorgekommenes Vermögen ist nach den Bestimmungen über die Nachtragsliquidation (Art. 139) zu verteilen. Bei den der Aufsicht der Stiftungsaufsichtsbehörde unterstehenden Stiftungen hat der Stiftungsrat diese über nachträglich hervorgekommenes Vermögen unverzüglich zu unterrichten. Die Befugnis zur Mitteilung steht auch dem gesetzlichen Repräsentanten zu.

L. Umwandlung

§ 41

Eine privatnützige Stiftung kann ohne Abwicklung oder Liquidation vom Stiftungsrat unter zwingender Wahrung des Wesens der Stiftung im Allgemeinen und des Stifterwillens im Besonderen in eine stiftungsrechtlich organisierte Anstalt oder ein stiftungsrechtlich organisiertes Treuunternehmen mit Persönlichkeit mittels formrichtiger Urkunde umgewandelt werden, wenn die Umwandlung:

1. unter Festlegung der Voraussetzungen in der Stiftungsurkunde vorbehalten ist; und
2. der Verwirklichung des Stiftungszwecks dienlich ist.

Art. 553 bis 570

Aufgehoben

Art. 955a Abs. 1

1) Einsichtnahme, Auszüge, Abschriften oder Zeugnisse von gemäss Art. 990 hinterlegten Akten und Schriftstücken sowie von Anmeldungen und Belegen

nicht im Öffentlichkeitsregister eingetragener Stiftungen und Treuhänderschaften oder von Gründungs- oder Änderungsanzeigen nicht im Öffentlichkeitsregister eingetragener Stiftungen können nur vom Hinterleger und demjenigen, der hierzu ermächtigt ist, sowie von Gesamtrechtsnachfolgern verlangt werden. Vorbehalten bleibt die Bekanntgabe des Repräsentanten oder Zustellbevollmächtigten an inländische Strafverfolgungsbehörden, die Stabsstelle FIU und die Finanzmarktaufsicht (FMA). Die Regierung regelt das Nähere mit Verordnung.

§ 66c SchlT

5. Anmeldungs-, Hinterlegungs- und Deklarationspflichten bei Stiftungen

1) Vom Landgericht kann auf Anzeige der Stiftungsaufsichtsbehörde im Rechtsfürsorgeverfahren mit einer Ordnungsbusse bis zu 10 000 Franken bestraft werden, wer als Mitglied des Stiftungsrats:

1. eine Stiftung beim Öffentlichkeitsregister entgegen Art. 552 § 19 Abs. 5 nicht anmeldet; oder
2. eine Gründungsanzeige entgegen Art. 552 § 20 Abs. 1 iVm Abs. 2 oder eine Änderungsanzeige entgegen Art. 552 § 20 Abs. 3 beim Grundbuch- und Öffentlichkeitsregisteramt nicht hinterlegt.

2) Die Ordnungsbusse nach Abs. 1 kann fortgesetzt verhängt werden, bis der gesetzliche Zustand hergestellt ist.

3) Wer vorsätzlich eine inhaltlich unrichtige Erklärung gemäss Art. 552 § 20 Abs. 1 iVm Abs. 2 oder gemäss Art. 552 § 20 Abs. 3 abgibt, wirdvom Landgericht wegen Übertretung mit einer Busse bis zu 50 000 Franken, im Nichteinbringlichkeitsfalle mit einer Freiheitsstrafe bis zu sechs Monaten, bestraft. Handelt der Täter fahrlässig, wird er vom Landgericht wegen Übertretung mit einer Busse bis zu 20 000 Franken, im Nichteinbringlichkeitsfalle mit einer Freiheitsstrafe bis zu drei Monaten, bestraft.

4) Ebenso ist nach Abs. 3 zu bestrafen, wer als Rechtsanwalt, Treuhänder oder Träger einer Berechtigung nach Art. 180a vorsätzlich oder fahrlässig eine unrichtige Bestätigung der Angaben gemäss Art. 552 § 20 Abs. 1 iVm Abs. 2 oder gemäss Art. 552 § 20 Abs. 3 vornimmt.

5) Disziplinäre Massnahmen bleiben vorbehalten.

II. Übergangsbestimmungen

Art. 1

Anwendung des neuen Rechts auf bestehende Stiftungen

1) Auf im Zeitpunkt des Inkrafttretens dieses Gesetzes bestehende Stiftungen findet das bisherige Recht Anwendung, soweit im Folgenden nichts anderes bestimmt ist.

2) Erfolgt erstmals nach Inkrafttreten dieses Gesetzes die Änderung einer Tatsache, die gemäss Art. 552 § 20 Abs. 3 dem Grundbuch-und Öffentlichkeitsregisteramt anzuzeigen ist, so ist von den Mitgliedern des Stiftungsrats eine Anzeige mit dem Inhalt nach Art. 552 § 20 Abs. 2 zu erstatten. Hinsichtlich der Pflicht und der Befugnis zur Anzeige sowie der Bestätigung der Richtigkeit der Angaben ist Art. 552 § 20 Abs. 1, hinsichtlich der Überprüfung der Richtigkeit ist § 21 sinngemäss anzuwenden. Auf alle folgenden Änderungen gelangt Art. 552 § 20 Abs. 3 zur Anwendung.

3) Wird eine Anzeige nach Abs. 2 erstattet oder ist eine solche bereits erstattet worden, so kann die Herausgabe der Stiftungsurkunde und der sonstigen Dokumente an die Stiftung begehrt werden, die gemäss Art. 554 in der bisher geltenden Fassung beim Grundbuch- und Öffentlichkeitsregisteramt hinterlegt wurden.

4) Die Art. 107 Abs. 4a und Art. 552 §§ 3, 5 bis 12, 21, 26, 27, 29 und 31 bis 35 sind auch auf Stiftungen anzuwenden, die vor Inkrafttreten dieses Gesetzes errichtet wurden. Die Mitglieder des Stiftungsrats haben Stiftungen, die gemäss Art. 552 § 29 der Aufsicht der Stiftungsaufsichtsbehörde unterstehen, der Stiftungsaufsichtsbehörde unter Vorlage eines Registerauszugs innerhalb von sechs Monaten nach Inkrafttreten dieses Gesetzes anzuzeigen. Der Stifter ist auch dann, wenn er sich dieses Recht nicht vorbehalten hat, berechtigt, ein Kontrollorgan nach Art. 552 § 11 Abs. 2 iVm Abs. 3 einzurichten. Wurde die Stiftung durch einen indirekten Stellvertreter errichtet (Art. 552 § 4 Abs. 3), so gilt der Geschäftsherr (Machtgeber) als Stifter; Art. 552 § 30 Abs. 3 ist sinngemäss anzuwenden. Ist der Stifter verstorben oder geschäftsunfähig, so kann ein Kontrollorgan gemäss Art. 552 § 11 Abs. 2 Ziff. 1 iVm Abs. 3 durch den Stiftungsrat eingerichtet werden. Die Einrichtung des Kontrollorgans muss innerhalb von sechs Monaten nach Inkrafttreten dieses Gesetzes erfolgen. Bei gemeinnützigen Stiftungen (Art. 552 § 2) und privatnützigen Stiftungen, die auf spezialgesetzlicher Grundlage ein nach kaufmännischer Art geführtes Gewerbe betreiben und

die nicht im Öffentlichkeitsregister eingetragen sind, ist jedes Mitglied des Stiftungsrats verpflichtet, die Stiftung innerhalb von sechs Monaten nach dem Inkrafttreten dieses Gesetzes zur Eintragung ins Öffentlichkeitsregister anzumelden; Art. 552 § 19 ist sinngemäss anzuwenden.

5) Wird ein Kontrollorgan gemäss Abs. 4 eingerichtet, so muss die Prüfung nach Art. 552 § 11 Abs. 4 oder Art. 552 § 27 Abs. 4 zum ersten Mal bis zum 30. Juni 2010 erfolgen.

Art. 2

Anpassung an das neue Recht

1) Erfüllt das Errichtungsgeschäft einer Stiftung, die vor dem 31. Dezember 2003 errichtet worden ist, nicht die Anforderungen nach Art. 552 § 16 Abs. 1 Ziff. 4, so ist der gesetzmässige Zustand nach den folgenden Bestimmungen bis zum 31. Dezember 2009 herzustellen.

2)Der Stifter ist auch dann, wenn er sich ein solches Recht nicht vorbehalten hat, berechtigt, die Stiftungserklärung so abzuändern, dass der gesetzmässige Zustand hergestellt werden kann. Wurde die Stiftung durch einen indirekten Stellvertreter errichtet (Art. 552 § 4 Abs. 3), so gilt der Geschäftsherr (Machtgeber) als Stifter; Art. 552 § 30 Abs. 3 ist sinngemäss anzuwenden.

3) Ist der Stifter verstorben oder geschäftsunfähig, so kann die Stiftungserklärung vom Stiftungsrat in einer dem Art. 552 § 16 Abs. 1 Ziff. 4 entsprechenden Weise geändert werden. Die Änderung durch den Stiftungsrat ist nur zulässig, wenn der Wille des Stifters festgestellt werden kann. Als Mittel zur Feststellung des Willens dürfen ausschliesslich Urkunden verwendet werden, die vom Stifter, einem bei der Gründung tätigen direkten oder indirekten Stellvertreter oder einem Stiftungsorgan stammen. Stammt das Dokument nicht vom Stifter, so dürfen nur solche Dokumente herangezogen werden, die vor dem 1. Dezember 2006 errichtet worden sind.

4) Der Stiftungsrat aller im Öffentlichkeitsregister nicht eingetragenen Stiftungen hat dem Grundbuch- und Öffentlichkeitsregisteramt durch ausdrückliche Erklärung zu bestätigen, dass die Stiftungsdokumente dem Art. 552 § 16 Abs. 1 Ziff. 4 entsprechen. Diese Erklärung darf erst abgegeben werden, nachdem der gesetzmässige Zustand gegebenenfalls hergestellt wurde. Auf die Überprüfung der Richtigkeit der Erklärung ist Art. 552 § 21 sinngemäss anzuwenden.

5) Wird der gesetzmässige Zustand bis zum 30. Juni 2010 nicht hergestellt, so hat der Stiftungsrat einen Auflösungsbeschluss gemäss Art. 552 § 39 zu fassen, der dem Grundbuch- und Öffentlichkeitsregisteramt anzuzeigen ist.

6) Wird die Anzeige nach Abs. 5 nicht bis zum 1. August 2010 erstattet, so hat das Grundbuch- und Öffentlichkeitsregisteramt den Stiftungsrat aufzufordern, innerhalb einer Nachfrist von sechs Monaten eine Erklärung nach Abs. 4 vorzulegen oder den Auflösungsbeschluss anzuzeigen. Verstreicht auch diese Frist ungenützt, so verständigt das Grundbuch- und Öffentlichkeitsregisteramt den Richter; dieser hat die Stiftung im Rechtsfürsorgeverfahren für aufgelöst zu erklären.

7) Wird eine Stiftung nach Abs. 5 oder 6 aufgelöst, so ist das Grundbuch- und Öffentlichkeitsregisteramt berechtigt, von sämtlichen Stiftungsorganen Auskünfte über den Fortgang der Liquidation zu verlangen. Erweist es sich, dass der Liquidator bei der Durchführung der Liquidation säumig ist, so kann der Richter im Rechtsfürsorgeverfahren auf Antrag von Stiftungsbeteiligten, des Grundbuch- und Öffentlichkeitsregisteramtes oder von Amts wegen den Liquidator seines Amtes entheben und eine andere geeignete Person zum Liquidator bestellen.

Art. 3

Strafbestimmungen

1) Wird eine Anzeige entgegen Art. 1 Abs. 2 nicht erstattet, so ist § 66c Abs. 1 und 2 SchlT sinngemäss anzuwenden.

2) Wer vorsätzlich eine inhaltlich unrichtige Erklärung nach Art. 1 Abs. 2 oder Art. 2 Abs. 4 abgibt oder eine Anzeige gemäss Art. 1 Abs. 4 vorsätzlich unterlässt oder zu Unrecht erklärt, nicht der Aufsicht der Stiftungsaufsichtsbehörde zu unterstehen oder wer als Rechtsanwalt, Treuhänder oder Träger einer Berechtigung nach Art. 180a vorsätzlich oder fahrlässig eine unrichtige Bestätigung der Angaben gemäss Art. 1 Abs. 2 iVm Art. 552 § 20 Abs. 1 PGR vornimmt, wird vom Landgerichtwegen Übertretung mit einer Busse bis zu 50 000 Franken, im Nichteinbringlichkeitsfalle mit einer Freiheitsstrafe bis zu sechs Monaten, bestraft. Handelt der Täter fahrlässig, wird er vom Landgericht wegen Übertretung mit einer Busse bis zu 20 000 Franken, im Nichteinbringlichkeitsfalle mit einer Freiheitsstrafe bis zu drei Monaten, bestraft.

3) Disziplinäre Massnahmen bleiben vorbehalten.

Art. 4

Anwendung des neuen Rechts auf bestehende Anstalten

1) Art. 107 Abs. 4a sowie Art. 552 § 2 Abs. 4, §§ 26, 27, 29, 31 bis 35, 36 Abs. 1 und 41 sind sinngemäss auch auf solche Anstalten gemäss Art. 551 Abs. 2 PGR anzuwenden, die vor Inkrafttreten dieses Gesetzes errichtet wurden.

2) Die Mitglieder der Verwaltung einer Anstalt, die gemäss Art. 551 Abs. 2 in Verbindung mit Art. 552 § 29 der Aufsicht der Stiftungsaufsichtsbehörde untersteht, haben dies der Stiftungsaufsichtsbehörde unter Vorlage eines Registerauszugs innerhalb von sechs Monaten nach Inkrafttreten dieses Gesetzes anzuzeigen.

3) Wer als Mitglied der Verwaltung die Anzeige gemäss Abs. 2 vorsätzlich oder fahrlässig unterlässt oder zu Unrecht erklärt, nicht der Aufsicht der Stiftungsaufsichtsbehörde zu unterstehen, ist nach Art. 3 Abs. 2 zu bestrafen.

III. Inkrafttreten

Dieses Gesetz tritt unter Vorbehalt des ungenutzten Ablaufs der Referendumsfrist am 1. April 2009 in Kraft, andernfalls am Tage der Kundmachung.

In Stellvertretung des Landesfürsten:
gez. Alois
Erbprinz

gez. Otmar Hasler
Fürstlicher Regierungschef

4. New law, valid from 1 April 2009 (in English)

216.0 (Systematic Codification)

Liechtenstein Law Gazette (Liechtensteinisches Landesgesetzblatt), 2008 Volume No. 220, Published on 26 August 2008.

Law of 26 June 2008 on the Amendment of the Persons and Companies Act.

I hereby grant My consent to the following Resolution taken by the Parliament:

I. Amendment of Present Law

The Persons and Companies Act of 20 January 1926, Liechtenstein State Gazette 1926, No.4, in the version currently in force, shall be amended as follows:

Art. 106, para.2, item 3

Repealed

Art. 107, para.4a

Where the Act refers to non-profit making (common-benefit) or charitable purposes, this shall include such purposes the fulfilment of which is of benefit to the general public. In particular, there is deemed to be a benefit to the general public if the activity serves the common good in a charitable, religious, humanitarian, scientific, cultural, moral, sporting or ecological sense, even if only a specific category of persons benefits from the activity.

Art. 182, para.2

It shall diligently manage and promote the enterprise of the legal entity and shall be liable for observing the principles of diligent management and representation. A member of the administration shall be deemed to act in harmony with these principles if in his commercial decision-making he is not governed by irrelevant interests and it must reasonably be assumed that he is acting for the good of the legal entity on the basis of appropriate information.

Art. 259, para.2

Repealed

Heading above Art. 552

Second Section

The Foundations

Art. 552

The following rules apply to foundations:

A. In General

I. Definition and Purpose

§1

1. Description and Delimitation

1) A foundation within the meaning of this Section is a legally and economically independent special-purpose fund which is formed as a legal entity (juristic person) through the unilateral declaration of will of the founder. The founder allocates the specifically designated foundation assets, stipulates the purpose of the foundation, entirely non-self-serving and specifically designated, and also stipulates the beneficiaries.

2) A foundation is only permitted to carry on business run along commercial lines if it directly serves the achievement of its common benefit purpose or if this is permitted on a special statutory basis. Insofar as the orderly investment and management of the foundation assets require, the setting-up of a commercial operation is permissible, even for private-benefit foundations.

3) If there is no case of para. 2), sentence 1, the foundation shall also not be permitted to be the shareholder with unlimited liability of a collective under personal law which runs a business along commercial lines.

§2

2. Foundation Purposes

1) Foundation purposes may include common-benefit or private benefit purposes.

2) A common-benefit foundation within the meaning of this Section is a foundation whose activity according to the declaration of establishment is entirely or predominantly intended to serve common benefit purposes in accordance with Art. 107, para. 4a, unless it is a family foundation.

3) A private-benefit foundation within the meaning of this Section is a foundation which according to the declaration of establishment is entirely or predominantly intended to serve private or personal purposes. Predominance is to be assessed according to the relationship between services provided to serve private-benefit purposes and those serving common-benefit purposes. If it is not certain that at any given time the foundation is entirely or predominantly intended to serve private-benefit purposes, it shall be treated as a common-benefit foundation.

4) The following in particular shall be regarded as private-benefit foundations:

1. pure family foundations; these are foundations whose assets exclusively serve the defrayal of costs of upbringing or education, provision for or support of members of one or more families or similar family interests;

2. mixed family foundations; these are foundations which predominantly pursue the purpose of a pure family foundation, but which supplementally also serve common-benefit or other private benefit purposes.

II. Foundation Participants

§3

1. Definition

The following are deemed to be participants in the foundation:

1. the founder;
2. the entitled beneficiaries;
3. the prospective beneficiaries;
4. the discretionary beneficiaries;
5. the ultimate beneficiaries;
6. the executive bodies of the foundation pursuant to §§ 11, 24, 27 and 28 as well as the members of these executive bodies.

§4

2. Founder

1) Founders may be one or more natural persons or legal entities. A foundation formed by way of last will and testament may only have one founder.

2) If a foundation has more than one founder, the rights to which the founder is entitled or which are reserved to the founder may only be exercised jointly by all founders, unless the declaration of establishment provides otherwise. If one of the founders ceases to hold office, in cases of doubt the above-cited rights shall lapse.

3) If the foundation is formed by an indirect representative, the principal (authorizer) shall be deemed to be the founder. If the latter also acts as indirect representative for a third party, the latter's principal (authorizer) shall be deemed to be the founder. In any event the indirect representative shall be under an obligation to notify the foundation council of the identity of the founder.

§5

3. Beneficiary

1) The beneficiary is deemed to be the natural person or legal entity that with or without valuable consideration in fact, unconditionally or subject to certain prerequisites or conditions, for a limited or unlimited period, with or without restrictions, revocably or irrevocably, at any time during the legal existence of the foundation or on its termination derives or may derive an economic benefit from the foundation (beneficial interest).

2) Beneficiaries within the meaning of para.1 are:

1. the entitled beneficiaries (§6, para.1);
2. the prospective beneficiaries (§6, para.2);
3. the discretionary beneficiaries (§7); and
4. the ultimate beneficiaries (§8).

§6

4. Beneficiary with a Legal Claim

1) An entitled beneficiary is a beneficiary who on the basis of the foundation deed, the supplementary foundation deed or the regulations has a legal claim to benefit, to a specified or specifiable extent, from the foundation assets or foundation income.

2) A prospective beneficiary is a beneficiary who after the occurrence of a condition precedent or at a specified time, in particular after the exclusion of a prior-ranking beneficiary, on the basis of the foundation deed, the supplementary foundation deed or a regulation has a legal claim to acquire an entitlement to a beneficial interest.

§7

5. Discretionary Beneficiary (Beneficiary without Legal Claim)

1) A discretionary beneficiary is a beneficiary who belongs to the category of beneficiaries specified by the founder and whose possible beneficial interest is placed within the discretion of the foundation council or another body appointed for this purpose. A person who only has an expectancy to such a future beneficial interest shall not be treated as a discretionary beneficiary.

2) A legal claim by the discretionary beneficiary to a specific benefit from the foundation assets or foundation income shall in any event not come into being until there is a valid resolution by the foundation council, or another executive body vested with this responsibility (§ 28), on an actual distribution to the relevant discretionary beneficiaries and such claim shall lapse on receipt of this distribution.

§8

6. Ultimate Beneficiary

1) An ultimate beneficiary is a beneficiary who in accordance with the foundation deed or supplementary foundation deed is intended to receive the remaining assets following the liquidation of the foundation.

2) If there is no designation of an ultimate beneficiary or no existence of the ultimate beneficiary, the remaining assets following the liquidation shall pass to the state.

3) If there is no specification of the appropriation of assets in the event of a revocation pursuant to § 30, para.1, the founder himself shall be deemed to be the ultimate beneficiary irrespective of whether he previously had the status of a beneficiary.

III. Rights of the Beneficiaries to Information and Disclosure

§9

1. In General

1) Insofar as his rights are concerned, the beneficiary is entitled to inspect the foundation deed, the supplementary foundation deed and possible regulations.

2) In addition, insofar as his rights are concerned, he is entitled to the disclosure of information, reports and accounts. For this purpose he has the right to inspect the business records and documents and to produce copies, and also to examine and investigate all facts and circumstances, in particular the accounting, personally or through a representative. However, this right must not be exercised with dishonest intent, in an abusive manner or in a manner in conflict with the interests of the foundation or other beneficiaries. By way of exception, the right may also be denied for important reasons to protect the beneficiary.

3) The ultimate beneficiary shall not be entitled to these rights until after the dissolution of the foundation.

4) The rights of the beneficiary shall be asserted in special non-contentious civil proceedings.

5) The exceptions pursuant to §§ 10 to 12 are reserved.

§ 10

2. The Founder's Right of Revocation

1) If in the declaration of establishment the founder has reserved for himself the right to revoke the foundation (§ 30) and he is himself the ultimate beneficiary, the beneficiary shall not be entitled to the rights pursuant to §9.

2) If the foundation has been formed by more than one beneficiary, these rights may be exercised by each individual founder who has reserved for himself the right of revocation.

§ 11

3. Setting-up of a Controlling Body

1) If in the declaration of establishment the founder has set up a controlling body for the foundation, the beneficiary may only demand disclosure of information concerning the purpose and organisation of the foundation, and concerning his own rights vis-à-vis the foundation, and may verify the accuracy of this information by inspecting the foundation deed, the supplementary foundation deed and the regulations.

2) The following may be setup as controlling body:

1. an audit authority, to which §27 shall be applied mutatis mutandis;
2. one or more natural persons specified by name by the founder, who have sufficient specialist knowledge in the sphere of law and business to be able to perform their duties; or
3. the founder.

3) The controlling body must be independent of the foundation. § 27, para. 2 applies mutatis mutandis.

4) The controlling body shall be under an obligation to verify once a year whether the foundation assets are being managed and appropriated in accordance with their purposes. The foundation council shall submit a report on the outcome of this audit. If there is no reason for objection, it shall be sufficient to provide confirmation that the foundation assets have been managed and appropriated in accordance with the purpose of the foundation and in conformity with the provi-

sions of the law and the foundation documents. If this is not the case, or while performing its duties the controlling body ascertains circumstances which jeopardize the existence of the foundation, it shall notify the beneficiaries and the court as soon as it is aware of these circumstances.
The court shall if necessary take action in accordance with § 35.

5) If a controlling body has been setup, the beneficiary may require from the foundation and the controlling body the forwarding of the reports pursuant to para.4.

6) If the beneficiary asserts his rights pursuant to §9, the foundation shall be under an obligation to prove that there exists a controlling body which satisfies the requirements of para. 2 in conjunction with para. 3.

§ 12

4. Supervised Foundations

The beneficiary shall not be entitled to the rights pursuant to §9 if the foundation is subject to the supervision of the foundation supervisory authority (§ 29).

§ 13

IV. Foundation Assets

1) The minimum capital of the foundation is 30'000 Swiss francs. It may also be contributed in euros or US dollars and shall then amount to 30'000 euros or 30'000 US dollars.

2) If there is an additional contribution of assets to the foundation by the founder after its legally valid formation, this shall be treated as a subsequent endowment.

3) If there is a contribution of assets to the foundation by a third party, this shall be treated as a donation. The donor shall not thereby acquire the status of a founder.

4) If the foundation does not become effective until the death of the founder or after the termination of a legal entity, with regard to the contributions of the founder it shall be deemed to have come into being before his death or before the termination of the legal entity.

B. Formation and Coming into Being

I. In General

§ 14

1. Foundation Inter Vivos

1) The foundation is formed through a declaration of establishment. This requires the written form and authentication of the signatures of the founders.

2) In the case of direct representation or indirect representation pursuant to § 4, para. 3, the signature of the representative shall be authenticated on the foundation deed.

3) For direct representation, the representative shall require a special power of attorney from the founder referring to this transaction.

4) Common-benefit foundations and private-benefit foundations carrying on business run along commercial lines on the basis of special law, shall be entered in the Public Registry and shall thereby acquire the right of legal personality.

5) Other private-benefit foundations may be entered in the Public Registry. However, there is no legal obligation to do so.

§ 15

2. Foundation Mortis Causa

1) The foundation may also be formed by way of last will and testament or contract of inheritance in accordance with the applicable formal rules.

2) The entry of a foundation or the deposition of a notification of formation of a foundation formed by way of last will and testament cannot be undertaken until after the death of the founder or, in the case of a contract of inheritance, unless the founder stipulates otherwise, after the death of one of the founders.

3) § 14, paras. 4 and 5 shall apply mutatis mutandis.

§ 16

1. Foundation Deed (Articles)

1) The foundation deed shall in any event include:

1. the intention of the founder to form the foundation;
2. the name or corporate name and domicile of the foundation;
3. the dedication of specific assets, which must amount to at least the statutory minimum capital;
4. the purpose of the foundation, including the designation of tangible beneficiaries, or beneficiaries identifiable on the basis of objective criteria, or of the category of beneficiaries, unless the foundation is a common-benefit foundation or the beneficiaries are evident from the purpose of the foundation, or unless there is instead express reference to a supplementary foundation deed regulating this;
5. the date of formation of the foundation;
6. the duration of the foundation, if this is limited;
7. regulations on the appointment, dismissal, term of office and nature of the management (adoption of resolutions) and power of representation (authority to sign)of the foundation council;
8. a provision concerning the appropriation of the assets in the event of the dissolution of the foundation, with the application mutatis mutandis of item 4. above;
9. the last name, first name and place of residence or corporate name and domicile of the founder or, in the case of indirect representation (§4, para. 3), the last name, first name and place of residence or corporate name and domicile of the representative. In this connection, there shall be express mention of the activity as indirect representative.

2) Insofar as the following contents are regulated, these shall likewise be recorded in the foundation deed:

1. the indication that a supplementary foundation deed has been drawn up or may be drawn up;
2. the indication that regulations have been issued or may be issued;
3. the indication that other executive bodies have been formed or may be formed; further particulars of the composition, appointment, dismissal, term of office as well as duties may be stated in the supplementary foundation deed or in regulations;

4. the reservation of the right of revocation of the foundation or amendment of the foundation documents by the founder;
5. the reservation of the right to amend of the foundation deed or supplementary foundation deed by the foundation council or by another executive body pursuant to §§ 31 to 34;
6. the exclusion of enforcement pursuant to §36, para.1;
7. the reservation of the right of conversion (§41);
8. the provision that the foundation, although a private-benefit foundation, is subject to supervision (§ 29, para.1, sentence 2).

3) The provisions in accordance with para.1, items 1, 3 and 4 are deemed to be material within the meaning of the voidability proceedings.

§ 17

2. Supplementary Foundation Deed (Internal Regulations)

The founder may draw up a supplementary foundation deed if he has reserved for himself the right to do so (§16, para. 2, item 1). This may include those integral parts of the declaration of establishment which do not have to be recorded in the foundation deed.

§ 18

3. Regulations

For the further execution of the foundation deed or the supplementary foundation deed, the founder, the foundation council or another executive body of the foundation may issue internal directives in the form of regulations (§16, para.2, item 2) if the right to do so has been reserved in the foundation deed. Regulations issued by the founder take precedence over those of the foundation council or another executive body of the foundation.

§ 19

III. Entry in the Public Registry

1) If the foundation is subject to the obligation to register, each member of the foundation council shall, irrespective of his power of representation, be under an obligation to make an application for the foundation to be entered in the Public

Registry. The application shall be submitted in writing together with the original or certified copy of the foundation deed. The foundation council shall confirm that the statutory minimum capital is at the free disposal of the foundation. The representative also has authority to make the application.

2) If the entry is made although there is no obligation to register (§ 14, para. 5), the foundation council must in any event confirm that the tangible beneficiaries, or beneficiaries identifiable on the basis of objective criteria, or of the category of beneficiaries, have been designated by the founder, unless this is evident from the notified purpose of the foundation.

3) The entry shall contain the following information:

1. name or corporate name of the foundation;
2. domicile of the foundation;
3. purpose of the foundation;
4. date of formation of the foundation;
5. duration of the foundation, if this is limited;
6. organisation and representation, stating the last name, first name, date of birth, nationality and place of residence or registered office, or the corporate name and domicile of the members of the foundation council as well as the form of the signatory's power;
7. the last name, first name, date of birth, nationality and place of residence or registered office of the legal attorney, or the corporate name and domicile of the audit authority;
8. the last name, first name, date of birth, nationality and place of residence or registered office of the legal attorney, or corporate name and domicile of the representative.

4) The entry can also, if necessary, be made on the basis of the foundation deed by order of the judge in special non-contentious civil proceedings:

a) on the application of foundation participants;
b) on notification from the Office of Land and Public Registration or the probate authority; or
c) ex officio.

5) If there is an amendment to the purpose of a foundation not entered in the Public Registry such that an obligation to register arises, the members of the foundation council shall be under an obligation to make an application within

30 days for the foundation to be entered in the Public Registry in accordance with paras.1 and 3. Para.4 shall apply mutatis mutandis.

6) Notification of the entry shall be made within the meaning of Art.957, para.1, item 1.

IV. Notification of Formation

§ 20

1. Deposition of Notification of Formation

1) If the foundation is not subject to an obligation to register, for the purpose of monitoring the obligation to register and prevention of foundations with an illegal or immoral purpose as well for preventing the circumvention of possibly required supervision, each member of the foundation council shall be under an obligation to deposit, within 30 days following formation, notification of formation at the Office of Land and Public Registration. The representative also has authority to make the deposition. The accuracy of the information pursuant to para.2 shall be certified in writing by an attorney at law admitted in Liechtenstein, trustee or holder of an entitlement in accordance with Art.180a.

2) The notification of formation shall contain the following information:

1. name of the foundation;
2. domicile of the foundation;
3. purpose of the foundation;
4. date of formation of the foundation;
5. duration of the foundation, if this is limited;
6. the last name, first name, date of birth, nationality and place of residence or registered office of the legal attorney or the corporate name of the members of the foundation council as well as the form of the signatory's power;
7. the last name, first name, date of birth, nationality and place of residence or registered office of the legal attorney, or the corporate name and domicile of the legal representative;
8. confirmation that the tangible beneficiaries, or beneficiaries identifiable on the basis of objective criteria, or of the category of beneficiaries, have been designated by the founder, unless this is evident from the notified purpose of the foundation;

9. confirmation that the foundation is not entirely or predominantly intended to serve common-benefit purposes;
10. indication of whether pursuant to a provision of the foundation deed the foundation is subject to supervision; as well as
11. confirmation that the statutory minim um capital is at the free disposal of the foundation.

3) On each amendment of a circumstance contained in the notification of formation and on the existence of a reason for dissolution pursuant to § 39, para.1, the members of the foundation council shall be under an obligation, within 30 days, to deposit a notification of amendment at the Office of Land and Public Registration. The representative also has authority to make the deposition. The accuracy of the information in the notification of amendment shall be certified in writing by an attorney at law admitted in Liechtenstein, trustee or holder of an entitlement in accordance with Art.180a.

4) On the application of the foundation the Office of Land and Public Registration shall, following each legally executed notification, issue an official confirmation of the deposition of the notification of formation. It shall not issue an official confirmation of deposition if:

1. the notified purpose is illegal or immoral; or
2. it is evident from the notification that the foundation is subject to an obligation to register.

§ 21

2. Authority to Examine and Measures

1) As foundation supervisory authority the Office of Land and Public Registration is entitled to verify the accuracy of the deposited notifications of formation and amendment. For this purpose it may demand information from the foundation and through the controlling body or, if no such body has been setup, through an authorised third party, inspect the foundation documents, insofar as this is necessary for verification purposes.

2) Duplicates and copies are only permitted to be drawn up if the verification indicates that the notification of formation or amendment is inaccurate.

3) If the verification shows that the foundation is pursuing an illegal or immoral purpose, it shall be dissolved, subject to application of the general rules concerning the legal entities. The provisions concerning the amendment of the purpose, which has subsequently become impermissible, are reserved (§§ 31 and 33). If it becomes evident that the foundation is subject to an obligation to register, the entry shall be made by the Office of Land and Public Registration with the application of § 19, para.4. If the verification shows that the foundation is subject to supervision pursuant to §29, the foundation supervisory authority shall if necessary take the appropriate measures.

4) If the courts, the Office of the Public Prosecutor or an administrative authority become aware that the notification of formation or amendment has not been submitted or that the submitted notification of formation or amendment is inaccurate in content, a report shall be drawn up and forwarded to the foundation supervisory authority.

5) The Government may, by way of Executive Order, issue more detailed provisions concerning the exercise of the capacity to examine as well as the setting and imposition of fees by the foundation supervisory authority.
C. Revocation of the Declaration of Establishment

§ 22

I. By the Founder

A revocation of the declaration of establishment is only permissible:

1. if the foundation has not yet been entered in the Public Registry, where entry is required for the formation of the foundation;
2. if an entry of the foundation is not required and this is intended to become legally effective during the lifetime of the founder, up until authentication of his signature in the foundation deed;
3. in the case of foundations formed by way of last will and testament or contract of inheritance, in accordance with the relevantly applicable rules under the law of inheritance.

§ 23

II. Exclusion of Heirs

1) In the case of foundations formed by way of last will and testament or contract of inheritance, the heirs themselves acquire no right to revoke the declaration of establishment after the death of the testator and the founder, even if the foundation has not yet been registered in the Public Registry.

2) The heirs likewise have no right of revocation if the founder, in the case of the foundation inter vivos, has drawn up the foundation deed but has died prior to the entry in the Public Registry.

D . Organisation

I. Foundation Council

§ 24

1. In General

1) The foundation council manages the business of the foundation and represents it. It is responsible for the fulfilment of the purpose of the foundation, in compliance with the provisions in the foundation documents.

2) The foundation council shall be composed of at least two members. Legal entities can be a member of the foundation council.

3) Unless otherwise provided in the foundation deed, the appointment of the foundation council shall be effective for a period of office of three years, whereby a reappointment is permissible and the members can perform their activity for or without remuneration.

4) The provisions drawn up for the members of the foundation council also apply to possible representatives.

5) The members of the foundation council shall sign in such manner that they append their signature to the name of the foundation.

6) If members of the foundation council act without remuneration, liability for minor negligence may be excluded in the declaration of establishment, unless the creditors of the foundation are adversely affected thereby.

2. Special Obligations

§ 25

a) Asset Management

1) The foundation council shall manage the foundation assets in compliance with the founder's intention, in conformity with the purpose of the foundation and in accordance with the principles of good management.

2) The founder may lay down specific and binding management criteria in the foundation deed, supplementary foundation deed or in a regulation.

§ 26

b) Accounting

Foundations carrying on business run along commercial lines are subject to the general rules on accounting. In the case of all other foundations the foundation council shall, in respect of the management and appropriation of the foundation assets and taking into consideration the principles of orderly book-keeping, maintain appropriate records of the financial circumstances of the foundation and keep documentary evidence presenting a comprehensible account of the course of business and movement of the foundation assets. In addition, the foundation council shall maintain a schedule of assets showing the asset position and the asset investments. A rt.1059 shall apply mutatis mutandis.

§ 27

II. Audit Authority

1) For each foundation subject to the supervision of the foundation supervisory authority pursuant to §29 the court shall in special non contentious civil proceedings appoint an audit authority in accordance with Art.191a, para.1. In these proceedings the foundation supervisory authority shall have the status of a party.

2) The audit authority must be independent of the foundation. It is under an obligation to notify the court and the foundation supervisory authority of reasons which rule out its independence. The foundation supervisory authority may demand from the audit authority the certification and evidence necessary for the assessment of independence. The following persons in particular shall be excluded as audit authority:

1. members of another executive body of the foundation;
2. persons with an employment relationship to the foundation;
3. persons with close family connections with members of executive bodies of the foundation; or
4. persons who are beneficiaries of the foundation.

3) The founder may submit two proposals for the audit authority, stating his preference. If the founder has not taken advantage of this right, the foundation council may refer such a proposal to the court. Subject to para.2, the court shall as a rule appoint the preferentially proposed audit authority.

4) As executive body of the foundation, the audit authority shall be under an obligation

to verify once a year whether the foundation assets are being managed and appropriated in accordance with their purposes. It shall submit to the foundation council and the foundation supervisory authority a report on the outcome of this audit. If there is no reason for objection, it shall be sufficient to provide confirmation that the assets have been managed and appropriated in accordance with the purpose of the foundation and in conformity with the provisions of the law and the foundation documents. If while performing its duties the audit authority ascertains circumstances which jeopardize the existence of the foundation, it shall also report on this. The foundation supervisory authority may demand from the audit authority disclosure of all facts of which it has become aware during the course of its audit.

5) In the case of common-benefit foundations, the foundation supervisory authority may on request dispense with the appointment of an audit authority if the foundation only manages minor-value assets or if this seems expedient for other reasons. The Government shall by way of Executive Order lay down the prerequisites for exemption from the obligation to appoint an audit authority.

§ 28

III. Additional Executive Bodies

1) The founder may designate additional executive bodies, in particular to specify a beneficiary from the category of beneficiaries, to specify the time, level and condition of a distribution, to manage the assets, to advise and assist the foundation council, to monitor the administration of the foundation in order to safeguard the purpose of the foundation, to reserve consents or issue instructions, as well as to safeguard the interests of the foundation participants.

These executive bodies shall have no power of representation.

2) § 24, para.6 shall apply mutatis mutandis.

§ 29

E. Supervision

1) Common-benefit foundations shall be subject to the supervision of the foundation supervisory authority. The same applies to private benefit foundations which are subject to supervision pursuant to a provision in the foundation deed.
2) The foundation supervisory authority is the Office of Land and Public Registration.

3) The foundation supervisory authority shall ex officio ensure that the foundation assets are managed and appropriated in accordance with their purposes. It shall for this purpose be entitled to demand information from the foundation and, through the audit authority, to inspect the books and documents of the foundation. If the appointment of an audit authority has been dispensed with pursuant to §27, para. 5, the foundation supervisory authority shall as a rule itself exercise the right of inspection. In addition, it may obtain information from other administrative authorities and the courts and may through special non contentious civil proceedings apply to the judge for the required orders, such as the control and dismissal of the executive bodies of the foundation, carrying out of special audits or cancellation of resolutions of executive bodies of the foundation.

4) Furthermore, to oppose asset management and appropriation by the executive bodies of the foundation conflicting with the purpose of the foundation, each foundation participant may through special non contentious civil proceedings ap-

ply to the judge for an order for the required measures in accordance with para. 3. If there is a strong suspicion of a punishable act by an executive body of the foundation, the judge may also intervene ex officio, particularly on the basis of a communication from the Office of the Public Prosecutor. In such proceedings the foundation supervisory authority shall have the status of a party.

5) Unknown beneficiaries shall be ascertained by way of public citation proceedings on the application of the foundation supervisory authority.

6) The Government may, by way of Executive Order, issue more detailed provisions concerning the activity of the foundation supervisory authority as well as the setting and imposition of fees by the foundation supervisory authority.

F. Amendment

§ 30

I. Rights of the Founder to Revoke or Amend the Foundation Documents

1) The founder may in the foundation deed reserve for himself the right to revoke the foundation or to amend the declaration of establishment. These rights cannot be assigned or bequeathed. Should one of these rights be exercised by a direct representative, this shall require a special power of attorney referring to this transaction.

2) If the founder is a legal entity, it cannot reserve for itself the rights in accordance with para.1.

3) If the rights in accordance with para.1 are exercised by an indirect representative (§ 4, para.3), the legal consequences shall revert directly to the founder.

II. Rights of the Executive Bodies of the Foundation

§ 31

1. Amendment of the Purpose

1) An amendment of the purpose of the foundation by the foundation council or another executive body shall only be allowed if the purpose has become unachievable, impermissible or irrational or if circumstances have changed to the

extent that the purpose has acquired a quite different significance or effect, so that the foundation is estranged from the intention of the founder.

2) The amendment must comply with the presumed intention of the founder and the power to amend must be expressly reserved to the foundation council or to another executive body of the foundation in the foundation deed.

§ 32

2. Amendment of Other Contents

An amendment of other contents of the foundation deed or the supplementary foundation deed, such as in particular the organisation of the foundation, is permissible by the foundation council or another executive body if and insofar as the power of amendment is expressly reserved in the foundation deed to the foundation council or to another executive body of the foundation. The foundation council shall, safeguarding the purpose of the foundation, exercise the right to amend if there is a substantially justified reason to do so.

III. Rights of the Judge

1. Supervised Foundations

§ 33

a) Amendment of the Purpose

1) If a foundation is subject to the supervision of the foundation supervisory authority, the latter may through special non-contentious civil proceedings apply to the judge for the amendment of the purpose of the foundation if:

1. the purpose has become unachievable, impermissible or irrational or if circumstances have changed to the extent that the purpose has acquired a quite different significance or effect, so that the foundation is estranged from the intention of the founder; and
2. the foundation deed has not entrusted the foundation council or another executive body of the foundation with the amendment of the purpose.

2) The amendment must comply with the presumed intention of the founder.

3) The foundation participants shall also be entitled to submit an application; in this case the foundation supervisory authority shall have the status of a party.

§ 34

b) Amendment of Other Contents

1) If a foundation is subject to the supervision of the foundation supervisory authority, the latter may through special non-contentious civil proceedings apply to the judge for the amendment of other contents of the foundation deed or the supplementary foundation deed, such as in particular the organisation of the foundation, if

1. this is expedient to safeguard the purpose of the foundation, in particular to safeguard the continuing existence of the foundation and to safeguard the foundation assets; and
2. the foundation deed has not entrusted the foundation council or another executive body of the foundation with the amendment of the other contents.

2) The foundation participants shall also be entitled to submit an application; in this case the foundation supervisory authority shall have the status of a party.

§ 35

2. Other Foundations

1) In the case of foundations not subject to the supervision of the foundation supervisory authority the judge may, on the application of a foundation participant and, in urgent cases, if necessary on the basis of a communication from the foundation supervisory authority (§21, para.3) or from the Office of the Public Prosecutor, also ex officio in special non-contentious civil proceedings exercise the powers pursuant to §§33 and 34, and pronounce the orders required pursuant to §29, para.3. There is deemed to be an urgent case in particular if there is a strong suspicion of a punishable act by an executive body of the foundation.

2) Unknown beneficiaries may on application be ascertained by the judge in public citation proceedings.

§ 36

G. Provisions under the Law of Enforcement

1) In the case of family foundations, the founder may provide that the creditors of beneficiaries shall not be permitted to deprive these beneficiaries of their entitlement to a beneficial interest or prospective beneficial interest acquired without valuable consideration, or individual claims arising from such an interest, by way of safeguarding proceedings, compulsory enforcement or bankruptcy. In the case of mixed family foundations, such a directive can only be issued insofar as the entitlement concerned serves the purposes of the family foundation.

2) If a creditor of the foundation can obtain no satisfaction from the foundation assets, and the founder has not yet fully provided the allocated assets, the foundation council shall be under an obligation to provide the creditor with the information he requires to take legal action. In the event of bankruptcy of the foundation, this applies mutatis mutandis with regard to the administrator of the estate.

§ 37

H. Liability

1) With regard to the creditors of the foundation, only the foundation assets serve as security for the debts of the foundation. There is no obligation to put up further security.

2) The foundation council is only permitted to make distributions to beneficiaries to fulfil the purpose of the foundation if claims by creditors of the foundation are not thereby curtailed.

§ 38

I. Challenge

1) The contribution of assets to the foundation may be challenged by the heirs or the creditors in the same manner as a gift.

2) The founder and his heirs may challenge the foundation on account of deficiencies of intention in the same manner as the rules concerning deficiencies in the conclusion of a contract, even after the registration of the foundation.

K. Dissolution and Termination

§ 39

I. Reasons for Dissolution

1) The foundation shall be dissolved if:

1. bankruptcy proceedings have been initiated in respect of the foundation assets;
2. the resolution, whereby the initiation of bankruptcy proceedings has been rejected due to the probable insufficiency of assets to cover the costs of the bankruptcy proceedings, has achieved legal force;
3. the court has ordered dissolution;
4. the foundation council has adopted a legally valid resolution on dissolution.

2) The foundation council shall adopt a resolution on dissolution as soon as:

1. it has received a legally admissible revocation by the founder;
2. the purpose of the foundation has been achieved or is no longer achievable;
3. the duration envisaged in the foundation deed has expired;
4. other grounds for dissolution are stated in the foundation deed.

3) The resolution on dissolution in accordance with para.2 shall be adopted unanimously unless otherwise provided in the foundation deed. In the case of foundations subject to the supervision of the foundation supervisory authority, the foundation council shall notify the supervisory authority of the resolution on dissolution.

4) If no resolution in accordance with para.2 is adopted despite the existence of aground for dissolution, in the case of foundations not subject to the supervision of the foundation supervisory authority the judge shall, on the application of foundation participants, dissolve the foundation in special non-contentious civil proceedings; in the case of other foundations, application for dissolution may also be made by the foundation supervisory authority.

5) If a resolution on dissolution is adopted in accordance with para.2 although there is no ground for dissolution, in the case of foundations not subject to the supervision of the foundation supervisory authority the judge shall, on the application of foundation participants, cancel the foundation council's resolution on dissolution in special non-contentious civil proceedings; in the case of other foundations, the foundation supervisory authority shall also be entitled to apply.

6) If the foundation carries on business run along commercial lines without complying with the prerequisites pursuant to § 1, para.2, the judge shall, on the application of a foundation participant or ex officio, adjudicate on the dissolution of the foundation if the foundation has not complied with a legally binding restraining order within a reasonable time limit.

§ 40

II. Liquidation and Termination

1) The general provisions on the legal entity shall apply to the liquidation and termination of the foundation.

2) The provisions concerning the public notice to creditors shall not apply to foundations not entered in the Public Registry.

3) On the termination of a foundation, the Office of Land and Public Registration shall issue a certificate of cancellation in the form of an extract from the Public Registry in the case of registered foundations, or an official confirmation in the case of unregistered foundations.
4) If the foundation is subject to the supervision of the foundation supervisory authority, the foundation council shall notify the foundation supervisory authority of the termination of the foundation. If the foundation is entered in the Public Registry, an extract from the Public Registry shall also be submitted. The legal representative also has authority to notify.

5) Subsequently discovered assets of a foundation shall be liquidated in accordance with the principles concerning subsequent liquidation (Art.139). In the case of foundations subject to the supervision of the foundation supervisory authority, the foundation council shall inform the authority without delay about subsequently discovered assets. The legal representative also has authority to notify.

§ 41

L. Conversion

Subject to the mandatory preservation of the essence of the foundation in general and the intention of the founder in particular, a private-benefit foundation can be converted, without being wound up or liquidated, into an establishment (Anstalt) organised in accordance with the law on foundations, or a trust enterprise with legal personality organised in accordance with the law on foundations, by way of a deed drawn up in due form, if the conversion:

1. is foreseen upon defining the conditions of conversion the in the foundation deed; and
2. is oriented to the realisation of the purpose of the foundation.

Arts. 553 to 570

Repealed

Art. 955a, para.1

1) **Inspection, extracts, copies** or certificates of files and **documents deposited** pursuant to Art. 990, as well as of notices and documentary evidence of foundations and trusts not entered in the Public Registry or of notifications of formation or amendment of foundations not entered in the Public Register, may only be demanded by depositors and the person authorised for this purpose, as well as by universal successors. The right is reserved to disclose to domestic criminal prosecution authorities, the Financial Intelligence Unit (FIU) and the Financial Market Authority (FMA) the identity of the representative or the person authorised to accept the post delivery. The Government shall issue more detailed provisions by way of Executive Order.

§66cSchlT (Final Heading)

5. Obligations of Foundations concerning Application to Register, Deposition and Declaration

1) On information from the foundation supervisory authority, the Court of Justice of Liechtenstein may in special non-contentious civil proceedings impose a fine of up to 10’000 Swiss francs on any person who as a member of the foundation council:

1. fails to apply for registration of a foundation in the Public Registry contrary to Art.552, §19, para.5; or
2. fails to deposit at the Office of Land and Public Registration a notification of formation contrary to Art.552, § 20, para.1 in conjunction with para.2 or a notification of amendment contrary to Art.552, §20, para.3.

2) The fine in accordance with para.1 may be repeatedly imposed until a lawful status is produced.

3) Any person who intentionally makes a declaration incorrect in substance pursuant to Art.552 §20, para.1 in conjunction with para.2 or pursuant to Art.552, § 20, para.3, shall be sentenced by the Court of Justice of Liechtenstein to pay a fine of up to 50'000 Swiss francs on account of a misdemeanour, and in the event of non-collectability to a term of imprisonment of up to six months. If the perpetrator acts negligently, he shall be sentenced by the Court of Justice of Liechtenstein to pay a fine of up to 20'000 Swiss francs on account of a misdemeanour, and in the event of non-collectability to a term of imprisonment of up to three months.

4) Any person who as an attorney at law, trustee or holder of an entitlement in accordance with Art. 180a intentionally or negligently provides an incorrect confirmation of the information pursuant to Art. 552, §20, para.1 in conjunction with para.2 or pursuant to Art.552, § 20, para.3 shall likewise be punished in accordance with para.3.

5) The right to take disciplinary measures is reserved.

II. Transitional Provisions

Art.1

Application of the New Law to Existing Foundations

1) Unless otherwise provided below, previous law shall apply to foundations existing at the time of entry into force of this Law.

2) If a change of circumstance, which pursuant to Art.552, §20, para.3 is to be reported to the Office of Land and Public Registration, initially occurs after the entry into force of this Law, the members of the foundation council shall submit a report containing the information in accordance Art.552, §20, para.2. With regard to the obligation and authority to report, as well as the confirmation of the particulars, Art. 552, §20, para.1 shall be applied mutatis mutandis, and with regard to the verification of accuracy §21 shall be applied mutatis mutandis. Art. 552, §20, para.3 shall apply to all subsequent amendments.

3) If a report is submitted in accordance with para.2, or if such a report had already been submitted, the foundation can be requested to surrender the foundation deed and the other documents which pursuant to Art.554 have, in their hitherto applicable versions, been deposited at the Office of Land and Public Registration.

4) Art.107, para.4a and Art.552, §§3,5 to 12,21,26,27,29 and 31 to 35 shall also apply to foundations which were formed prior to the entry into force of this Law .The members of the foundation council shall, within six months after the entry into force of this Law and enclosing an extract from the Public Registry, report to the foundation supervisory authority foundations which pursuant to Art.552, §29 are subject to the supervision of the foundation supervisory authority. The founder shall be entitled to setup a controlling body in accordance with Art.552, § 11, para.2 in conjunction with para.3, even if he has not reserved this right for himself. If the foundation has been formed by an indirect representative (Art.552, §4, para.3), the principal (authorizer) shall be deemed to be the founder; Art.552, §30, para.3 shall be applied mutatis mutandis. If the founder is deceased or is without legal capacity to contract, a controlling body can be setup by the foundation council pursuant to Art.552 §11, para.2, item 1 in conjunction with para.3. The controlling body must be set up within six months following the entry into force of this Law. In the case of common-benefit foundations (Art.552, §2) and private-benefit foundations which on a special statutory basis carry on business run along commercial lines and are not entered in the Public Registry, every member of the foundation council shall be under an obligation to apply for registration in the Public Registry within six months following the entry into force of this Law; Art.552, §19 shall apply mutatis mutandis.

5) If a controlling body is setup pursuant to para.4, the audit in accordance with Art.552, §11, para.4 or Art.552, §27 para.4 must initially take place by 30June2010.

Art.2

Adaptation to the New Law

1) If, with regard to a foundation formed prior to 31 December 2003, the formation documents do not satisfy the requirements in accordance with Art.552, §16, para.1, item 4, a lawful status shall be produced by 31 December 2009.

2) The founder shall be entitled to amend the declaration of establishment in order to produce a lawful status, even if he has not reserved for himself such a right. If the foundation has been formed by an indirect representative (Art. 552, §4, para.3), the principal (authorizer) shall be deemed to be the founder; Art.552, §30, para.3 shall apply mutatis mutandis.

3) If the founder is deceased or is without legal capacity to contract, the declaration of establishment can be amended by the foundation council in a manner in conformity with Art.552, §16, para.1, item 4. Amendment by the foundation council is only permissible if the intention of the founder can be ascertained. As a means of ascertaining the intention of the founder, only documents originating from the founder, a direct or indirect representative involved in the formation or an executive body of the foundation shall be permitted to be used. If the document does not originate from the founder, only documents drawn up prior to 1st December 2006 shall be permitted to be used.

4) The foundation council of all foundations not entered in the Public Registry shall, by way of express declaration, provide the Office of Land and Public Registration with express confirmation that the foundation documents comply with Art.552, §16, para.1, item 4. Insofar as applicable, this declaration shall not be permitted to be submitted until a lawful status has been produced. Art.552, §21 shall apply mutatis mutandis to the verification of the accuracy of the declaration.

5) If a lawful status has not been produced by 30th June 2010, the foundation council shall adopt a resolution on dissolution pursuant to Art.552, §39, which shall be reported to the Office of Land and Public Registration.

6) If the report in accordance with para.5 has not been submitted by 1st August 2010, the Office of Land and Public Registration shall request the foundation council to submit a declaration in accordance with para.4 within a period of grace of six months or to report the resolution on dissolution. If this time limit also expires without submission, the Office of Land and Public Registration shall notify the judge; the latter shall in special non-contentious civil proceedings declare the foundation dissolved.

7) If a foundation is dissolved in accordance with para.5 or 6, the Office of Land and Public Registration shall be entitled to demand all executive bodies of the foundation to provide information on the progress of the liquidation. If it proves that the liquidator is dilatory in carrying out the liquidation, the judge can, in

special non-contentious civil proceedings, on the application of foundation participants, the Office of Land and Public Registration or ex officio, remove the liquidator from office and appoint another suitable person as liquidator.
Art.3

Penal Provisions

1) If, contrary to Art.1, para.2, a report is not submitted, §66c, paras. 1 and 2 SchlT shall apply mutatis mutandis.

2) Any person who makes a declaration incorrect in substance in accordance with Art.1, para.2 or Art.2, para.4 or intentionally fails to submit a report pursuant to Art.1, para.4 or who wrongfully declares that he is not subject to the supervision of the foundation supervisory authority, or who as an attorney at law, trustee or holder of an entitlement in accordance with Art.180a intentionally or negligently provides an incorrect confirmation of the information pursuant to Art.1, para.2 in conjunction with Art.552, §20, para.1 of the Persons and Companies Act, shall be sentenced by the Court of Justice of Liechtenstein to pay a fine of up to 50'000 Swiss francs on account of a misdemeanour, and in the event of non-collectability to a term of imprisonment of up to six months. If the perpetrator acts negligently, he shall be sentenced by the Court of Justice of Liechtenstein to pay a fine of up to 20'000 Swiss francs on account of a misdemeanour, and in the event of non-collectability to a term of imprisonment of up to three months.
3) The right to take disciplinary measures is reserved.

Art.4

Application of the New Law to Existing Establishments

1) Art.107, para.4a as well as Art.552, §2, para.4, §§26,27,29,31 to 35,36, para.1, and 41 shall also be applied mutatis mutandis to those establishments pursuant to Art.551, para. 2 of the Persons and Companies Act which were formed prior to the entry into force of this Law.

2) The members of the management of an establishment, which pursuant to Art.551, para.2 in conjunction with Art.552, §29 is subject to the supervision of the foundation supervisory authority, shall report this to the foundation supervisory authority, enclosing an extract from the Public Registry, within six months following the entry into force of this Law .

3) Any person who as a member of the management pursuant to para.2 intentionally or negligently fails or wrongfully declares that he is not subject to the supervision of the foundation supervisory authority, shall be punished in accordance with Art.3, para.2.

III.

Entry into Force

Subject to the expiration of the referendum time limit without a referendum having been taken, this Law shall enter into force on 1st April 2009, or otherwise on the date on which it is announced.

On behalf of the Reigning Prince:

signed Alois, Hereditary Prince

signed Otmar Hasler, Prime Minister

Bibliography

ABT Daniel / WEIBEL Thomas, Praxiskommentar Erbrecht: Nachlassplanung, Nachlassabwicklung, Willensvollstreckung, Prozessführung, Basel 2007.

ACHERMANN Hubert, Studien zu Auslegungsproblemen des Abkommens zwischen der Schweizerischen Eidgenossenschaft und dem Fürstentum Liechtenstein über die Anerkennung und Vollstreckung von gerichtlichen Entscheidungen und Schiedssprüchen in Zivilsachen vom 25. April 1968, (Diss.Bern 1983) Zollikerberg 1983.

AEBI-MÜLLER Regina Elisabeth, Die optimale Begünstigung des überlebenden Ehegatten: Güter-, erb-, obligationen- und versicherungsrechtliche Vorkehren, unter Berücksichtigung des Steuerrechts, 2. A., Bern 2007.

AEPLI Hans, Das Treuhandgeschäft, in: Vertragsverhältnisse im Treuhandwesen, Treuhändertagung '95 Luzern, Luzern 1995.

ALEXANDER Lukas, Anstalten und Stiftungen, verselbständigte Vermögensmassen im Römischen Recht, Köln 2003.

ARTER Oliver, Commercial Trust, in: Entwicklungen im Gesellschaftsrecht II, Bern 2007, 307-343.

ARTER Oliver / JOERG Florian S., Stimmbindung mit Aktionärbindungsvertrag: Voting Trusts als Alternative, STH 81, 2007, 474-476.

BAECHINGEN Patricia, Die Reformbestrebungen der EU im Berich des Erbrechts – Lösungsansätze in Anlehnung an die Fragestellung des Grünbuchs, AJP 16, 2007, 1532-1541.

BAKER Andrew, Ein Vergleich zwischen der liechtensteinischen Treuhänderschaft und der liechtensteinischen Stiftung, aus dem Blickwinkel des common law, Diplomarbeiten 2000 (Recht) des Nachdiplomstudiengangs Treuhandwesen der Fachhochschule Liechtenstein, (Schriften zum liechtensteinischen Recht, Band 8), Vaduz 2000, 7-44.

BARBETTA Gian Paolo, Foundations in Italy, in: ANHEIER / TOEPLER (Hg.), Private Funds, Public Purposes, New York, 1999.

BARTHOLD Beat, Aussonderung von Treugut im schweizerischen Partikularkonkurs, (Schweizer Studien zum internationalen Recht, Band 99) Zürich 1997, (3. Kapitel: Fürstentum Liechtenstein), 58-119.

BATLINER Heinz, Die Stiftung im Fürstentum Liechtenstein, 4. A., Vaduz 1986.

–, Die privatrechtliche Anstalt im Fürstentum Liechtenstein, Vaduz 1985.

BATLINER Herbert, Die Stiftung im Fürstentum Liechtenstein, Vaduz 1996.
–, Die Treuhänderschaft: einschliesslich das Treunternehmen im Fürstentum Liechtenstein, Vaduz 1996.
BAUER Carsten, Trust und Anstalt als Rechtsformen liechtensteinischen Rechts, (Wirtschaftsrecht und Wirtschaftsverfassung, Band 15) Frankfurt am Main/ Berlin/Bern/New York/Paris/Wien 1995.
BAUMANN Hanspeter, Psychologische und organisatorische Aspekte der Nachfolge in Familienunternehmen, STH 81, 2007, 323-327.
BAUMGARTNER Hans / BUEHLER Simon, Nachfolgemanagement im KMU als interdisziplinäre Herausforderung: Generationenwechsel oder Eigentumsübergang in KMU erfordern aktives Management und die richtigen Partner, STH 81, 2007, 348-351.
BAUR Georges, Beitritt des Fürstentums Liechtenstein zum Haager TrustÜbereinkommen, Jus & News 2002, 263-278.
BAUR Leonid, Der IPO-Prozess im Überblick, ST 81, 2007, 360-363.
BECK Emil, Zur Frage des Impedimentum ligaminis im liechtensteinischen internationalen Privatrechts, Vaduz 1962.
BECK Wilhelm, Unternehmungen und selbständige Vermögensverwaltungen im Fürstentum Liechtenstein, Vaduz 1931.
BETSCHART Philipp, Grundzüge der Trustbesteuerung – dargestellt anhand der Praxis des Kantons Zürich, StR 62, 2007, 158-164.
BEUSCH Michael, Von der Erbschaftssteuer für Pflegekosten bis zur Integrations- und Infrastruktursteuer für Unternehmen: ein Blick auf aktuelle steuerrechtliche Nebenschauplätze und Kuriositäten, StR 82, 2007, 303-317.
BIEDERMANN Klaus, Trust (Treuhänderschaft), establishment (Anstalt) and foundation (Stiftung) under Liechtenstein law, Vaduz 1983.
–, Die Treuhänderschaft des liechtensteinischen Rechts: dargestellt an ihrem Vorbild, dem Trust des Common Law: Unter Berücksichtigung des Gesetzes betreffend das Treuunternehmen, (Abhandlungen zum schweizerischen Recht, Neue Folge Band 470) Bern 1981.
BIEDERMANN Klaus / PEASE Richard, The Law of Trusts in Liechtenstein, Geneva/Vaduz 1980.
BIERI René, Abgrenzung der Erbschafts- und Schenkungssteuer von der harmonisierten Einkommenssteuer, dargestellt am Beispiel der Leistungen aus der reinen Risikoversicherungen im Todesfall, StR 62, 2007, 93-108.
BOECKLE Hermann, Gründung, Vewaltung, Auflösung von Stiftungen und Abgrenzung zu anderen Verbandspersonen, LJZ 2001, 63-72.
BOECKLE Hermann / GRABHER Heinz, Die Entstehung und Überwachung der Stiftung, Festschrift für Peter Marxer, Vaduz 1993, 35.

BOECKLI Peter, Der angelsächsische Trust: Zivilrecht und Steuerrecht, Zürich/ St. Gallen 2007, Sonderdruck aus der Zeitschrift Gesellschafts- und Kapitalmarktrecht 2007, 209-235, STR 62, 2007, 710-730 und 774-795.

BOEHMER Justus Henning, Ius ecclesiasticum protestantiom, Halae Magdeburgicae, 1743-45

BOESCH Harald, Liechtensteinisches Stiftungsrecht, Bern 2005.

–, Zur Anwendung der allgemeinen Vorschriften des Personen- und Gesellschaftsrechts auf die Stiftung, Festschrift für Herbert Batliner, Vaduz 2004, 193-233.

–, Auskunfts- und Rechnungslegungsanspruch des Pflichtteilsberechtigten gegenüber einer liechtensteinischen Stiftung, LJZ 2003, 55-63.

–, Stiftungsrecht im Fürstentum Liechtenstein, Heft 3 des Instituts für Stiftungsrecht und das Recht der Non-Profit-Organisationen der Bucerius Law School Hamburg, Hamburg 2003.

–, Liechtensteinische Trustrezeption und Anwendungsbereich der Bestimmungen über die Treuhänderschaft: Neue Erkenntnisse oder nur alter Wein in neuen Schläuchen, LJZ 2001, 42-54, 73-92.

–, Judikaturwende im liechtensteinischen Treuhandrecht: Eine Nachlese und ein Ausblick, LJZ 2000, 87-93.

–, Bemerkungen zur Haftung des Treuhänders für falsche Angaben und zu anderen aktuellen Fragen des liechtensteinischen Treuhandrechts, LJZ 1999, 73-81.

–, Schweizerische Spuren im liechtensteinischen Treuhandrecht, ZSR 119, 2000, 175-220.

–, Trust und Fiduzia im Liechtensteinischen Recht, Jus & News 1997, 12 ff.

–, „Stifterrechte" wie Gründerrechte bei der Anstalt übertrag- und vererbbar?, Jus & News 1997, 265-280.

–, Die liechtensteinische Treuhänderschaft zwischen trust und Treuhand: Eine rechtsdogmatische und -vergleichende Untersuchung aufgrund der Weisungsbestimmung des Art. 918 liecht. PGR, (Schriften zum liechtensteinischen Recht, Band 2) Mauren 1995.

BOUTIN Gilberto, La fundacion de interes privado en el derecho panameño y comparado, Panamá 2000.

BRAUCH Philip Kurt, The charitable company im englischen Recht, Frankfurt am Main 2001.

BREITSCHMID Peter, Das Bankkonto im Erbgang – Probleme rund um die Vermögensverwaltung vor und nach dem Tod, Successio 1 (2007) 220-238.

–, Erben in der Schweiz, Glück oder Last, verdient oder unverdient, mit Bemerkungen über den beschränkten Neuigkeitswert von Studien, Successio 1, 2007, 202-210.

–, Das Erbrecht im 19. und 21. Jahrhundert: der Konflikt zwischen Status, Realbeziehung und erblasserischer Freiheit, Successio 1, 2007, 6-18.

–, Die Erbschaftssteuer im verfassungsrechtlichen Schussfeld, Successio 1, 2007, 136-137.

–, Das Gut rinnt wie das Blut, oder Wie Gesellschaft, Gesetz oder Individuen es wollen: Fragen zu Erben und (Kenntnis der) Abstammung, Successio 1, 2007, 142-149.

–, Formvorschriften im Testamentsrecht *de lege lata / de lege ferenda*, rechtsvergleichend, dargestellt insbesondere am Beispiel des eigenhändigen Testaments, Diss. Zürich 1982.

BRUCK Eberhard, Über Römisches Recht im Rahmen der Kulturgeschichte, Berlin/Heidelberg 1954.

BRUNS Carl, Fontes iuris romani antiqui, Tübingen 1909.

BUECHLER Andrea, Eingetragene Partnerschaft, Bern 2007.

BUEHLER Alfred, Die Stiftung nach dem Recht des Fürstentums Liechtenstein, Hamburg 1980.

–, Die Anstalt: eine privatrechtliche Gesellschaftsform im Fürstentum Liechtenstein, Hamburg 1977.

BUEHLER Theodor, Wann beginnt das Jahr, nach dessen Ablauf die erbrechtliche Ungültigkeits- bzw. Herabsetzungsklage verjäht? SJZ 69, 1973, 21.

BUEHRER Gerold, Unternehmensnachfolge – Steuerpolitik im Dienste der KMU und unserer Volkswirtschaft, STH 81, 2007, 310-313.

BUNDESVERBAND DEUTSCHER STIFTUNGEN, Zahlen, Daten, Fakten, Berlin 2001.

BURCKHARDT Jean-Louis, Leitfaden für Stiftungen und die Funktion der Bank bei deren Errichtung und Verwaltung: unter Berücksichtigung des schweizerischen und liechtensteinischen Rechts, (Publikation der Swiss Banking School Zürich, Nr. 129) Bern/Stuttgart/Wien 1996.

BUSCHOR Thomas, Nachlassplanung (‚estate planning‘) nach schweizerischem internationalem Erbrecht, Diss. Zürich 1994.

CANDRIAN Daniel, Scheidung und Trennung im internationalen Privatrecht der Schweiz: unter Berücksichtigung des deutschen, österreichischen, französischen, italienischen, spanischen und liechtensteinischen Rechts, (Diss. St.Gallen) St. Gallen 1994.

CASNER James, Estate planning, Fifth Edition, Boston/Toronto/London 1988.

CASPERS Wolfgang / WAGNER Jürgen / KUENZLE Hans Rainer, Die Liechtensteinische Stiftung: Referate der Tagung „Stiftungsnovellierung: wohin geht die Reise?“ vom 27. Juni 2002 and der Fachhochschule Liechtenstein, (Schweizer Schriften zur Vermögensberatung und zum Vermögensrecht, Band 4) Zürich 2002.

CHCL FIDUCIARY GROUP, The Republic of Panama as a Jurisdiction, Panama 2005.
CLAUSS Jörg / BLOCKWITZ Manuela, Leitfaden zur Stiftungserrichtung in der Schweiz, Checkliste und Musterverträge, Herausgeber: Handelskammer Deutschland-Schweiz, Zürich 2003.
COING Helmut, Handbuch des Stiftungsrechts, München 1986.
CRETTI Sibilla, Le Trust – Aspects fiscaux, 2. ed., Basel/Genf/München 2007.
DANON Robert, Note sur le statut du trust en droit fiscal suisse, StR 82, 2007, 376-379.
–, Switzerland's direct and international taxation of private express trusts: with particular references to US, Canadian and New Zealand trust taxation, (Droit fiscal Suisse et international, vol. 1) Zürich 2004.
DE GIORGI Maria Vita, Stiftungen im italienischen Recht, Hopt/Reuter, Europäisches Stiftungsrecht, Köln 2001.
DE POVER Marie-France, Trust, fiducie administratiekantoor, foundation du Liechtenstein, Bruxelles 2001.
DEVISME Marjorie, Présentation synthétique de la réforme du droit des Successions en France, ZBGR 88, 2007, 253-262.
DREXEL Cornelia, Die Sorgfaltspflichten des liechtensteinischen Treuhänders, Diplomarbeiten 2000 (Recht) des Nachdiplomstudiengangs Treuhandwesen der Fachhochschule Liechtenstein, (Schriften zum liechtensteinischen Recht, Band 8) Schaan 2000.
DRUEY Jean Nicolas, Der Anspruch der Erben auf Information, BJM 1988, 113.
–, Grundriss des Erbrechts, 3. Auflage, Bern 2002.
DUDEN Gustav, Vorschriften und Tatsachen zur deutschen Stiftung, Die Stiftung, 21. Tagung der DACH in Wien vom 16.-18.9.1999, Wien 2000.
EHRAT Felix R. / FREY Thomas, Nachfolgeplanung aus ehegüter- und erbrechtlicher Sicht, STH 81, 2007, 328-333.
EHRENZWEIG Armin, System des österreichischen allgemeinen Privatrechts, Band 2: Obligationen-, Familien- und Erbrecht, 4. A., Wien 1907.
EICHNER Mark, Die Rechtsstellung von Treugebern und Begünstigten aus Trust und Treuhand: unter besonderer Berücksichtigung des Haager Trust Übereinkommens und des Aussonderungsanspruchs, Basel 2007 (Schriftenreihe für Internationales Recht Nr.107).
EISELBERG Maximilian, Die österreichische Privatstiftung – privatnütziges System ohne staatliche Aufsicht, in: Achermann/Künzle/Roth, Die Liechtensteinische Stiftung „Stiftungsnovellierung – wohin geht die Reise?“, Schweizer Schriften zur Vermögensberatung und zum Vermögensrecht, Schriftenreihe von KPMG private, Vaduz 2002.

EITEL Paul, Hundert Jahre Begünstigung des Ehegatten nach Art. 473 ZGB, in: ZGB: gestern – heute – morgen, Festgabe zum Schweizerischen Juristentag 2007, hrsg. v. Daniel Girsberger und Michele Luminati, Zürich/Basel/Genf 2007, 139-180.
–, Aktuelle Entwicklungen im türkischen Erbrecht aus schweizerischer Sicht, in: Rezeption und Autonomie, hrsg. v. Roland von Büren, Susan Emmenegger und Thomas Koller, Bern 2007, 125-146.
–, Die Nacherbeinsetzung in Theorie und Praxis, Successio 1, 2007, 82-107.
–, Das Recht der Errungenschaftsbeteiligung als „Steinbruch" für das Recht der Nacherbeneinsetzung, in: Festschr. für Bruno Huwiler, hrsg. von Pascal Pichonnaz, Nedim Peter Vogt und Stephan Wolf, Bern 2007, 205-218.
–, Die Stiftung als Instrument zur Perpetuierung von Aktiengesellschaften?, in: Festschr. für Hans Michael Riemer, hrsg. v. Peter Breitschmid, Wolfgang Portmann, Heinz Rey und Dieter Zobl, Bern 2007, 79-97.
–, Zivilrechtliche, insbesondere erbrechtliche Aspekte der Unternehmensnachfolge, in: Weiterbildungsanlass Unternehmensnachfolge, hrsg. v. Luzerner Notarenverband, Luzern 2007.
ELKUCH Ivo, Personen- und Gesellschaftsrecht des Fürstentums Liechtenstein, 4. A., Schaan 2001.
–, Sachenrecht des Fürstentums Liechtenstein, Schaan 1999.
–, Ehegesetz des Fürstentums Liechtenstein, Schaan 1998.
ESTRIBÍ Ch., Heriberto, Fundaciones de Interés Privado, Guía Práctica, Panamá, 2002.
FEENSTRA Robert, L'histoire des fondations, in Tjidschrift voor Rechtsgeschiedenis, Bd. 24, 1956, 381 ff.
FELBER Markus, Jusletter 23. Juli 2001, *www.weblaw.ch/jusletter*.
FELD Daniel E / CATHERALL John, Exempt Organisations Tax Digest, 2. Edition, Valhalla 1996.
FERID Murad / SONNENBERGER Hans-Jürgen, Das französische Zivilrecht, 2. Aufl., Heidelberg 1994.
FERREIRA Francisco Pérez, Las fundacioes de interés privado en Panamá, Portobelo, Panamá 1998.
FERRER-MORGAN Eduardo, Introduction and Analysis of the Origin and Intent of each article of the new Panamanian law on Private Foundations, „The Private Foundation under Panamanian Law", Morgan & Morgan, Panamá 1995.
FISCHER Monika, Was tun, wenn jemand stirbt: ein Ratgeber der Stiftung für Konsumentenschutz, Bern 2007.
FISHMAN James / SCHWARZ Stephen, Non-profit Organizations, 2. Aufl., New York 2000.

FORBES-JAEGER David / GSTOEHL Martin, Liechtenstein Foundation and Anglo-Saxon Trust Compared, Trusts & Trustees 3, 1997, No. 10, 6-12.

FRANKHAUSER Roland, Gesetzliches Ehegattenerbrecht in der (Ehe-) Krise, Familienpraxis Schweiz 8, 2007, 229-255.

FREEMAN Douglas, The handbook on Private Foundations, New York 1991.

FRICK Mario, Lugano-Übereinkommen: Vor- und Nachteile für den liechtensteinischen Finanzdienstleistungssektor (am Beispiel der Banken), Jus & News 205, 275-294.

–, Sind ausländsiche Urteile taugliche Urkunden für eine Rechtsöffnung in Liechtenstein?: Anmerkungen zum Beschluss den liechtensteinischen Obergerichts vom 22.08.2002 zu 7 Rö 2002.3, Jus & News 2003, 7-16.

–, Die Anerkennung und Vollstreckung ausländischer Entscheidungen in Zivilsachen im Fürstentum Liechtenstein: unter Berücksichtigung des schweizerischen, österreichischen und deutschen Rechts, (St. Gallen Studien zum internationalen Recht, Band 11) St. Gallen 1992.

FRICK Rony, Die Aktienarten nach liechtensteinischem Aktienrecht, (Diss. Bern 1975) Schaan 1977.

FRICK-TABARELLI Marion, Die besondere Bedeutung der Treuhänderschaft gemäss Art. 897 ff. PGR für die privatrechtliche Stiftung nach liechtensteinischem Recht, (Schriften zum liechtensteinischen Recht, Band 1) Mauren 1993.

GALGANO Francesco, Le associazioni, le fondazioni, i comitati, Padua 1996.

–, Delle persone giuridiche, nel Commentario del Codico Civile a cura di Scialoja e Branca, Libro primo, Delle persone e delle famigli, Bologna/Roma 1969.

GASSER Johannes, Neues zum Internationalen Insolvenzrecht in Liechtenstein, LJZ 2004, 24-36.

–, Quo vadis Trust im Stiftungsrecht, in: Festschr. Herbert Batliner, hrsg. v. First Advisory Group, Vaduz 2004, 150-173.

GASSMANN Richard, Asset Tracing trotz Bankgeheimnis: Die Bank im Visier des Gläubigers ihres ausländischen Kunden, in: Festschr. für Kurt Siehr, hg. v.Peter Johannes Weber, Marc Weber, Riccardo Seitz und Hans Rainer Künzle, Zürich 2001, 25-43.

GEISER Thomas, Partnerschaftsgesetz und Notariat, AJP 16, 2007, 3-12.

–, Sorgfalt in der Vermögensverwaltung durch den Willensvollstrecker, Successio 1, 2007, 178-184.

GEISER Thomas / GREMPER Philipp, Zürcher Kommentar zum Partnerschaftsgesetz, Zürich 2007.

GIRSBERGER Daniel / HEINI Anton / KELLER Max / KREN Jolanta / SIEHRT Kurt / VISCHER Frank / VOLKEN Paul, Zürcher Kommentar zum IPRG, Zürich/Basel/Genf 2004.

GLAUS Hannes, Irrtumsanfechtung und Auslegung beim Testament, Diss. Zürich 1982.
GRETER Jürg, US-Quellensteuern bei Liechtensteiner Stiftungen und Offshore Trusts: Neue Regeln – Offene Fragen, STH 2001, 111-114.
GROEHS Bernhard / STARINGER Claus, Österreichische und liechtensteinische Stiftung in rechtsvergleichender Sicht, in: Handbuch zum Privatstiftungsgesetz, hg. v. Peter Csoklich, Michael J. Müller, Bernhard Gröhs und Franz Helbich, Wien 1994, 293-316.
GROSSFELD Bernhard, Gläubigeranfechtung und Druchgriff. Das Problem der liechtensteinischen Anstalt, IPRax 1981, 116-117.
GRUENINGER Harold, Aktuelles aus dem Stiftungs- und Gemeinnützigkeitsbereich: Fälle, Entscheide, Literatur, Successio 1, 2007, 124-128.
–, Besteuerung von Trusts – Kreisschreiben 30 der Schweizerischen Steuerkonferenz vom 22. August 2007, Successio 1, 2007, 260-267.
GUBLER Friedrich, Besteht in der Schweiz ein Bedürfnis nach Einführung des Instituts der angelsächsischen Treuhand (trust)?, ZSR 73, 1954, 215.
GUBSER Anton, Outline of the Liechtenstein Company law reform of 1980, Vaduz 1981.
–, Grundriss der Liechtensteinischen Gesellschaftreform 1980, Vaduz 1980.
GUILLAUME Florence, Aspects successoraux de la transmission d'une entreprise à un descendant. La transmission d'une entreprise de famille, STH 81, 2007, 334-338.
GUTZWILER Peter Max, Schweizerisches Internationales Trustrecht, Kommentar zum Haager Übereinkommen über das auf Trusts anzuwendende Recht und über ihre Anerkennung (HTÜ) vom 1. Juli 1985 und zur schweizerischen Umsetzungs-Gesetzgebung vom 20.Dezember 2006, Basel 2007.
–, Trusts für die Schweiz, Anwaltsrevue 2007, 156-159.
–, Zur Bedeutung der Urteilsfähigkeit im Rahmen des „Vorsorgeauftrages“: zum Vorschlag des Bundesrates vom 28.6.2006, AJP 16, 2007, 556-560.
GUTZWILER Peter Max / SCHLEIFFER Patrick, Offenlegung von Beteiligungen im Falle eines Trusts (Trustees) als Aktionär, GesKR 2, 2007, 61-67.
GUEGGI Bruno, Die Familienstiftung im liechtensteinischen Recht, 13. A., Vaduz 2000.
–, La fondation de familie dans le droit liechtensteinois, 9e éd., Vaduz 2000.
–, La fondazione di famiglia nel diritto die Liechtenstein, 9a ed., Vaduz 1997.
HAAB Dieter, Aktionärbindungsvertrag: Vereinbarung zur Ergänzung des Aktienrechts und Mittel für eine massgeschneiderte Nachfolgeregelung, STH 81, 2007, 383-386.

HAAS-LEIMBACHER Christelle, Journée d'étude de droit comparé (CDCE Lausanne) du 5 Mars 2007: „Nouveautés en matière de pactes successoraux en droit français, italien et espagnol, Successio 1, 2007, 150-154.

–, Droit successoral et droit fiscal français: interdépendance dans les situations internationales, Bâle, 11 septembre 2007, Successio 1, 2007, 292-296.

–, Une réforme importante du droit successoral français: vers plus de liberté, Successio 1, 2007, 58-73.

HARDEGGER Ida, Geltendes Pflichtteilsrecht wird mehr und mehr zum Anachronismus – Ein Votum für angemessene Möglichkeiten autonomer Nachlassdispositionen, NZZ Nr.267, 16. November 2007, 18.

HÄUSLER Tom, Erbschaftsratgeber Deutschland-Schweiz, Herausgeber: Handelskammer Deutschland-Schweiz, März 2003.

HASENBOEHLER Franz, Sittenwidrige Verfügungen von Todes wegen, BJM 1980, 1-21.

HEEB Eugen, Tolley's Tax Havens. Tolley Publishing Co. Ltd., Liechtenstein 1990.

HEGNAUER Cyril, Grundriss des Kindesrechts und des übrigen Verwandschaftsrechts, 5.Aufl., Bern 1999.

–, Der Vater im Ausland als Beistand seines Kindes in der Schweiz, ZVW 1988, 61 ff.

–, Der Ausschluss des Pflichtteils des unmündigen Erben von der elterlichen Verwaltung (Art.322 ZGB), Festschrift für Frank Vischer, Zürich 1983.

–, Zur Verwendung der Erträge des Kindsvermögens gemäss Art.319 ZGB, ZVW 1979, 14.

–, Kann der Pflichtteil des Kindes nach Art.294 ZGB von der elterlichen Verwaltung und Nutzung befreit werden? SJZ 1967, 310.

HEINI Anton, Zu einem Urteil des Schweizerischen Bundesgerichts über das Personalstatut ausländischer juristischer Personen (Ungültigkeit einer liechtensteinischen Stiftung), IPRax 1984, 166-168.

HEISS Helmut, Zur Sanierung fehlerhafter Stiftungsstatuten – kein Handlungsbedarf des liechtensteinischen Gesetzgebers infolge des Urteils des StGH vom 18.11.2003, Az. StGH 2003/65, LJZ 2004, 80-83.

HEISS Helmut / LORENZ Bernhard, Der erstarrte Stifterwille, Aktuelle Fragen zum Finanzplatz Liechtenstein, Marxer & Partner, Vaduz 2004, 123-139.

HEPBERGER Rainer, Die Liechtensteinische Stiftung unter besonderer Berücksichtigung der Rechte des Stifters nach deren Errichtung, (Schriften zum liechtensteinischen Recht, Band 13) Schaan 2003.

HEPBERGER Rainer / MAUTER Wolfgang, Die Besteuerung der liechtensteinischen Familienstiftung aus der Sicht der Schweiz, StR 2004, 586-603.

HEROLD Hans / BRAXATOR Camillus, Das Rechtsinstitut der Stiftung, Zu den Einsatzmöglichkeiten für die Gesellschafternachfolge und die Führung von Wirtschaftsunternehmen, RIW 1993, 397.
HONSELL Heinrich / MAYER-MALY Theo / SELB Walter, Römisches Recht, Berlin 1988.
HIER Karl Josef, Die Unternehmensstiftung in Liechtenstein, (Schriften zum liechtensteinischen Gesellschafts-, Steuer- und Bankenrecht, Band 1) Vaduz 1995.
HOOP Gerold, Die Liechtensteinische Stiftung: Rechtliche Aspekte und Grenzen der Flexibilität, in: Die Liechtensteinische Stiftung, hg. v. Wolfgang Caspers, Jürgen Wagner und Hans Rainer Künzle, (Schweizer Schriften zur Vermögensberatung und zum Vermögensrecht, Band 4) Zürich 2002, 67-75.
HOPKINS Bruce, The Law of Tax-Exempt Organizations, 6. Ed., New York 1992, in Cumulative Supplement, New York 2001.
HOPKINS Bruce / BLAZEK Jody, Private Foundations, Tax Law and Compliance, New York 1997.
HOPT Klaus / REUTER Dieter, Stiftungsrecht in Europa, Köln 2001.
HORN Norbert, Aequitas in den Lehren des Baldus, Forschungen zur neueren Privatrechtsgeschichte, Bd. 11, Köln 1968.
–, Das französische Gesellschaftsrecht im 19. Jh., in: Coing (Hg.), Handbuch der Quellen und Literatur der neueren europäischen Privatrechtsgeschichte, München 1986, 3188 ff.
HOERNIG Martin, Grundzüge des liechtensteinischen Erbrechts und des IPR, Grenzenloses Erbrecht – Grenzen des Erbrechts, hrsg. v. DACH Europäische Anwaltsvereinigung e.V., Köln 2004, 201-216.
HUX Thomas, Die Anwendbarkeit des Auftragsrechts auf die Willensvollstreckung, die Erbschaftsverwaltung, die Erbschaftsliquidation und die Erbenvertretung, Entlebuch 1985 (Diss. Zürich 1985).
JACOB Dominique, Das Stiftungsrecht der Schweiz im Europa des dritten Jahrtausends, SJZ 104, 2008, Nr.22, 533 f.
JAUSSI Thomas / PFIRTER Markus, Unternehmensnachfolge – Steuerliche Aspekte und Stolpersteine. Von der steuerlichen Risikominimierung zur steuerlichen Chancennutzung, STH 81, 2007, 390-395.
JEEVES Bryan, Liechtenstein company law, the prevalent revised sections from the Personen- und Gesellschaftsrecht also relevant laws issued since publication ot the first edition, 2. ed., Vaduz 1999.
JOHNSTON David, The Roman Law of Trusts 1988.
JONES Neil, Trust in England after the Statute of Uses. A View from the 16th Century, Helmholz / Zimmermann, Itinera Fiduciae, Berlin 1998.
KASER Max, Das römische Privatrecht, München 1975.

KEICHER Werner, Die privatrechtliche Stiftung im Liechtensteinischen Recht, Diss. Zürich 1975.
KIEBER Daniel, Die Beendigung der Stiftung, Festschrift für Peter Marxer, Vaduz 1993, 193.
KIEBER Walter, Die treuhänderische Errichtung von Familienstiftungen, Festgabe für Herbert Batliner, hg. von Rita Batliner, Vaduz 1988, 273.
KLATIL Julia, Die Auskunftspflicht der Banken im Verlassenschaftsverfahren, LJZ 2004, 188-123.
KNELLER Michael, Die Haftung der Verwaltung einer liechtensteinischen Stiftung unter besonderer Berücksichtigung von Art. 159 IPRG, (Zürcher Studien zum Privatrecht, Band 101) Zürich 1993.
KOHLEGGER Karl, Möglichkeiten und Grenzen der Vollstreckung ausländischer zivilgerichtlicher Entscheidungen im Fürstentum Liechtenstein, in: Festschr. Herbert Batliner, Vaduz 2004, 111-125.
–, Liechtenstein – Steueroase oder Wirtschaftszentrum?: Rechtsfälle aus der Praxis des Fürstlich Liechtensteinischen Obersten Gerichtshofes, ÖJZ 1990, 577.
KOHLER Christian, Kodifikation und Reform des internationalen Privatrechts in Liechtenstein, Jus & News 1997, 281-286.
KRUG Walter, Die aktuelle deutsche Erbrechtsreform (2008) – eine Übersicht, Successio 1, 2007, 276-287.
KRÜGER Gerda, Die Rechtsstellung der vorkonstantinischen Kirchen, Stuttgart 1935, Reprint Amsterdam 1969.
KUHN Hans, Der Renvoi im internationalen Erbrecht der Schweiz. Eine Analyse internationaler Erbfälle im Verhältnis der Schweiz zu Deutschland, Frankreich, Italien, Oesterreich, dem Fürstentum Liechtenstein, Griechenland, England und den Niederlanden (Schweizer Studien zum internationalen Recht, Band 107) Zürich 1998.
KULMS Rainer, Ist das liechtensteinische Personen- und Gesellschaftsrecht kapitalmarktfähig?, LJZ 2004, 6-15.
–, 75 Jahre Liechtensteinische Treuhänderschaften. Die Art. 897 ff. PGR im Lichte europäischer Grundsätze zum Trustrecht, ZEuP 2001, 653.
KUNKEL Wolfgang, Herkunft und soziale Stellung der römischen Juristen, Köln 1967.
KUENZLE Hans Rainer, Familienstiftung – Quo vadis? Festschr. für Hans Michael Riemer, hrsg. v. Peter Breitschmid, Wolfgang Portmann, Heinz Rey und Dieter Zobl, Bern 2007, 173-198.
–, Unternehmensstiftung – Quo vadis?, STH 81, 2007, 369-373.
–, Konturen des Stiftungsbegriffs aus der schweizerischen Sicht, in: Achermann/ Künzle/Roth, Die Liechtensteinische Stiftung „Stiftungsnovellierung – wohin

geht die Reise?", Schweizer Schriften zur Vermögensberatung und zum Vermögensrecht, Schriftenreihe von KPMG, Private, Vaduz, 2002.
–, Revision des liechtensteinischen Stiftungsrechts, Private 2004, 22.
KUSTER Peter, Anhang Checkliste und Anhang Willensvollstreckung, in: Praxiskommentar Erbrecht (PraxKomm Erbrecht), hrsg. v. Daniel Abt und Thomas Weibel, Basel 2007.
LAMBSDORFF Hans-Georg, Liechtensteinische Stiftung und angelsächsischer Trust als Instrumente der Vermögensanlage in der Praxis, Vaduz 1989.
LAMPERT Siegbert / TAISCH Franco, Stiftungen im liechtensteinischen Recht, Stiftungsrecht in Europa, hg. v. Klaus J. Hopt und Dieter Reuter, Köln/Berlin/Bonn/München 2001, 521-540.
LANTER Marco, Was die Schweizer Stiftung kann – Ein kurzer zivilrechtlicher Überblick über da schweizerische Stiftungsrecht, in: Die Stiftung, 21. Tagung der DACH in Wien vom 16.-18.9.1999, Wien 2000.
LIERMANN Hans, Geschichte des Stiftungsrechts, 2.Aufl., Tübingen 2002.
LORETZ Dietmar, Die Rechtsstellung des Treuhänders einer liechtensteinischen Treuhänderschaft, Diplomarbeiten 2000 (Recht) des Nachdiplomstudiengangs Treuhandwesen der Fachhochschule Liechtenstein, (Schriften zum liechtensteinischen Recht, Band 8), Schaan 2000, 91-120.
–, Liechtensteinische Stiftungen. Anerkennung und Besteuerung in Österreich, (Diss. Wien) Wien 1993.
LOMBARDI Carlo, Gestion de fortune: Deux intéressants arrêts du Tribunal Fédéral, Relevant 2005 Nr. 2, 1.
MAROK Graziella, Die privatrechtliche liechtensteinische Anstalt, unter besonderer Berücksichtigung der Gründerrechte, (Schweizer Schriften zum Bankenrecht, Band 22) Zürich 1994.
MARXER Benedikt / REICHERT Fritz / SCHNYDER Anton, Gegenwartsfragen des liechtensteinischen Privat- und Wirtschaftsrechts. Referate und Diskussionsberichte des rechtsvergleichenden Kolloquiums in Vaduz vom 30. September und 1. Oktober 1996, Tübingen 1998.
MARXER Florian, Das Internationale Erbrecht Liechtensteins. Ein Vergleich mit dem österreichischen und schweizerischen Recht, (Schriftenreihe zum liechtensteinischen Gesellschafts-, Steuer- und Bankenrecht, Band 2) Vaduz 2002.
MARXER Ludwig, Die liechtensteinische Familienstiftung, ihre Eigenart im Verhältnis zum schweizerischen Recht, (Diss. Freiburg i.Ue. 1990) Freiburg i.Ue. 1990.
MARXER Peter, Die liechtensteinische Familienstiftung – Ihre Eigenart im Verhältnis zum schweizerischen Recht, Vaduz 1990.
–, Liechtenstein in International Estate Planning, Matthew Bender, 2.ed., New York 1999.

–, Mandatum Post Mortem. Auftrag auf den Todesfall und Todesvollmachten im liechtensteinischen Recht, Schaan 1996 (Diss. St. Gallen).

MAITLAND Frederic William, Trust und Korporation, Zeitschrift für das Privat- und öffentliche Recht der Gegenwart, Bd. 32, 1905, 1.

MANTHE Ulrich, Das senatus consultum Pegasianum, München/Freiburg 1985.

MATTHEUS Daniela, Gläserne Stiftungen? Eckpfeiler einer stiftungsrechtlichen Publizität, in: Achermann/Künzle/Roth, Die Liechtensteinische Stiftung „Stiftungsnovellierung – wohin geht die Reise?“, Schweizer Schriften zur Vermögensberatung und zum Vermögensrecht, Schriftenreihe von KPMG private, Vaduz 2002.

MATTHEWS Paul, Die Gefahren der Über-Klassifikation im Trustrecht, LJZ 2001, 109.

MAYER Thomas, Der Trust und das auf ihn anwendbare Recht aus Schweizer Sicht, Recht 25, 2007, 64-68.

MEDIUCUS Dieter, Pflichtteilsergänzung wegen Zuwendungen an Stiftungen, Festschr. für Helmut Heinrichs, hg. v. Andreas Heldrich, Peter Schlechtriem, Eike Schmidt, München 1998, 381-396.

MEIER Guido, La fiducie (trust) dans le droit des personnes et des sociétés du Liechtenstein, 2e éd., Vaduz 1997.

–, The trust in the Liechtenstein law on persons and companies, 2nd ed., Vaduz 1989.

–, Grundstatut und Sonderanknüpfung im IPR des liechtensteinischen Gesellschaftsrechts: erläutert anhand ausländischer Kollisionsrechtslehre und -praxis, (Schriftenreihe des Instituts für Internationales Recht und Internationale Beziehungen, Heft 27) Basel 1979.

MEIER Otto, Die Liechtensteinische Privatrechtliche Anstalt, (Zürcher Beiträge zur Rechtswissenschaft, Neue Folge Heft 341) Zürich 1970.

MEIER Philippe, Le consentement des autorités de tutelle aux actes du tuteur, Fribourg 1994.

MILLIOT Louis, Introduction à l’étude du droit Musulman, Paris 1953.

MOOSMANN Kurt, Der angelsächsische Trust und die liechtensteinische Treuhänderschaft, unter besonderer Berücksichtigung des wirtschaftlich Begünstigten. Eine rechtsvergleichende Studie mit Erkenntnissen für das Schweizer Treuhandrecht, (Schweizer Schriften zum Bankenrecht, Band 56) Zürich 1999.

MORENO-PUJOL José Martín, Constitución Política de la República de Panamá, incl. Indice Analítico actualizado, Hg. Mizrachi & Pujol, 6.Auflage, Panamá 2005.

MORGAN Eduardo E., La Fundación de Interés privado y su incorporación en la legislación panameña, Resumen de Tésis de Graduación para optar al Título de licenciado en derecho y ciencias políticas, Panamá 1992.
MORGAN & MORGAN, Morgan & Morgan Group, La fundación de interés privado bajo la legislación de la república de Panamá, Ley N° 25 de 12 de junio de 1995, Análisis y Comentarios por artículos de la Ley Modelo de una fundación privada y su reglamento, Panamá 1995.
MOSER Jean-Pierre, La protection du patrimoine du mineur soumis à l'autorité parentale, Diss. Lausanne 1977.
MOOSER Michel, Eingetragene Partnerschaft: Erbrecht, in: Rechte der Lesben und Schwulen in der Schweiz, hrsg. v. Alexander R. Ziegler, Martin Bertschi, Alexandre Curchod, Nadja Herz und Michel Montini, Bern 2007, 285-296.
–, Partenariat enregistré: droit successoral, in: Droit des gays et lesbiennes en Suisse, éd. par Alexander R. Ziegler, Martin Bertschi, Alexandre Curchod, Nadja Herz et Michel Montini, Berne 2007, 271-281.
MUELLER Franz / GENNA Gian Sandro, Die Haftung des Notars für Rechtsbelehrung in Steuerfragen, BN 68, 2007, 1-17.
MUELLER-TIBERINI Franziska, Vom Erben und Ver(d)erben: Heikle Themen konstruktiv angehen. Familie und Unternehmen, Zürich 2007.
NIGG Thomas, Liechtensteinische und schweizerischer Vereinsrecht im Vergleich, (Diss. Zürich 1996) Vaduz 1996.
OBERHUBER Herbert, Liechtenstein / Capital, Taxes and Estate Planning in Europe, hrsg. v. Timothey J. Lyons, London 1999, 2901-2955.
PAPEIL Anne-Sophie, Doit on laisser la possibilité au futur de cujus de choisir la loi applicable à la succession?, Successio 1, 2007, 108-123.
PICENONI Vito, Die Verjährung der Testamentsgültigkeits- und Herabsetzungsklage gemäss Art.521 und 533 ZGB, SJZ 1967, 101.
PIOTET Denis, Les inefficacités des dispositions à cause de mort en droit suisse. Quelques actions en annulation, éd. par François Bohnet, Neuchâtel 2007, 51-83.
–, La substitution fidéicommissaire pour le surplus au détriment de la réserve du grevé incapable de discernement dans le projet de révision du droit de la protection de l'adulte, Successio 1, 2007, 240-247.
PLÜSS Adrian, Die Stiftungsrechtsreform in der Schweiz. Achermann/Künzle/Roth, Die Liechtensteinische Stiftung „Stiftungsnovellierung – wohin geht die Reise?“, Schweizer Schriften zur Vermögensberatung und zum Vermögensrecht, Schriftenreihe von KPMG private, Vaduz 2002.
PRAST Peter, Anerkennung liechtensteinischer Gesellschaften im Ausland. Eine rechtsvergleichende Untersuchung nach deutschem, schweizerischem und ös-

terreichischem Recht, (St. Galler Studien zum internationalen Recht, Band 22) Lachen 1997.
PUEMPIN Cuno, Nachfolgeplanung und Private Equity, STH 80, 2007, 352-354.
QUADERER Roger, Die Rechtsstellung der Anwartschaftsberechtigten bei der liechtensteinischen Familienstiftung. Dissertation an der Universität Innsbruck/Schaan, 1999.
RABEL Ernst, Grundzüge des römischen Rechts, in: Holtzendorff/Kohler, Enzyklopädie der Rechtswissenschat in systematischer Bearbeitung, Bd. 3, 1892.
RASELLI Nicolo, Erklärter oder wirklicher Wille des Erblassers? AJP 1999, 1262.
RAMATI, U. E., Liechtenstein's uncertain foundations: anatomy of a tax haven, Dublin 1993.
RAWERT Peter, Der Stiftungsbegriff und seine Merkmale, in: (Hg) HOPT/REUTER, Stiftungsrecht in Europa, Köln 2001, 109.
RAWERT Peter / KATSCHINSKI Ralf, Stiftungserrichtung und Pflichtteilsergänzung, ZEV 1996, 161-166.
REGELSBERGER Ferdinand, Pandekten, Leipzig 1893.
REGIERUNG des Fürstentums Liechtenstein, Grundlagenbericht zu einer liechtensteinischen Ehe- und Familienrechtsreform, Vaduz 1987.
REICHERT Daniel, Prozessrechtliche und kollisionsrechtliche Fragen des umgekehrten Durchgriffs, Gegenwartsfragen des liechtensteinischen Privat- und Wirtschaftsrechts, Tübingen 1998, 27-34.
REICHERT Fritz, Durchgriffshaftung des liechtensteinischen Gesellschaftsrechts, Gegenwartsfragen des liechtensteinischen Privat- und Wirtschaftsrechts, Tübingen 1998, 15-25.
REITHNER Nicolas, Die Auskunftsfplicht der Banken im Verlassenschaftsverfahren – Replik, LJZ 2005, 91-95.
RESCIGNO Pietro, Le fondazioni: prospettive e linee de riforma. Le fondazioni in Italia e all'estero, Padua 1989.
RICHTER Andreas, Germann and American Law of Charity. Helmholz/Zimmermann (Hg.), Itinera Fiduciae, Berlin 1998, 427.
RIEMER Hans Michael, Verwaltung von Kindesvermögen durch Dritte gemäss Art.321 und 322 ZGB und Beistandschaft gemäss Art.325 ZGB, insbesondere in Gestalt der ‚mehrfachen Vermögensverwaltung' und der ‚mehrfachen Beistandschaft', ZVW 2001, Sonderausgabe, 84-89.
–, Bedingungen und Auflagen, namentlich bei Schenkungen und Verfügungen von Todes wegen, Weblaw, Jusletter vom 17. Juli 2000, www.weblaw.ch
–, Anfechtungs- und Nichtigkeitsklage im Schweizerischen Gesellschaftsrecht, Bern 1998.

–, Nichtige (unwirksame) Testamente und Erbverträge, Festschrift für Max Keller, Zürich 1989, 245-259.
–, Kommentar zum Schweizerischen Privatrecht, Band I: Einleitung und Personenrecht, 3. Abteilung: Die juristischen Personen, 3. Teilband: Die Stiftungen, Bern 1993.
RITTER / WOHLWEND / WOLFF, Liechtenstein, International Succession, Louis Garb, The Hague 2001.
ROTH Patrick, Die Beendigung und Liquidation von Körperschaften des liechtensteinischen Personen- und Gesellschaftsrechts, (Schriften zum liechtensteinischen Recht, Band 9) Schaan 2001.
RUFFNER Markus, Financial Planning, Rechtliche Einbindung und Haftungsrisiken, AJP 26, 2007, 869-884.
RUMO-JUNGO Alexandra, Tafeln und Fälle zum Erbrecht unter Berücksichtigung des internationalen Erbrechts, des Ehegüterrechts und des Partnerschaftsgesetzes, Zürich 2007.
–, Vorschlagszuweisung an den überlebenden Ehegatten als Rechtsgeschäft unter Lebenden: eine Qualifikation mit weitreichenden Folgen, Successio 1, 2007, 158-167.
RUSCH Arnold, Konten für Dritte, AJP 16, 2007, 561-574.
SACHAU Eduard, Mohamedanisches Recht, Berlin 1897.
SALEILLES Raymond, Les „piae causae“ dan le droit de Justinien. Mélanges Girardin, Paris 1907, 513.
SANTO-PASSO Rolf, Family Estate Planning, Achermann/Künzle/Roth, Die Liechtensteinische Stiftung „Stiftungsnovellierung – wohin geht die Reise?“, Schweizer Schriften zur Vermögensberatung und zum Vermögensrecht, Schriftenreihe von KPMG private, Vaduz 2002.
SATTAR Shaista, Il trust e la fondazioni di famiglia del Liechtenstein, di Panama e delle Antille Olandesi quali strumenti per la pianificazione fiscale internazio-nale, Lugano 1999.
SCHAERER Jürg Christian, Der Grundsatz der materiellen Höchstpersönlichkeit der letztwilligen Verfügung, Zürich 1973, Diss. Bern 1973.
SCHAUER Martin, Die liechtensteinische Stiftung im internationalen Vergleich unter Berücksichtigung der Familien- und Unterhaltsstiftung, Aktuelle Fragen zum Finanzplatz Liechtenstein, Vaduz 2004, 67-121.
–, Erbrechtliche Aspekte des Entwurfs eines Privatstiftungsgesetzes, RdW 1993, 170
–, Privatstiftung und Erbrecht, Aktuelle Fragen des Privatstiftungsrechts, Peter Doralt und Susanne Kalss, Wien 2001, 13.

–, Erbrechtliche Probleme der Privatstiftung, Handbuch zum Privatstiftungsgesetz, Peter Csoklich, Michael J. Müller, Bernhard Gröhs und Franz Helbich, Wien 1994, 107-143.

–, Privatstiftung und Pflichtteilsrecht, NZ 1993, 251.

SCHLÜTER Alexander, Stiftungsrecht zwischen Privatautonomie und Gemeinwohlbindung. Ein Rechtsvergleich Deutschland, Frankreich, Italien, England und die Vereinigten Staaten, München 2004.

SCHLÜTER Alexander / THEN Volker / WALKENHORST Peter, Foundations in Europe, London 2001.

SCHMID Roger, Die Unternehmensstiftung im geltenden Recht, im Vorentwurf zur Revision des Stiftungsrechts und im Rechtsvergleich, (Schweizer Schriften zum Handels- und Wirtschaftrecht, Band 181) Zürich 1997.

SCHNEIDER Michael, Anstalt und Treuunternehmen des liechtensteinischen Rechts als Unternehmensformen für Sitz- und Holdinggesellschaften, Göttingen 1970.

SCHNEIDER Nadine, Der Mythos Liechtensteinische Stiftung, ein Rechtsvergleich zur Schweizerischen Stiftung, Stiftung und Gesellschaft, Basel 2006, 171-191.

SCHNYDER Anton, Trust, Pflichtteilsrecht, Familienfideikomiss, Festschrift für Hans Michael Riemer, hrsg. v. Peter Breitschmid, Wolfgang Portmann, Heinz Rey und Dieter Zobl, Bern 2007, 331-350.

SCHOENBLUM Jeffrey, Multistate and multinationale estate planning, Boston/Toronto 1982.

SCHOENLE Herbert, Die Gründerrechte im Falle privatrechtlicher Anstalten, Aktuelle Fragen des Liechtensteinischen Gesellschaftsrechts, Vaduz 1967.

SCHURR Francesco, Vermögensnachfolge durch Stiftungserrichtung in Italien, Probleme des Pflichtteils- und Nacherbrechts, Zeitschrift für Rechtsvergleichung Internationales Privatrecht und Europarecht (ZfRVergl), 2001, 19-26.

SCHWENZER Ingeborg, Gesetzliche Vertretungsmacht der Eltern für unmündige Kinder. Notwendigkeit oder Relikt patriarchalischer Familienstruktur? Festschschfrift für Bernhard Schnyder, Freiburg 1995, 679.

SCHYLE Michael, Brennpunkte des liechtensteinischen Stiftungsrechts im Lichte der neueren Rechtsprechung, LJZ 2004, 181-216.

SEEGER Norbert, Die Verantwortlichekit gemäss Art. 218 bis 228 des liechtensteinischen Personen- und Gesellschaftsrechtes, (Abhandlungen zum schweizerischen Recht, Neue Folge Band 504) Bern 1987.

SEIFART Werner / VON CAMPENHAUSEN Axel Freiherr, Handbuch des Stiftungsrechts, München 1999.

SENN Heinrich, Mündelsichere Kapitalanlagen, Diss. Zürich 1972.

SIEDERER Nigel, Foundation Law in the United Kingdom, London 2002.

SIGNER Martin, Vermögenssicherung über Generationen. Praxisfälle, STH 81, 2007, 462-465.

SMITH James / BORGMANN Allen, Foundations in Europe, the Historical Context. Schlüter/Then/Walkenhorst, Foundations in Europe, London, 2001, 2.

SOERGEL Hans Theodor / NEUHOF Klaus, Kommentar zum Bürgerlichen Gesetzbuch, Band 1: Allgemeiner Teil, 13. A., Essen 2000.

SONNEVELDT Frans / VAN MENS Harrie, The trust, bridge or abyss between common and civil law jurisdiction?, Deventer 1982.

SPIELVOGEL Christina, Die schweizerische und österreichische Privatstiftung im Vergleich, Wien 1998.

SPRECHER Thomas / VON SALIS-LÜTOLF Ulysses, Die schweizerische Stiftung, Zürich 1999.

STAEHLIN Valo / GANTENBEIN-AFFRUNTI Susanne, Nachbesteuerung in Erbfällen und die Einführung der straflosen Selbstanzeige, STH 81, 2007, 117-120.

STETTLER Martin, Das Kindsrecht. Schweizerisches Privatrecht, Band III, Basel/Frankfurt 1992.

STOTTER Heinz Josef, Ausgewählte Entscheide des Fürstlich-Liechtensteinischen Obersten Gerichtshofes zum liechtensteinischen Stiftungsrecht. Festschrift für Herbert Batliner, Vaduz 2004, 174-192.

STRAUB Hans, Über das Treuhandrecht unter besonderer Berücksichtigung des liechtensteinischen Gesetzes betreffend Treuunternehmen, (Diss. Bern 1939) Zug 1940.

STRUB Wolfgang, Der Geheimnisschutz im liechtensteinischen Treuhandwesen, 2. A., (Bankwirtschaftliche Forschungen, Band 104) Bern 1988.

STUTZ Heidi / BAUER Tobias / SCHMUGGE Susanne, Erben in der Schweiz. Eine Familiensache mit volkswirtschaftlichen Folgen, Zürich 2007.

SUMMER Markus, Vertrauen ist gut, Kontrolle ist besser. Die Auskunftsrechte von Begünstigten im liechtensteinischen Stiftungs- und Treuhandrecht, LJZ 2005, 36-53.

SUEDEL Inken, Das landwirtschaftliche Erbrecht in Norddeutschland (am Beispiel von Schleswig-Holstein und Mecklenburg-Vorpommern) und in der Schweiz: Gemeinsamkeiten, Unterschiede, Zukunftstauglichkeit, Frankfurt am Main 2007 (Europäische Hochschulschriften, Reihe 2: Rechtswissenschaft, Band 4566).

TAISCH Franco, Diskretion am Bankschalter oder Persönlichkeitsschutz und Bankgeschäft. Aspekte aus liechtensteinischer Sicht, (Schriftenreihe der Liechtensteinischen Landesbank, Band 19) Vaduz 1996.

–, Privatplacierungen, insbesondere im Hinblick auf Notes, (Schweizer Schriften zum Handels- und Wirtschaftsrecht, Band 101) Zürich 1987.

TAISCH Franco / MUELLER Urs, Der Fondsstandort Liechtenstein. Einführung, gesetzliche Grundlagen, Sachregister, (Schriftenreihe der Liechtensteinischen Landesbank, Band 22) Vaduz 1997.

TAMM Gaby, Die Liechtensteinische Privatrechtliche Anstalt im Todesfall des Gründers unter besonderer Berücksichtigung der deutsch-liechtensteinischen Rechtsbeziehungen, Osnabrück 2003.

TETIWA Werner, Grundzüge, Entstehung und Bedeutung des ‚estate planning' (Nachlassplanung) im Recht der USA, Münster 1975.

THORENS Justin, L'article 335 CCS et le trust de common law. Mélanges Henri-Robert Schüpbach, Basel/Genf/München 2000, 155-166.

–, Le trust de common law et les institutions de substitution en pays de droit civil, Fiscalité européenne 18, 1987, 3-18.

TOGGLER Hellwig, Die österreichische Privatstiftung im Spannungsfeld der Interessen. 21. Tagung der DACH in Wien vom 16.-18.9.1999, Wien 2000.

TOLLEY'S Administration of Trusts, ed. STEP (Society of Trust and Estate Practitioners, London). London 2002,

TRIBALDOS-ALBA Rogelio, Die Panama-Stiftung, ed. Panazur, a Member of the Morgan & Morgan Group, Zurich Branch, Zürich 1999.

UMLAUFT Manfred, Die Anrechnung von Schenkungen und Vorempfängen im Erb- und Pflichtteilsrecht, (Habilitation Innsbruck 2001) Wien 2001.

UNDERHILL Hayton, Law relating to Trusts and Trustees, 15th edition 1995.

VERNEHMLASSUNGSBERICHT der Regierung zur Abänderung de Stiftungsrechts, Art. 552-570 des Personen- und Gesellschaftsrechts, PGR, Ressort Justiz, Vaduz 2004.

VOGEL Urs, Die Person des Beistandes, ZVW 2003, 331-337.

VOGT Nedim Peter, Trusts und schweizerisches Recht (das Haager Trust-Übereinkommen und die neuen Art. 149a-e IPRG), Anwaltsrevue 2007, 199-203.

VON BURG Roger, Der Trust in der Schweiz. Auswirkungen der Ratifikation des Haager Trust Übereinkommens. Aktuelle Probleme des europäischen und internationalen Wirtschaftsrechts, Band 9, Basel 2007, 463-517.

VON CAMPENHAUSEN Axel Freiherr, Geschichte des Stiftungswesens. Handbuch Stiftungen, Wiesbaden 1998, 23.

VON HIPPEL Thomas, Konturen des Stiftungsbegriffs aus deutscher Sicht. Achermann/Künzle/Roth, Die Liechtensteinische Stiftung „Stiftungsnovellierung – wohin geht die Reise?", Schweizer Schriften zur Vermögensberatung und zum Vermögensrecht, Schriftenreihe von KPMG private, Vaduz 2002.

VON LOEWE Christian, Familienstiftung und Nachfolgegestaltung: Deutschland – Österreich – Schweiz – Liechtenstein, (Diss. Stuttgart 1998) Düsseldorf 1999.

WACHTER Michael, Liechtensteinische Ermessensstiftung zum Wohle Begünstigter. Schweiz-Deutschland CH-D Wirtschaft 56, 2007, 15-16.

WEBER Roger, Gerichtliche Vorkehren bei der Nachlassabwicklung, AJP 1997, 550.

WENGER Jean-Claude, Der Anwalt als Willensvollstrecker. Das Anwaltsgeheimnis, Zürich 1997, 51.

WERRO Franz, Le mandat et ses effets, Une étude sur le contrat d'activité indépendente selon le Code suisse des obligations, Analyse critique et comparative. Travaux de la Faculté de Droit de l'Université de Fribourg, Suisse. Habil. Fribourg 1993.

WETZEL Claude, Interessenkonflikte des Willenvollstreckers unter besonderer Berücksichtigung des Anspruchs auf Erbschaftsverwaltung gemäss Art.554 Abs.2 ZGB, Diss. Zürich 1984.

WAGNER Jürgen, Bankenplatz Liechtenstein, Zürich 2004.

WAGNER Jürgen / HEPBERGER Rainer, Neues Stiftungsrecht in Liechtenstein (Teil 1): Schritte zur Reform, Jus & News 2005, 295-305

WAGNER Jürgen / PLUESS Adrian, Handels- und Wirtschaftrecht in der Schweiz und in Liechtenstein, (Schriftenreihe Recht der internationalen Wirtschaft, Band 59) Heidelberg 2000.

WANGER Markus, Stiftungen/Foundations, Offshore Trust Yearbook, International Money Marketing, Liechtenstein 1993.

–, Liechtenstein in Foundations in Europe. Andreas Schlüter, Volker Then, Peter Walkenhorst, London 2001, 179-185.

–, Liechtensteinisches Wirtschafts- und Gesellschaftsrecht: Aktiengesellschaft, Anstalt, Stiftung, Trust und Treuunternehmen: mit einer Einführung in das liechtensteinische Schiedsgerichtsverfahren, 3. A., (Abhandlungen und Kommentare zum liechtensteinischen und internationalen Recht, Band 1) Vaduz 1998.

WANNER Georges, Die Anstalt nach liechtensteinischem Personen- und Gesellschaftsrecht, Diss. Basel 1959.

WENAWESER Stefan, Ausgewählte Fragen zum liechtensteinischen Treuhänder-schaftsrecht, LJZ 2005, 7-16.

–, Zur Rezeptionsfrage der Treuhänderschaft und ihrem Anwendungsbereich nach liechtensteinischem Recht, LJZ 2001, 1-23.

WIENBRACKE Mike, Die erbschafts- und schenkungssteuerliche Behandlung von trusts in Deutschland, StR 82, 2007, 490-503.

WITZ Claude, La fiducie es ses applications dans plusieurs pays européenns: Allemagne, Angleterre, Liechtenstein, Luxembourg, Suisse: colloque organisé par le Centre d'Etudes Juridiques Françaises 29 novembre 1990, Paris 1991.

WYLER Marcus, Über das Treuhandrecht: mit besonderer Berücksichtigung der Regelung im Fürstentum Liechtenstein, ZSR 56, 1937, 293.

ZAECH Roger, Die Stellvertretung gemäss Art.32-40 OR. Kommentar zum Schweizerischen Privatrecht, Band VI, Das Schweizerische Obligationenrecht, Bern 1990.

ZELGER Ulrich, Die Nachlassabsonderung nach liechtensteinischem Recht, LJZ 2004, 217-223.

ZELLWEGER Jakob, Die Verantwortlichkeit der vormundschaftlichen Organe aus der Vermögensverwaltung. Diss. Bern 1939.

ZINDEL Mario, Problemanalyse im Zusammenhang mit der Benachteiligung von Erbeninteressen durch Gründung eines liechtensteinischen Vermögensträgers, (Diss. Zürich 1982) Vaduz 1982.

ZOBL Dieter, Probleme im Spannunsfeld von Bankrecht, Erbrecht und Schuldrecht, AJP 2001, 1007.

–, Die Aussonderung von liechtensteinischem Treuhandgut in der schweizerischen Zwangsvollstreckung, (Schweizer Schriften zum Bankenrecht, Band 21) Zürich 1994.

ZWIEFELHOFER Susanne, Das liechtensteinische Recht betreffend die Investmentunternehmen vergleichen mit dem schweizerischen Anlagefondsrecht, (Schweizer Schriften zum Bankenrecht, Band 68) Zürich 2002.

Bochumer Studien zum Stiftungswesen

Herausgegeben von Karlheinz Muscheler

Der Verein „Fundare e.V., Gemeinnütziger Verein zur Förderung des Stiftungswesens“ hat sich zum Ziel gesetzt, zu einer aufblühenden Stiftungskultur in Deutschland beizutragen. Auch die von Prof. Dr. Karlheinz Muscheler im Auftrag von Fundare herausgegebene Schriftenreihe „Bochumer Studien zum Stiftungswesen“ dient diesem Ziel. In ihr sollen Arbeiten aus grundsätzlich allen wissenschaftlichen Disziplinen erscheinen, die sich mit dem Stiftungswesen im weitesten Sinne beschäftigen. Einen Schwerpunkt bilden Arbeiten zum Zivil-, Verwaltungs- und Steuerrecht der Stiftung. Veröffentlicht werden insbesondere Dissertationen, Habilitationen und sonstige Monographien.

Bochumer Studien zum Stiftungswesen

Herausgegeben von Karlheinz Muscheler

Band 1 Irena Braxator: Grundlagen der Panama-Stiftung. 2009.

Band 2 Frank Schuck: Die Doppelstiftung. Instrument zur Gestaltung der Unternehmensnachfolge. 2009.

Band 3 Sang-Hyun Ko: Errichtung einer Stiftung nach deutschem und koreanischem Recht. 2009.

Band 4 Jonas Arnhold: Die selbständige Stiftung und der Testamentsvollstrecker. 2010.

Band 5 Sebastian Trappe: Unternehmensmitbestimmung und unternehmensverbundene Stiftungen. 2010.

Band 6 Irena Braxator: Fundamental Principles of Panamanian Foundations. 2011.

www.peterlang.de

www.ingramcontent.com/pod-product-compliance
Ingram Content Group UK Ltd.
Pitfield, Milton Keynes, MK11 3LW, UK
UKHW021831100926
8556IPUK00004B/285

9 783631 613320